Saving Main Street

Saving Main Street

*Small Business in the Time
of COVID-19*

Gary Rivlin

**HARPER
BUSINESS**

An Imprint of HarperCollinsPublishers

HarperCollins books may be purchased for educational, business,
or sales promotional use. For information, please email the Special
Markets Department at SPsales@harpercollins.com.

FIRST EDITION

Map by Nick Springer, copyright © 2022 Springer Cartographics

Library of Congress Cataloging-in-Publication Data has been applied for.

ISBN 978-0-06-306596-3

22 23 24 25 26   LSC   10 9 8 7 6 5 4 3 2 1

For

Daisy, Oliver, and Silas

with love

Contents

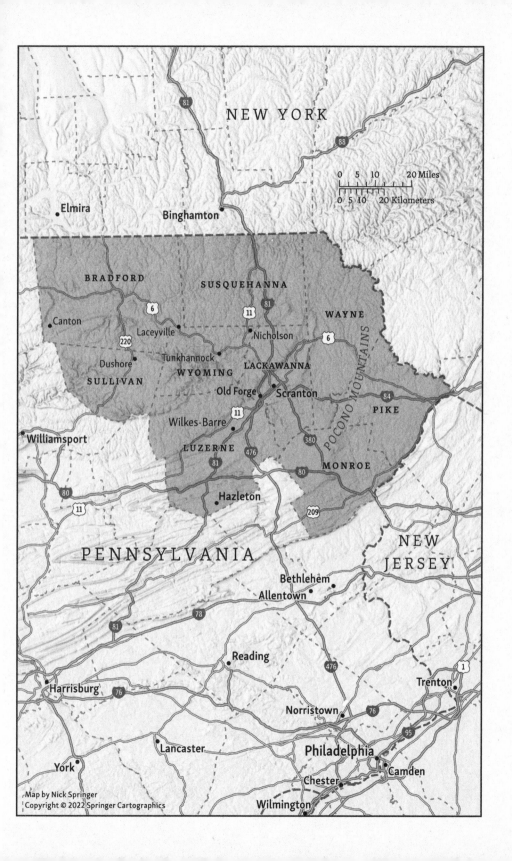

Saving Main Street

Introduction

January had been a terrific month inside Cusumano's, an Italian restaurant in Old Forge, Pennsylvania, a town of eight thousand a few miles south of Scranton. The dining room was packed every weekend, despite temperatures that sometimes dipped down into the single digits. So, too, was a downstairs bar area called the Cellar. TJ Cusumano, a thickly built thirty-four-year-old, had started cooking when he was in grade school. His wife, Nina, two years his junior, had been working in restaurants since the age of sixteen. There had been moments since they first opened Cusumano's in 2013 when the couple regretted ever getting into the restaurant business. The food was delicious, and they had the accolades to prove it. But the couple sometimes went months without drawing a salary. They lived off the tips Nina earned serving the food.

By January of 2020, though, they were drawing crowds even on Wednesdays and Thursdays. The good times continued into February. Valentine's Day that year fell on a Friday. The restaurant had probably its best Friday night in its seven-plus years of operation, making for a blockbuster three-day weekend that ranked among their top grossing since they first opened.

"We felt like we were really making it," TJ said.

The crowds thinned in the second half of the month, and the Cusumanos told themselves that a drop-off was inevitable. Yet

February turned into March, and one or the other of them glanced at the binder they left open by the phone for writing down reservations. There were few names listed even on a Friday or Saturday night. "Just the winter blues," the Cusumanos reassured each other. They chalked up the slowdown to the cyclical nature of the restaurant business and a population tired of trekking outside at the end of a long winter. On some nights, they seemed more like weather forecasters than restaurateurs. "Low of twenty-five tonight," one said to the other to explain a dining room barely half-full on the last Saturday night of February. Another night it was "freezing rain turning to ice."

Reservations remained down even as the temperature outside warmed up in early March. TJ kept up with current events and had read about this new strain of coronavirus spreading around the globe. At that point, though, the virus had barely reached the shores of the US. Even then, only a few cases had been reported on either coast—far from their modest-sized burgh. Neither mentioned the pending pandemic as a possible explanation for the steep drop-off in reservations.

The date stamps on the food the restaurant was getting from their suppliers were another early sign of the calamity about to hit Old Forge and the rest of the world. Cusumano's was one of a half-dozen Italian eateries on Main Street in Old Forge, an old coal miner's town. Phyllis Mischello, the owner-chef of Anthony's down the street, phoned. So, too, did Russell Rinaldi at Cafe Rinaldi next door and other restaurant owners in town. All of them asked the same question: Were his purveyors sending him older product? TJ noticed the difference in the fish. The catch that typically had been caught within forty-eight hours was now several days out of the water.

"I'm starting to make the correlation," TJ said. He began to see the impact of the coronavirus on their business.

"We stopped spending money in any way we could," he said.

"Ordering less food. Cutting down on our alcohol purchase. Cutting people's hours."

On the second Friday of March—Friday the thirteenth—temperatures hit a high of sixty-four. The crowd that night was still sparse. That Saturday Scranton would have held its annual St. Patrick's Day parade. In normal times, that would mean an overflow crowd and fat bar bills both in the main dining room and downstairs in the Cellar. "This place would have been a total zoo," Nina said. But Scranton canceled its parade. Bob Mulkerin was behind the bar in the Cellar that night. Mulkerin was a lifelong Old Forger who'd started bartending on Saturday nights in 2017, after serving a single term as town mayor. ("I care about my kids" was his rationale both for running and deciding not to run for reelection.) Normally, Mulkerin pocketed a couple of hundred dollars in tips on a busy Saturday night. He was lucky if he made $50 that night. A small surprise party was up in the air until a few hours before the guests slated to arrive. They went ahead with the celebration, but the only other people there that night were the battered regulars who parked themselves on the same bar stools night after night. In a room that in normal times practically vibrated with good cheer, the mood was more that of a wake.

On Sunday, the mayor of Philadelphia, two hours to the south, suspended indoor dining. The governor put the same restrictions on restaurants in the suburbs surrounding Philadelphia and also in Allegheny County, which includes Pittsburgh. TJ recalled the night as a last hurrah, as if people sought one more night out before the inevitable. "It was kind of a good Sunday, which kind of shocked us," TJ said. At the end of the shift, he sat with Jessica Barletta, a waitress who had been with him and Nina since they first opened their doors. She was herself a small business operator with her own dance studio in Scranton.

"TJ's like, 'I'm pretty sure we're not going to be open this Wednesday,'" Barletta recalled. (Cusumano's is closed on Mondays and Tuesdays.) "I was like, 'Yeah.'" Pennsylvania's governor, Tom Wolf, made it official that Monday. Restaurants could still offer takeout and delivery. But Wolf signed an order shutting down indoor dining everywhere in the state.

TJ's first hours in lockdown were spent largely on his phone, texting or talking with the restaurant's two dozen employees. The servers and bartenders tended to have other sources of income but not his kitchen staff, who needed a paycheck to pay the rent and buy food. That would be his first hard decision: Whom could he afford to keep, if anyone, and whom would he lay off?

TJ tried not to think about the timing. A landmark moment for any business is establishing a retirement program for its employees. Finally, he and Nina were making enough to start a 401(k) for themselves and several longtime employees. They were only a couple of weeks from finalizing a small benefits package that matched an employee's contributions to a retirement fund when the governor issued his shutdown order. The 401(k) would be added to the list of things that needed to be put on hold for who knew how long.

"We had been very blessed," TJ said. "Coming into our seventh year, we were really hitting our stride." In the prior fifty-two weeks, he figured that they had experienced two or three slow weeks. Yet suddenly he was looking at an indefinite closure.

"Things had really been going great," he said.

And like that, they weren't.

* * *

Fifty minutes south of Cusumano's on the interstate lies Hazleton, another old coal mining town. Both Hazleton and Old Forge date back two centuries to when northeastern Pennsylvania's coal and iron ore helped power the Industrial Revolution. Yet the modern-day version of each stands as a polar opposite of the other. What distinguishes Old Forge is how little the town has changed over the years. Old Forge was Italian one hundred years ago just as it is Italian today, even as it has the "Polish Alps," a hilly neighborhood where those of Polish ancestry first settled, and a token Irish pub. People commute to jobs in Scranton or work in town. There are warehouse jobs at a wholesale beer and soda distributor that ranks as one of Pennsylvania's biggest and more to be found at the sprawling lumber and kitchen supply warehouse just off the main road into town. Many find work inside one of the Italian eateries that for generations have drawn people to Old Forge.

Hazleton, by contrast, has been in great flux for decades. The Hazleton area—the city of Hazleton, with its thirty thousand people, and the surrounding "patch towns" that popped up each time a new mine was opened—has always been a melting pot. The Italians arrived to work its mines (or sell their goods and services to the coal miners, as Cusumano's people have been doing in Old Forge for several generations) but so did the Irish, the Welsh, the Poles, the Slovaks, the Germans, and, more recently, the Dominicans.

In 1959, the coal industry closer to Scranton collapsed in a single day, after the Knox Coal Company dug too close to the Susquehanna River. What locally is known as the "Knox disaster" flooded mines for miles, all but putting an end to mining in the area. The fall of coal came more slowly to Hazleton but no less emphatically. By the early 2000s, 70 percent of its downtown's storefronts were sitting empty. For Hazleton, salvation was its proximity to Interstate 80, though some would come to think of that as the source of its problems. This east-west colossus that connects New York City to San Francisco (and also Cleveland, Chicago, and a long list of large cities along the way) cuts past the city only a few miles to the north. Today a massive Amazon fulfillment center occupies one of several industrial parks that a civic group financed just outside of town. Cargill Meat Solutions operates a giant slaughterhouse in that same park. There are also distribution centers there for AutoZone, American Eagle Outfitters, Hershey, and dozens of other brands.

Jobs were again plentiful in the area, which helped resuscitate the local economy. The occupancy rate of the small shops on Broad

Street, Hazleton's main commercial strip—its Main Street—was up around 75 percent at the time of the pandemic. Yet the same easy access to New York (two hours to the east) and New Jersey that drew Amazon and Cargill also attracted workers, most with roots in the Dominican Republic, to the area. Less than 5 percent of Hazleton's population were Latino in 2000. By the pandemic, more than half were. The English and the Welsh and the Irish who worked the mines in the mid-nineteenth century had banned from their unions the Italians and Eastern Europeans who arrived after them. They made the newcomers feel uncomfortable entering their banks and some businesses. Yet the lessons of that ugly bit of history apparently were lost on the descendants of those who were on the receiving end of that discrimination. They, in turn, have given a hostile reception to this newest immigrant group sharing their small city.

Birmania Hernandez—Vilma to family, friends, and customers—was part of that first big wave of Dominicans to arrive in Hazleton. Born in the Dominican Republic, Vilma moved to New York City when she was nineteen. She married Leonardo Reyes, a fellow Dominican native. He delivered soft drinks and other beverages for a local distributor while Vilma cut hair—first for a salon, then out of their Bronx apartment. They were a family of five stuffed into a two-bedroom place on September 11, 2001. Within six months of the terrorist attack that brought down the Twin Towers, the family bought a house in Hazleton. There, Vilma would finally fulfill her dream of owning her own salon in the United States. On Broad Street, only a few blocks from the Altamont Hotel, where JFK had famously addressed a large crowd in the waning days of the 1960 election, she opened Vilma's Hair Salon.

Like TJ, Vilma struggled through her early years in business. Unlike him, she faced the extra burden of prejudice against those perceived as interlopers. Her salon had been open for several years when, in 2006, Hazleton passed what some in the national press cast as maybe the country's harshest anti-immigration measure.

Among other provisions, a business would lose its license if it was caught hiring an undocumented immigrant, and landlords would be fined $1,000 a day if they rented to one. Vilma, who spoke little English, had her citizenship papers but the measure scared off many newcomers to town. What she referred to simply as *"la ordinancia"* cost her salon, she figured, roughly half its business.

The industrial parks on the edge of town, however, continued to flourish, expanding the customer base for a hairstylist eager to grow her business. Vilma added chairs and cutting stations and hired people to fill them. She had eight people working for her when the pandemic hit. Six cut hair, and the other two did the shampooing and swept up around the shop.

Vilma, who turned fifty-four in 2020, was a fit woman with a kind and open face. She wore her dark hair pulled back and had bright, mirthful eyes behind stylish glasses. She spoke to friends still living in the Bronx, who scared her with stories of hairdressers and others in her old neighborhood sick with the disease. There was also the Spanish-language media to frighten her. Still, she could not imagine COVID showing up in faraway Hazleton and resisted the idea that she might have to close her shop, even after the governor banned indoor dining. When three days later Governor Wolf ordered the closure of "all non-life-sustaining businesses in Pennsylvania," she still did not seem able to fully process the news. Her daughter, Genesis, phoned to make sure her mother had heard Wolf's announcement. "She tells me, '*Mami*, the governor says you need to close,'" Vilma said. "And I was like, 'How could this be? It can't be true.'" Vilma had lived through September 11 and still cut hair the next day and the day after that. In seventeen years of business, she had never closed the shop once, even for vacation. "I didn't want to believe it," she said of the shutdown order.

Vilma, despite her disbelief, was relieved to have an excuse to close her shop. Her people hovered over customers at the shampoo bowl and leaned into people's faces while cutting their hair. Health experts at that point stressed the possibility of picking up the virus touching a doorknob or another infected surface. Vilma and her staff started wearing gloves during work. They disinfected their workstations after every client. But the salon itself was a communal and intimate space. Like TJ, Vilma felt disaster coming even if she could not have articulated it at the time. Inside her normally busy shop, her staff were standing around, waiting for customers who apparently didn't feel comfortable stopping by for their usual weekly or biweekly visit to the beauty parlor. The governor only made official what in retrospect had seemed inevitable for at least a week.

"People were scared," Vilma said. "*I* was scared." The coming days did nothing to calm her fears. The industrial parks and Hazleton's connection to New York City meant the virus was spreading rapidly through her small, working-class city. Soon Hazleton was posting what local officials believed were the highest COVID numbers in all of Pennsylvania. A disproportionate share of the essential workers staffing the Amazon fulfillment center and Cargill meat processing plant were Latino, and many were going back and forth to New York. Some in town blamed the area's Latinos for the town's high numbers, just as they would blame them for the curfew the mayor, a Republican, imposed on all residents. On the national stage, Donald Trump was whipping up hate against Asian Americans by calling COVID-19 the "Chy-na virus" and the "kung flu." In Hazleton, Vilma and others were braced for a possible fallout against Latinos.

Vilma phoned each of her eight employees to let them know she had to lay them off. She had always been skilled at filling out government forms and offered any help they might need navigating the state's unemployment system. Two of her people would not qualify for unemployment because they had only recently started to work at her shop. She paid them what she could and felt thankful that she and Leonardo had savings. They would need any reserves to pay the mortgage on the shop and cover other business expenses while they were closed.

Vilma worked at not fretting about her long-term prospects. Yet the hours she burned each week talking to her employees did not help. "They're calling, worried about their future, worried they won't have a job," she said. She did her best to hide her deepest fears but also couldn't bring herself to reassure them that everything would be okay.

"They're asking me, 'When we will be back?' 'What is going to happen?' I had to tell them I didn't know," Vilma said.

"No one knows anything."

* * *

The story of small business has always been one of survival. Technology evolves, tastes change, markets shift, new competitors emerge. Technology rendered blacksmiths and buggy whip makers obsolete, and later video rental stores and twenty-four-hour photo shops. Neighborhoods morph, causing closures, and recessions wipe out businesses that had been limping through good times. The internet created opportunities for entrepreneurs but also represented a new kind of threat. Sometimes pint-sized enterprises are collateral damage when goliaths trample them in pursuit of big piles of money, like when the financial manipulations by Wall Street giants caused the 2008 subprime meltdown. Nearly ten years passed before the small business sector recovered from the resulting deep recession.

Survival has only gotten harder in recent decades. Walmart and other big-box stores popped up on the edges of Main Streets around the country. Chains continue to chew up entire sectors of the economy. Private equity firms and other deep-pocketed investors with national or global ambitions hired teams of MBAs to implement just-in-time inventory management systems and other efficiencies at their restaurants, retail outlets, or manufacturing plants, driving down prices. Meanwhile, the rent a small business paid soared along with insurance premiums and the price of practically everything. Those independents that managed to keep their doors open have stared down Amazon and the internet. They've navigated their way through any number of sweeping trends, including globalization and offshoring. One in three small businesses in the United States fails before celebrating a second anniversary. Half close within five years of opening. Seventy percent are dead within a decade. Floods, hurricanes, fires, broken supply chains, dishonest brokers, banks that discriminate against small businesses in general and those owned by women and people of color in particular: it's a wonder that any small business survives.

Initially, COVID seemed as if it might deliver a temporary blow to businesses large and small—a lousy March and an equally bad April. A few weeks would pass, we'd flatten the curve, and everything would return more or less to normal. "I'd love to have it open by Easter, OK?" Donald Trump said during a Fox News town hall at the end of March. Yet five days later, even Trump, who minimized COVID, acknowledged that the country was looking at a lockdown of indeterminate length.

A coronavirus does not discriminate. Large businesses as well as small would suffer through a shutdown. But unlike their larger cousins, independents tended to have almost no financial buffer, and therefore were more fragile and vulnerable during a downturn. A 2019 study by JPMorgan Chase looked at more than 750,000 small businesses in a cross section of US cities. Half had two weeks or less of cash on hand to cover their bills. The average white business owner had just nineteen days of reserves. Black owners had even less: twelve days of cash in the bank. Added to the worries of many who cared about the fate of the country's small businesses was the concern that the man in the White House was not up to the immense challenges presented by a once-in-a-century global pandemic.

Pundits warned of the carnage to come. Sifting through data from the first two months of the pandemic, the Hamilton Project, an economic policy initiative inside the Brookings Institution, declared COVID-19 "the greatest existential threat to American small business in memory." That spring, some were predicting that one out of every four small businesses would permanently close because of the pandemic. Others put that figure at one in three—or higher if the pandemic stretched into the fall and beyond, as epidemiologists were warning. Those hearing directly from small business owners received an even more pessimistic assessment of their chances. Only 30 percent of restaurateurs thought they could survive if the pandemic lasted four months, according to an April 2020 study by the National Bureau of Economic Research. Only 15 percent saw their operations surviving if it stretched for more than six months. Local chambers of commerce and trade associations around the country surveyed their people. Rural, urban, suburbs, exurbs—it made no difference: more than half the local businesses in almost any poll taken in the spring of 2020 said they were at risk of closing permanently.

Most of the country's brand-name chains and other corporate giants would survive. Generally, they had months of cash reserves and options for raising money should they need it. Even giant retailers that declared bankruptcy in the first months of the pandemic (JCPenney, Neiman Marcus, Brooks Brothers, Ann Taylor, Lane Bryant) arranged the financing they needed to continue operations. For some small businesses, an understanding landlord or mortgage banker was the only thing that stood between them and solvency. By the end of March, revenue at salons like Vilma's and barbershops was down more than 80 percent. One month into the pandemic, clothing and apparel sales were down more than 90 percent, according to an electronic payment firm used by sixty thousand small businesses across the US. Credit card transactions at bars and restaurants across the country were down 43 percent, though that included the transaction volumes at pizza places, Asian restaurants, and others that prepared foods well suited to delivery. Sit-down restaurants like TJ's saw a much steeper drop in their business.

Olive Garden, Applebee's, and Supercuts would be fine. So, too, would the big-box retailers that were permitted to remain open because they sold groceries, pharmaceuticals, hardware supplies, or other essential items. The concern among those advocating on behalf of small business was that COVID would prove a giant opportunity for the economy's bigger players to expand market share. Every abandoned storefront meant a potential spot for another Chick-fil-A, Panda Express, Foot Locker, or Payless. "These are times when the strong can get stronger," the CEO of Nike told a group of financial analysts several months into the pandemic. That was no doubt the mind-set at a long list of retail and restaurant chains for which expansion seemed a constant, even if their top executives were circumspect enough not to articulate that during earnings calls.

* * *

The travails and risks of running a small business are well-known to me and a core part of my childhood. My father was a small businessman his entire adult life. He was just eighteen and a Jewish immigrant from England (a year younger than Vilma when she arrived in New York City) when he and his father set up a business importing bolts of cloth from Savile Row for making men's suits. A decade later, he was running a small manufacturing plant that he'd opened with a partner. That morphed into a pet food company and ultimately a half-dozen pet stores called Pet Pavilion that he owned and operated with my two brothers.

The election of Ronald Reagan in 1980 eventually torpedoed his manufacturing business (they sold mainly to universities and research centers, and Reagan slashed the dollars the government devoted to scientific research). A larger company that bought the pet food business betrayed my father and his partner, offsetting what otherwise would have been a healthy payout. Venture capital played a central role in the demise of Pet Pavilion (he and my brothers didn't have deep-pocketed investors, and a competitor did), though ultimately the business was done in by the recession that helped elect Bill Clinton president in 1992. Pet Pavilion was falling apart when my father died of a heart attack at age sixty-four. In every way that mattered, he was a success, providing well for his family and living a very comfortable life. But always it was hard, and never quite generated the payout he was seeking. My front-row seat on the ups and downs of my father's various businesses gave me the utmost respect for any small operator who survives the treacherous waters they must navigate.

Business owners were generally receptive in the spring of 2020 when I asked to spend time with them. Only in time did I realize that by hanging out with small businesses, I was writing about the broader pandemic. Some, like Joe Lech of Lech's Pharmacy, were essential workers who did not have the luxury of closing their doors even if there were times when Joe, who was in his early sixties, wished he could. Small businesses were on the front lines of the mask wars. They enforced, or did not enforce, the rules requiring a face covering, just as they were the arbiters of social distancing rules. Eventually, there was also the question of vaccinations. Whether they require employees to get vaccinated was not an inconsequential question for a business owner in the food or haircutting business.

Oddly, disasters had become something of a specialty of mine. Water still covered most of New Orleans after Hurricane Katrina in 2005 when my then-employer, the *New York Times*, dispatched me there to find a small business hit particularly hard by the flooding and episodically chronicle its struggle to rebuild. For the next decade, I followed Liberty Bank, which was down to around seventy-five employees after Katrina yet rebuilt itself into one of the country's largest black-owned banks. My portfolio expanded to include the rebuilding of the entire city, where six months after the collapse of the levees, twenty-one thousand of New Orleans's twenty-two thousand businesses were still shuttered. Every homeowner I was talking with found that the decision of whether to rebuild depended in part on the future of small businesses in their drowned-out neighborhoods. Was it prudent to rebuild with no guarantee that the grocery store was coming back, or the pharmacy, or a dry cleaner or gas station? Small businesses didn't determine the fate of a community but New Orleans after Katrina showed that they were central to people's perception of what it meant to live in a place. A few years later, I was writing about the 2008 housing crisis that caused nearly ten million foreclosures in the US alone. I spent part of my time in distressed communities where those merchants of misery that thrive when times are hard (payday lenders, rent-to-own stores, pawnbrokers) had set up shop. Mom-and-pop businesses struggling at the start of the recession invariably went out of business. The payday lenders or pawnbrokers moved in, or maybe one of the big wireless carriers. Otherwise, it was likely that storefront sat empty for a long time.

A dark vision of empty storefronts in her town haunted Glenda Shoemaker, who owns a gift and card shop in Tunkhannock, a town of 1,700 in a rural stretch of Pennsylvania called the Endless Mountains. In April of 2020, sitting alone in her store, Glenda contemplated not only the death of her business, which her mother had started more than thirty years earlier, but also her town and countless ones like it. COVID, she feared, might mean "the end of the American way of life. Small town America will be over as we know it."

It was hard to argue her point. One-quarter or one-third fewer small businesses would have a profound effect on a place, whether a small town, a big city, or a locale of any size in between. A small business die-off of that magnitude would further hollow out Main Streets and retail strips across the country already diminished by the big-box retailers and other chains. The center of gravity in communities would shift even further to a mall anchored by a Lowe's or a Target or a Best Buy. COVID-19 had the potential to change the geography of commerce in the country. Stores and restaurants on Main Streets with character and charm would close; locales would lose what Jane Jacobs in *The Death and Life of Great American Cit-*

ies called "the ballet of the good city sidewalk." Invariably, people would end up eating and shopping on strips that have the generic feel of a service road off the interstate. COVID-19 had the potential to decimate local economies. More dollars going to some faraway corporate office meant less cash recycling through a community. It also threatened a broader economic slowdown. In every community where I spent time, I found people who had been working hard to revive their faded Main Streets, battered and diminished from years of competing with corporate giants. The pandemic added a tragic element to that fight, and an urgency. "If we all close," Glenda said, "what's left for people except the Walmart, a dollar store, or the internet?"

"Diversity" was my watchword when seeking out businesses with which to spend time. That included the type of business, of course, along with the age, gender, and race of the business owners. Geographic diversity was also important and, in these hyperpartisan, fractious times, also political affiliation. I live in New York City, which at the start of the pandemic was home to more than two hundred thousand small businesses. There was no shortage of interesting micro-enterprises from which to choose. But New York hardly seemed typical, as the country's largest city and one of its most expensive. Here, the dominant issue is the exorbitant rent and crazy cost of living. Nigel was my dry cleaner downstairs, but the landlord raised his monthly rent from $8,500 to $13,000 for a tiny hole-in-the-wall barely big enough for a counter and hook to hang a customer's clean clothes. He shuttered his shop, and a local franchise that specialized in low-priced pastries, sandwiches, and coffee drinks moved in. The restaurant I look at from my work window, the Consulate, pays more than $20,000 a month for its space.

I found my small manufacturer in New York: Sol Cacao, a chocolate maker based in an industrial stretch of the Bronx. Otherwise, the businesses that serve as the focal point of this book are in northeastern Pennsylvania, specifically three counties: Luzerne (Hazleton), Lackawanna (Old Forge and Scranton), and Wyoming

(Tunkhannock). Pennsylvania meant looking at small businesses away from the coasts and offered a nice cross section of settings. I liked that northeastern Pennsylvania had neither a major metropolis (I had my own hometown) nor sprawling suburbs but instead something less familiar—what James and Deborah Fallows, in their 2018 book and the HBO documentary *Our Towns*, describe as "small or smaller places" that rarely get noticed unless the media is there to report on something bad. The alpha city in the region, Scranton, may punch above its weight in pop culture, but, with a population of seventy-seven thousand, it's hardly a big city. Hazleton, home to Vilma's salon, was a once-grand city whose population had shrunk to thirty thousand and where many small businesses were suffering because of the lack of workers occupying the office buildings along Broad Street. To the west, in Tunkhannock, I found Glenda Shoemaker and also a small group of independent pharmacists fighting to keep their stores open in places where, without them, people would have to drive as many as fifty miles just to pick up a medicine.

Countless other locales might have served as the setting for a book about small businesses confronting COVID. "Its Main Street is the continuation of Main Streets everywhere," the writer and social critic Sinclair Lewis wrote about the fictional burgh of Gopher Prairie, Minnesota, in *Main Street*, published in 1920. "The story would be the same in Ohio or Montana, in Kansas or Kentucky or Illinois, and not very differently would it be told . . . in the Carolina hills." The plight of Cusumano's in Old Forge was not much different from that of an upscale eatery in almost any other town. The same could be said of Vilma's Hair Salon, or Lech's Pharmacy, or Glenda Shoemaker's gift and card shop in Tunkhannock. But heading into an election year, battleground Pennsylvania promised something else. Only California, Texas, New York, and Florida offered more electoral votes than Pennsylvania, a state Donald Trump had won in 2016 by just forty-four thousand votes—a margin of less than 1 percent. Trump captured 70 percent of the vote in the various counties that make up the Endless Mountains, and Luzerne (Hazleton) and Lackawanna (Scranton) had seen the two largest swings to Trump among Pennsylvania's counties. Luzerne was a so-called boomerang county—one of 206 in the US that twice had gone for Obama but flipped to Trump in 2016. Joe Biden was Joe from Scranton, of course, and Trump even stepped into my narrative when he showed up in Old Forge to give a speech at the big sprawling lumber and kitchen supply warehouse in town. Already I had been talking with TJ Cusumano for several months when, following the speech, the Beast—the heavily armored, oversized limousine that the Secret Service flies around to ferry a president—parked on Main Street, directly in front of Cusumano's. Trump, though, was not stopping for a meal at a high-end Italian restaurant but instead walked into the popular pizza restaurant across the street, run by a reliably Republican set of families. Trump picked up several trays of Old Forge pizza—a unique (and quite delicious) rectangular version with a spongier, lighter crust—for the Air Force One ride back to Washington.

* * *

A note about "small business," a term that has become so elastic as to be rendered nearly meaningless. The federal government preposterously defines a small business as one with as many as 499 employees, which by any measure would be a medium-sized enterprise if we didn't live in a time of mega-businesses with tens of thousands of employees, if not head counts in the hundreds of thousands. (Walmart employed 2.2 million people at the start of 2021, Amazon 1.3 million, and Lowe's 300,000.) Academics and think tankers came up with the term "microbusinesses" because our modern-day economy demanded a new extra-small size designation to preserve this idea of smaller mom-and-pop operations. The businesses I approached had two, five, or ten but never more than two dozen employees.

Hypocrisy is a big part of the story of small businesses in America. They are heroes in the American narrative: rugged individuals who strike out on their own rather than work for someone else. That small businesses are essential to the health of the US economy is one of the few things elected officials can agree upon. Job growth in the US is fueled almost entirely by small businesses and not larger ones, which as a group tend to shed as many jobs as they create. On the left, right, and in the center, politicians repeat the same line: "Small business is the backbone of America." Yet even as they offer those words, they implement policies that favor the large, powerful, and well-connected at the expense of the bantamweight enterprises they supposedly believe are essential. There's a Small Business Administration, but the SBA is the government's smallest cabinet-level agency—by a lot—with an annual operating budget smaller than what the Department of Defense spends in a day. Much of its money ends up in the coffers of businesses with hundreds of employees, if not sometimes enterprises in excess of five hundred people. Even the Paycheck Protection Program, the very rescue plan Congress in the spring of 2020 created to help small businesses survive the pandemic, was rigged in favor of the large and dominant. A long list of larger entities (most famously, Shake Shack and Ruth's Chris) capitalized on a loophole that had been written into the original legislation, causing the funds to vanish before most small operators could access money that the government had ostensibly set aside for them. The money was replenished and the rules changed, but even then the PPP favored these larger small businesses to the detriment of microbusinesses with only a few employees—those often facing the greatest need—and especially those owned by women and people of color.

Yet it's not just the politicians who speak out of both sides of the mouth. Almost all of us are living the same contradictions in relation to small businesses. No matter how much we might cherish this notion of the mom-and-pop shop or family-owned restaurant, the data is unmistakable: with each passing year, we spend a greater share of our dollars with corporate giants. We recognize that small businesses animate our towns and cities. That cute little shop or old-fashioned drugstore or charming family-run restaurant lends a locale personality. Yet we're too busy, so we log on to shop or drive to the parking lot of some retail colossus in search of cheaper prices. We may all agree that independently owned businesses help make up the fabric of our communities, but then people patronize a LensCrafters (part of a $10-billion-a-year conglomerate) or log on to Warby Parker ($394 million in revenues in 2020). We get a bargain cut at a hair-clipping chain or buy cut-rate flowers at a giant supermarket.

I include myself among the hypocrites. There's a CVS two blocks from our apartment on the Upper West Side of Manhattan, but we use Park West Pharmacy, an independent pharmacy a few blocks the other way. Yet we order staples such as soap and toothpaste online because it's cheaper to buy them that way, and I'll confess to more than once dropping into the CVS for a bottle of aspirin or shaving cream. We buy our eyeglasses at one of two independent shops in our neighborhood. But convenience and the 20-percent-off coupons Office Depot ($10 billion in revenues in 2020) regularly sends me keeps me ordering most of my work supplies from them, not the local stationery store six blocks from our apartment. Recently, I purchased a desk at Wayfair, the online home furnishings giant ($14 billion in revenues in 2020). We wouldn't dream of ordering from the Domino's Pizza ($4 billion in revenues in 2020) three blocks from us, but that's more of a culinary decision: why anyone in the vicinity of our place would phone them is a mystery when we've got several alternatives far superior to Domino's, including the excellent Pizza Pete's on our block. Still, occasionally I'll pass by any number of independently owned restaurants to grab a quick lunch at a nearby Chipotle, and, on the road, I'm pleased when I see signs for Panera Bread and Subway. Two things are simultaneously true about my family and Amazon: we try to avoid Amazon, yet we spend an embarrassingly large amount of money at its site. We support the Strand, an independent bookstore that recently took over a failing shop down the street. My go-to alternatives are Powell's Books, an independent shop based in Portland, Oregon, with a large online presence, and ThriftBooks. But our health insurance carrier gives us a dollar redeemable at Amazon whenever we exceed a daily goal for steps, and it seems there are at least two or three Amazon gift cards in the bounty of gifts that arrive whenever one of our boys celebrates a birthday. And, of course, sometimes we want the convenience of one-stop shopping and two-day delivery, which is free because we have Amazon Prime for its streaming service.

Finally, a word about my presence in the book. I started talking with small business operators in April of 2020 but did not meet people face-to-face until that summer, which is when I (sparingly) enter the narrative. I still feared I would be chronicling a great die-off when I hit the road in August. Instead, I found something at once surprising and more interesting and, perhaps, even uplifting.

Chapter 1

Heavy Is the Crown

Glenda Shoemaker imagined someone who really understood business going through her books. The thought made her recoil in horror. "I'd die of embarrassment," she said. For years, J.R.'s Hallmark, a gift and card shop in Tunkhannock, Pennsylvania, had turned a decent profit. Glenda's mother and her mother's partner lived well off the extra cash J.R.'s generated. There was money to invest in the store and sometimes extra cash to salt away for the future. But for the past decade—more or less since Glenda took charge; just her luck—J.R.'s sometimes generated so little cash she worried about covering that month's bills.

Glenda is a sturdy white woman of above average height. She has a broad, open face with blue eyes, a high forehead, and a mane of blonde hair pulled back, lioness-style, giving her the look of an aging British rocker. Long before COVID, she described herself as a "physical wreck" and also an emotional one.

"I'm not going to lie," Glenda said. "We were barely making it before this happened."

Glenda knew she spent too much time contemplating her doom. It didn't help her state of mind that hers was a seasonal business, based on gifts, cards, and special occasions. The spring wouldn't be bad, with Easter and Mother's Day and graduations, but when summer hit, she endured weeks so slow she wondered if she would survive to endure another one. Every year, the fall proved her savior. The store booked nearly half its sales between Thanksgiving and Christmas. But New Year's Day came, and the cycle repeated itself. "I'm still here"—that was her stock answer when anyone asked her how business was going. She'd managed to last another year. To her, that was success.

The year 2020 had started like every other since she took over the store. She had had a strong Christmas to end 2019, but then the spigot turned off. Business ticked up ahead of Valentine's Day, as it always did, but then it was about hunkering down until the spring. People went out more when the weather thawed. Women put away their winter boots and heavy clothes and started browsing the racks of clothes she sold alongside cards and gifts. Customers came not just from town and the farms in the surrounding areas but also from adjoining counties. Her store "carried the gold crown," as Glenda put it, invoking the iconic logo Hallmark stamps on the back of each of its greeting cards. When the weather warmed up, people seemed more inclined to drive as much as an hour or more to J.R.'s to stock up on cards and see what Glenda was carrying in the rest of the store.

J.R.'s was one of the tens of thousands of small businesses in Pennsylvania that temporarily closed when Pennsylvania's Democratic governor, Tom Wolf, ordered the shutdown on March 19 of all "non-life-sustaining" activity. Millions more small shops, restaurants, and other enterprises around the country were similarly shut down as nonessential. Glenda was among those angry that Wolf had closed her down. She had never particularly liked the governor, and that was before she watched him grant himself the right to do whatever he wanted just by declaring something an emergency. She sided more with Trump, who warned the country against overreacting to a virus he assured everyone he had under control. Glenda was also angry at the media, blaring endlessly about a virus landing people in the hospital, if not the graveyard. But her shop was deemed a nonessential business, and she would close, as ordered.

Glenda phoned the ten part-timers she had working for her and told each the same thing: *The governor has shut us down. Don't come into the store until future notice.* And then she sent herself home. Only after a week of watching *Good Morning America* and CNN and Fox did the reality hit her: COVID-19 had the potential to take a wrecking ball to her business. If she stayed home much longer, Glenda realized, she might no longer have a store to return to.

* * *

Glenda was five years old when her father went to work for IBM. The job was in Oswego, New York, a college town along Lake Ontario where the computer giant manufactured specialized equipment for the military. They moved the three hours north from Tunkhannock to Oswego, a place that offered the family a chance at the middle class. "I don't think my father really went to college but he was always good with numbers," Glenda said. "This was his big break."

Yet Oswego served as home for barely five years. Cancer took Glenda's father at the age of forty-two, and mother and daughter moved back home to Tunkhannock, where they had family and friends. Glenda attended the local elementary school and her mother, Janet Shoemaker, took a job as a salesclerk at Fitze's, a clothing store in town. "It's basically been just the two of us since," Glenda said.

Eventually, Glenda's mother secured a better-paying job as a secretary in Clarks Summit, a bigger town in the hills closer to Scranton. Glenda graduated high school but then was in a bad car accident before she could even begin the rest of her life. The femur (the thigh bone) is the thickest and longest bone in the human body and considered the most painful if broken. Glenda broke both. Because of the accident, she's had both knees replaced and a hip replacement, and she's suffered from back pain her entire adult life. "One leg is shorter than the other," she said, "screwing up everything in my body." Glenda was twenty when she finally felt strong enough to work. She donned a "puke brown uniform and ridiculous visor" each day to work at the McDonald's in town. She started as a "lobby girl," a job that had her clearing tables, keeping the bathrooms clean, and mopping the floor. She worked the fryer machines, flipped burgers, and manned the drive-through window, a job reserved for a store's most capable crew members. Eventually, she was running the place on behalf of an out-of-town couple who owned franchises scattered throughout northeastern Pennsylvania.

For some, opening a small business is born of a passion. An animal-loving couple opens a pet store; the art enthusiast opens her own craft studio for children. Janet Shoemaker fell in that other category of people for whom owning a business is more an expression of independence, if not also a way of granting themselves a raise. Doing her research, Janet learned that while Hallmark had its own corporate-owned stores dotted around the country, most that carried the company name were independently owned. The Kansas City–based greeting card giant required no franchise fee, nor did it charge royalties. Instead, carrying the gold crown meant that an operator agreed to a "minimum product footage requirement." At least half of a store's shelves need to be devoted to selling Hallmark products, including greeting cards but also Christmas ornaments, stuffed animals, and a branded line of products stamped with inspirational sayings. What the company called its Gold Crown agreement also included rules about proper lighting and cleanliness. Until J.R.'s, people had to drive to Scranton or Wilkes-Barre if seeking a boutique gift store. Those living in the more rural areas west and north of Wyoming County, in the rest of the Endless Mountains, needed to travel even farther.

Glenda was in her twenties and still working her way up the McDonald's hierarchy when J.R.'s Hallmark opened in 1988. Janet

Shoemaker (the "J" in "J.R.'s") was in her early fifties and, Glenda said, "one of the rare women Hallmark owners at the time." A local Realtor in town, Rachel Raker (the "R"), provided the seed money that let her get started, but it was Janet's to run. To keep expenses down, they rented a narrow storefront in the Towne Plaza, a strip mall three-quarters of a mile from the center of town. The memory of those first years of J.R.'s made Glenda nostalgic for the Tunkhannock of her childhood.

"It's a beautiful little town," she said. "It's just sad what's happened to it. It's the story of small towns everywhere."

* * *

Tunkhannock (pronounced "ton-can-nick") is from the Native American word for "little stream." The center of town is where the Tunkhannock Creek hits the Susquehanna River, the East Coast's longest river and the longest in the US that cannot be commercially navigated. Officially, the state of Pennsylvania has designated this town of 1,700 founded in 1841 a "borough." Hillary Clinton spoke of summer nights there as a girl, licking ice-cream cones and strolling along the river with her grandparents, who had a summer home eight miles away. The town's main commercial strip sits along Tioga Street ("Tioga" is derived from the Iroquois word for "at the forks," where two rivers meet) and stretches for around six blocks. The town's other main thoroughfare is Bridge Street (Route 29), which bisects Tioga and connects Tunkhannock to the boroughs and townships to the north and south. Supposedly, Elvis had been a guest at the Prince Hotel, a once stately three-story brick-and-stucco building at the corner of Tioga and Bridge Streets. Across the street sat the Dietrich Theater, an Art Deco jewel that George Dietrich opened in 1936.

Tunkhannock and the rest of Wyoming County lies tantalizing close to but outside the coal fields that enriched much of northeastern Pennsylvania. The Susquehanna offered a similar tease: good for fishing and swimming and walking along but not for commerce. Agriculture and logging were the main industries there until 1966. That's when Procter & Gamble built a giant plant ten miles west of town. It's there, at a site the company describes as its largest manufacturing site in the United States, that P&G produces its Pampers and Luvs diaper brands, Bounty paper towels, and the packages of Charmin toilet paper that the country was clamoring for in the spring of 2020. Somewhere around 2,200 people work there—nearly 10 percent of the county's total population, said Wyoming County Chamber of Commerce president Gina Suydam, including her husband.

The Dietrich had grown shabby by the time Glenda was a school kid growing up in Tunkhannock in the 1970s. But the theater still showed a movie every night and, to her mind, bestowed an extra bit of glamor on the town. Glenda's grandmother worked as a ticket taker there, "sitting behind this little window out front, like in the big city," she said. The town had two department stores. Fitze's, the shop where her mother had worked, was one of two clothing stores in town. The town also had its own shoe store. "You could dress yourself all year round without leaving town," Glenda said. "And it was really nice stuff, too."

In the 1980s, rumors started about Walmart coming to town. Judy and David Mead, who had purchased Fitze's from an aging Cleve Fitze in 1980, had recently started a downtown merchants' association. The Wyoming County Chamber of Commerce had only recently been created. "But the prospect of a Walmart coming in really raised the heat and gave these organizing efforts a lot more momentum," said Joe Lech, a local pharmacist who served as the chamber's second president. The two groups reached out to those in other towns that had resisted Walmart, or at least tried to, and assigned people the jobs of researching the zoning laws and other legalities. When rumors became requests by the retail giant for building permits, a group sued, citing the environmental impact of so large a store built so close to the Susquehanna. The two business associations, however, chose not to fight. "There was basically nothing we could do about it," Judy Mead said. The environmental lawsuit failed, and construction began on a giant box fronted by a football field–sized parking lot. Like other merchants in town, Mead took a deep breath and kept moving forward. "We tried to go with it as best we could," she said.

The opening of the Walmart in 1994 proved a double blow to the town. Retailers on Tioga, of course, lost shoppers drawn to Walmart's lower prices, but the town coffers suffered as well. Walmart built its store one mile south of Tunkhannock, in Eaton Township. The tax revenues the Walmart siphoned off from the Tioga Street shops benefited Eaton, not Tunkhannock, which saw its revenues shrink. Walmart also did what it could to minimize the taxes it did pay, said Judy Mead, who served as a Wyoming County commissioner for twelve years.

"Walmart has this group of lawyers who go from town to town, claiming they're being overassessed, saying they should be paying less in property taxes," Mead said. Every few years, the same fight took place. Walmart brought in outside appraisers, who invariably concluded the county was overcharging the company, and a fight ensued that might even save this company that booked $549 billion in revenue in 2020 one or two thousand dollars a year in property taxes. (Walmart declined comment.)

Fassett's department store, housed in a handsome Victorian-style building at Tioga and Bridge, was an early casualty of Walmart. A second department store held on longer, but it, too, closed. "All of us were getting squeezed by Walmart," Mead said. To illustrate, she brought up the three-packs of Hanes men's underwear they sold at Fitze's. Theirs was a small operation that could not buy Hanes by the gross, so they relied on a wholesaler in Scranton who bought Hanes in bulk and replenished their supply of underwear as they needed it. Mead glimpsed her fate the first time she walked into the new Walmart. They sold three-packs of Hanes for the same price she paid her wholesaler.

"We kept Hanes in stock for a while because we'd have customers come in and ask for it," Mead said. But she felt as if she were cheating people and wondered if they had the same thought. They sold Woolrich, Northern Isles, and other higher-quality brands the Walmart did not carry, but the sale of jeans and other essentials plummeted. They tried adding a shoe department to Fitze's after the local shoe store closed, "but with all the sizes and styles you have to carry, we couldn't keep up in a small store," Mead said. They dropped shoes and added gift items. The other clothing store in town went out of business, but Fitze's limped along. "We were trying to think of anything that would keep us going," she said.

The town's low point came in the 1990s. The Dietrich had gone dark in the late 1980s, and the building fell into disrepair. The Prince Hotel across the street was also in decline. A town survey conducted a few years after the Walmart opened counted thirteen empty storefronts on Tioga. The beloved Gable's Bakery had shuttered its doors. So, too, had the town's only butcher shop. Stalwarts such as Greenwood's Furniture Store, a fixture on Tioga since 1916, still stood. But people found fewer reasons to come downtown. Allison Schultz, the events coordinator at the chamber of commerce, was a teenager in the 1990s. "When we were growing up, you left Tunkhannock if you wanted to do anything," Schultz said. "It got to the point where you couldn't even eat downtown." In 1960, Tunkhannock had been home to 2,300 people. By the end of the 1990s, it's population barely reached 1,900.

The town battled back. Judy Mead was one of a trio of women behind a Tunkhannock streetscape committee. None of the three had written a grant application in her life, but they managed to raise $1 million. That was enough to plant trees up and down Tioga, fix its broken sidewalks, and add handsome metal lampposts that evoked olden times. Simultaneously, a citizens' group had formed to rescue the Dietrich. They raised money from townspeople for a down payment to buy the property, and then used government grants and donations from small businesses and wealthy individuals in the area to return the theater to its former glory (and also add a second screen to better compete with the multiplexes). The theater's green-and-red neon marquee once again brightened its corner of Tioga in the spring of 2001.

The Dietrich's revival was one critical inflection point for Tunkhannock. The construction of a highway bypass was another. After the Pennsylvania Turnpike was completed in the 1950s, state mapmakers in Harrisburg redirected Route 6 through town. Route 6 was the country's second-longest highway, connecting Provincetown, Massachusetts, to Bishop, California. State transportation officials hoped the rerouting would drive more tourists to the area, but instead the change caused a near-constant traffic jam on Tioga Street, including trucks going to and from the big P&G plant. When construction finally began on a new roadway that rerouted traffic around Tioga, the mood was captured by a headline in the local newspaper: "Drivers Wait 36 Years for Pennsylvania Bypass."

The revival of the Dietrich gave people a reason to visit downtown, and the bypass removed the excuse for avoiding the center of Tunkhannock. Slowly, businesses returned to Tioga, demonstrating that the desire of humans to free themselves by starting their own business seems to require only a healthy environment in which to realize that dream. For thirteen years, Jerry Bogedin made a good living working at the P&G factory, but in 1999, he quit to open a restaurant called Twigs, one block from the Dietrich. A second restaurant, the Tioga Bistro, opened across the street from the Dietrich, inspired, one of its cofounders said, by the "renaissance started by the Dietrich."

The Dietrich added another two screens, bringing the number to four, and created space to hold cultural events, workshops, and classes for kids. More businesses followed: a florist, a barbershop, a martial arts studio, a tattoo shop. The Downtown Deli opened next to the Bistro, and another restaurant called Seasons. Samarios, a popular pizza place in Scranton, opened an outpost in the storefront next to the Dietrich. A diner opened a block away. A store called the Spice Shoppe rented the storefront next to Twigs.

Yet the headwinds confronting small businesses were still strong. Malls and big-box stores mushroomed in and around Scranton and Wilkes-Barre, both around forty-five minutes away by car. Chains moved into Clarks Summit, twenty-five minutes away on Route 6, and the internet devoured an ever-larger portion of the retail market. Weis Markets, a regional grocery chain, opened a giant supermarket just south of town, also in Eaton Township. Walmart built an even larger box across the road from its original store. The opening of the new Walmart Supercenter in 2011 meant a second giant grocery store in the area, along with a garden center, an expanded pharmacy, and a small furniture department. A Dollar Tree moved into the old Walmart and a Dollar General opened across the street from J.R.'s Hallmark. Besides the McDonald's in town, there was also a Pizza Hut, a Subway, a Burger King, a Dunkin' Donuts, and a Perkins, a chain that promotes itself as "the nation's leading family restaurant."

The recession sparked by the dot-com crash hurt sales in the early 2000s, as did the deeper recession that followed the 2008 financial crisis. The Susquehanna River flooded in 2011, causing extensive damage to many downtown businesses. "The water came in through both the front and back [doors]," said Erica Rogler, the Dietrich's executive director. Once again, the community pitched in to save the theater. Three hundred volunteers gutted the building and raised money for reconstruction.

Mead and her husband closed Fitze's in 2012, shortly after the flood. In retrospect, Mead said, they probably should have called it quits three or four years earlier. "We kept thinking times were going to turn around," she said. She called the closing "a sign of the times," adding, "Small businesses were going out and it was our turn." A CVS had moved into town, as had a Rite Aid. Like Mead, Joe Lech, of Lech's Pharmacy, also said he had held on longer than he should have before closing his pharmacy in town not long after

Fitze's shut down. Other shops closed, including the town's three grocery stores. The last of the three to close was Brick's Market, a good-sized store with a meat counter and large produce section that for decades had stood on the east end of the downtown shops. Bricks had employed close to forty people when it shuttered its doors a few years before COVID.

"That's just how the times are," one shopper told a Scranton television crew that had come to report on the closing. "The moms and pops are going away."

* * *

COVID, of course, would prove another threat to those mom-and-pop stores. On the second-to-last day of 2019, a thirty-four-year-old emergency room doctor working at a hospital in Wuhan, China, logged on to an online chat group to share what he knew about a mysterious respiratory virus spreading through this city of eleven million in central China. Initially, this new pathogen was considered only moderately contagious, much like the SARS virus, which had been contained by isolating those showing symptoms. Yet medical professionals quickly recognized that the asymptomatic could serve as super-spreaders. By the time the Chinese government restricted travel from Wuhan, on January 21, 2020, it was too late. An estimated seven million people had traveled from the city since the first patient showed up at a hospital with symptoms. On January 30, the World Health Organization declared this novel coronavirus a global emergency. By then, at least ten thousand people in twenty countries had been infected, including the United States.

Public health officials in the United States sounded the alarm. Members of the Obama administration's National Security Council had created a sixty-nine-page guide that it had helpfully titled "Playbook for Early Response to High-Consequence Emerging Infectious Disease Threats and Biological Incidents." Yet rather than follow this detailed step-by-step guide, Trump and his people pursued a policy of wishful thinking. The president repeatedly floated the idea that the virus would disappear with the warmer weather ("A lot of people think that it goes away in April with the heat," Trump told a group of governors) and dismissed COVID as another "hoax" advanced by political foes looking to derail his re-election. Near the end of February, the CDC's top respiratory disease chief warned that a widespread outbreak in the US was inevitable. "Disruptions to everyday life may be severe," she said, including school closures. Trump, however, knew better. The next evening, during a meeting at the White House, he said, "One day—it's like a miracle—it will disappear."

By March 3, hospitals in parts of Italy were overwhelmed and select cities went into lockdown. In the US, that was Super Tuesday, a night dominated by Joe Biden, who increasingly seemed like he would be Trump's foe that November. Two days later, Trump traveled to Scranton to troll a victorious Biden in his hometown. A hastily arranged town hall sponsored by Fox News was held at the Scranton Cultural Center—what would be the president's last campaign appearance for a couple of months. The first question was from a self-described undecided voter, who asked the president about his plan for combating the coronavirus. Instead, Trump spoke of his "rave reviews" and declared, "We've done a great job."

Cindi Heyen was among those attending that night's town hall. Heyen ran a small, Scranton-based pool supplies company with her husband and lived in Old Forge. She was active in the National Federation of Independent Business, one of several major advocacy groups that declare themselves the voice of the country's small business operators. The Trump campaign had reached out to the NFIB in search of bodies to fill seats. Heyen was a bona fide undecided, a Republican who believed in low taxes and deregulation but was troubled by Trump's comportment ("he says such stupid things"). She was eager to find reasons to vote for Trump but primarily what she remembers of the night was the president's cavalier attitude, and that of event organizers, toward the virus itself. "They bunch us all together in line," she said. "No one told us to stand apart from each other." The CDC was already urging people to practice social distancing and avoid shaking hands. "But there was Trump onstage, shaking hands with people, acting like nothing was going on," she said.

Chapter 2

Governor Richie Rich

S tanding at a narrow lectern adorned with the Pennsylvania state seal, Tom Wolf, a seventy-one-year-old Democrat in his second term as governor, sought a reassuring tone. It was March 6, 2020, and Pennsylvania had just recorded its first two cases of the coronavirus. Bearded, bespectacled, and bald, with his tie slightly askew, Wolf looked and sounded like the academic he had once dreamed of becoming. He was a dull speaker but a calming presence with a just-the-facts, restrained style. Five weeks earlier, the governor explained, his administration had set up an Incident Command Center in the state's Emergency Management headquarters, a three-story glass-and-brick building a few miles from the Capitol in Harrisburg. There, they'd been "working diligently to develop a plan for when this virus inevitably arrived in Pennsylvania," he said.

The country's Centers for Disease Control's *Field Epidemiology Manual* dictates that an elected official's primary job in an epidemic is one of reinforcing the main communication objectives as public health officials lay them out. That was Wolf's approach. He gave advice that would become standard in the coming weeks. To mitigate the spread of COVID-19, he counseled, wash your hands for as long as it takes to sing the "Happy Birthday" song two times. Cough into your elbow. Stay home if you feel sick.

Wolf shared his podium with Secretary of Health Dr. Rachel Levine. She repeated the same wash-your-hands message and reassured people that the administration was on top of the problem. Behind the scenes, though, Levine had been monitoring the spread of COVID with growing concern. She had been warning Wolf and his staff that this highly contagious virus might require that they suspend large indoor gatherings and shut down businesses. Standing at the podium, however, the only hint either gave of the extraordinary measures they were considering was Wolf's announcement that he had signed a statewide disaster order that granted the executive branch broad powers to issue orders "as is deemed necessary to cope with this emergency situation."

* * *

Tom Wolf was born in the borough of Mount Wolf—a place named for his great-great-grandfather. This son of privilege and old money attended an elite boarding school in eastern Pennsylvania that counts US senators and cabinet secretaries among its alumni (and also Trump's two eldest sons, Don Jr. and Eric), and then went on to Dartmouth. There was a two-year stint in India for the Peace Corps, and then, after earning a master's at the University of London, a doctorate in political science at MIT. Instead of teaching, like he had planned, he returned to Mount Wolf. Just as four previous generations of Wolfs had done, he eventually went into the family business: making and selling kitchen and bath cabinets.

There was something quaint and old-fashioned about the Wolf family business that invoked a different time. Each summer growing up, his grandfather hosted a dinner for the employees of Wolf Supply Company. Wolf and his cousins were enlisted to serve as car valets. Wolf's father implemented a profit-sharing program that set aside 20 to 30 percent of the company's earnings each year to be split among the workers. In this patrician family business, the new generation bought out the previous one if they wanted the keys to the operation. Back in his ancestral home, Wolf worked as a forklift driver and then managed a local True Value hardware store. Seven years passed before his father apparently thought he was ready to take the helm. Wolf and two cousins took over as copresidents of a company they renamed the Wolf Organization and, over the next twenty years, they grew it into a giant of the kitchen-cabinet business that generated nearly $400 million a year in revenue.

The former Peace Corps volunteer never gave up on community. He championed an effort to clean a local waterway, and he pushed for the reform of the area's underperforming public schools. He raised money for the nearby public radio station and chaired the board of trustees at the local college. When he became more serious about political office, he and his wife, Frances, became major political donors in the state. Over a five-year period, the pair gave more than $250,000 in campaign contributions to Ed Rendell, the state's Democratic governor.

Apparently, the next generation of Wolfs were uninterested in running a cabinet supply company. Wolf was approaching sixty years old when he and his two cousins reached out to a Boston-based private equity firm. A leverage buyout was arranged in 2006 that burdened the company with tens of millions of dollars in debt but made Wolf and his two cousins rich. Each pocketed around $20 million and kept an 11 percent stake in the company. One year later, Rendell named Wolf his new secretary of revenue. Eighteen months after that, Wolf stepped down as the state's revenue chief to run for governor in 2010.

That first try at governor ended before Wolf even made his candidacy official. The 2008 global financial meltdown battered a business that specialized in building supplies, and the ensuing credit crisis threatened its existence. He and his cousins still owned one-third of the Wolf Organization, and there were also the ramifications for his political career of a five-generation operation declaring bankruptcy largely because of the huge debts it had racked up when they had sold the company. Wolf returned to his namesake business. Meanwhile, a Republican named Tom Corbett moved into the governor's mansion in Harrisburg.

Wolf was a sixty-five-year-old political neophyte when he entered the 2014 governor's race. His statewide name recognition was near zero, and he favored the bland, careful language of the business executive he was. His advantage was the money he had made selling the family business. Wolf and his wife chipped in $10 million for a primary campaign that played out largely on TV sets across the state. Long before rivals could even consider television commercials, Wolf bombarded Pennsylvania with a series of ads that longtime political observers would declare some of the best they had ever seen. The first cast him as a kid from central Pennsylvania who, after starting there as a forklift driver, transformed the family business into one of the country's largest kitchen cabinet suppliers. The ad included a snippet of workers cheering the company's profit-sharing program. In another ad, he proposed a new fracking tax to help a school system decimated by the austerity measures that Corbett had implemented. Wolf won the primary with 58 percent of the vote and that fall became the sole Democrat to defeat a sitting Republican governor in 2014. Speaking at his inauguration, Wolf declared, "I'm going to be an unconventional governor."

* * *

On March 11, the World Health Organization officially declared the coronavirus outbreak a global pandemic. The number of confirmed cases in the US crossed one thousand. The NBA suspended its season that day, and Tom Hanks announced that he and his wife, Rita Wilson, had both tested positive for the coronavirus. The stock market fell by more than 5 percentage points. That night, Donald Trump addressed the nation from the Oval Office. "My fellow

Americans," he began—and for once he may have sounded presidential. Wash your hands frequently, he counseled. Wipe down frequently used surfaces and avoid large gatherings. "If we are vigilant," he said, "the virus will not have a chance." Yet at a press conference two days later, on Friday the thirteenth, Trump was anything but vigilant. He shook hands and leaned into people's faces for a word. Standing at the podium, however, he had good news for the country's small businesses. He proclaimed the COVID-19 pandemic a national emergency. By doing so, he freed up tens of billions in low-interest emergency loans to help small businesses hurt by the virus's spread.

The country began shutting down. Disneyland closed its theme parks; the NCAA canceled its annual March Madness college basketball tournament. Colleges began sending students home. At that point, the goal was to slow the transmission of the virus—to "flatten the curve," as if in a matter of a few weeks we could contain this plague spreading through our communities. That weekend, Dr. Anthony Fauci, the head of the National Institute of Allergy and Infectious Diseases, warned during a television interview that hundreds of thousands could die in the US unless every American did his or her part to blunt the impact of the coronavirus. At a press conference that same day, Trump contradicted his chief infectious disease expert. "It's something we have tremendous control over," Trump said of COVID.

In Pennsylvania, Tom Wolf ordered the schools closed on Friday the thirteenth. For two weeks, the governor said, there would be no in-person learning for the 1.7 million children attending public or private schools in the state. That would give his emergency response team time to "reevaluate and decide whether continued closure is needed." That Monday, he ordered every restaurant and bar in the state to close its doors to customers and "strongly urged" nonessential businesses to act before officials found it "necessary to compel closures." He asked people to cancel any gatherings they had planned in the coming eight weeks.

The Pennsylvania Liquor Control Board ordered every liquor store in the state to shut down indefinitely by nine p.m. on Tuesday—St. Patrick's Day. The next day, the state registered its first death from the virus. On Thursday, Wolf returned to the Emergency Management headquarters. His request that businesses close their doors became an order. The governor shut down all "non-life-sustaining businesses" across the state.

The speed of Wolf's response ranked him in the middle of the pack among governors. He was earlier than most in his decision to close the schools but lagged in initiating other sweeping emergency orders. California, the country's most populous, was the first state to do the unthinkable and issue a stay-at-home order on the same day Wolf shut down all non-life-sustaining businesses. More than thirty states had imposed a statewide stay-at-home order before Wolf, on April 1, did the same in Pennsylvania. People could take a walk or a run if they maintained social distancing, and of course were free to leave the house to visit a pharmacy or go to a job, but otherwise they were to remain at home.

There was no guidebook to help the state grapple with a pandemic. "It's not like the governor and his people could say, 'Oh, here, let's go to page 47 and see how we handle business closures,'" said Gene Barr, the longtime head of the Pennsylvania Chamber of Business and Industry. "They were feeling their way through this like we all were." The first time the governor laid out the state's criteria for business closures, he distinguished between "essential" and "nonessential." Yet when the state made it official that it was shutting down most businesses, the criteria shifted to those that were "life-sustaining" and those that were not. Pharmacies and food stores were life-sustaining, but hardware stores? Garden supply centers and nurseries? A bike shop? "I understand they're figuring this out while they're going," said John Longstreet, the head of the Pennsylvania Restaurant & Lodging Association, "but the governor's information was very, very cloudy."

The first flurry of decrees the governor signed in the early days of the pandemic inadvertently shut down every hotel in the state—a confusing, potentially catastrophic edict when people were instructed to shelter in place. Had his members followed the governor's order as written, Longstreet said, "they would have been forced to evict tens of thousands of guests across the state." The big hotel chains had their contacts in Harrisburg, who could reassure them that a fix was in the works. The smaller operators, however, were on their own as they tried to make sense of contradictory orders. The state quickly corrected its mistake, but, Longstreet said, "that should have foreshadowed our experience dealing with this governor."

Presumably, the Wolf administration also did not intend to favor big-box retailers over the state's small businesses. But that was the upshot of its shutdown order. A Walmart could remain open because it operated a pharmacy and sold groceries, yet virtually every small retailer in Pennsylvania was forced to lock its doors. "I was on the phone, sometimes ten times a day, with people in the state government trying to get this changed," Gene Barr said. Others were waging the same fight. Maybe the rules could be rewritten to allow that small florist to do curbside delivery or permit retailers selling the same goods as a Walmart (a garden center, a furniture outlet, a jewelry store) to see customers by appointment. Yet the order stood as written. Pennsylvania was hardly alone. Other governors, too, imposed COVID-related restrictions that favored large chains over small business owners. In the unequal fight between small and large businesses, and in the midst of a national crisis, the largest of the giants once again had an advantage.

*   *   *

Wolf had been a businessman for most of his adult life. The hope among those working for the various groups representing business in the state was that Wolf's experience running the family business would give them an inside track through the pandemic. They looked next door to Ohio, where Governor Mike DeWine, a Republican, created a task force heavy with businesspeople who could provide him guidance through the crisis. Other governors of both parties did the same.

Yet Wolf's style was to lock himself inside the governor's office with a small coterie of key aides and department heads, and then inform the state about the decisions they had reached. The restaurant and hotel association represented more than twenty-six thousand food and drinking establishments around the state, as well as Pennsylvania's fifteen hundred hotels—two industries particularly hard hit by the pandemic. Yet weeks passed before the association's CEO, John Longstreet, was able to secure thirty minutes on the governor's calendar.

Gordon Denlinger felt similarly rebuffed. Denlinger was the Pennsylvania director of the National Federation of Independent Business. Denlinger had served six terms in the state legislature before going to work for the NFIB, an organization whose membership tilts heavily Republican. "I think a lot of the missteps resulted from the fact that they didn't draw on people who actually knew something about the businesses they were impacting," Denlinger said. "All of our offers of help were met with silence."

The Pennsylvania Chamber of Business and Industry's Gene Barr was the exception. His organization represented a full range of enterprises, from the largest chains and manufacturers operating in the state to its smallest shops. Barr stood onstage with the governor when he announced the first business shutdowns in Pennsylvania, and later felt like a prop.

"I thought it was appropriate even though I knew what he was asking of businesses," Barr said. "But at that point, I thought, 'Hey, it'll be a few weeks, we'll let this thing burn out and we'll get back up and running.'"

—————

Chapter 3

Fearless

TJ Cusumano was just a baby when his parents got into the grocery store business. His father, Tom Cusumano, had been a pipe fitter who worked on power plants, condominium complexes, and other oversized projects. He was a tradesman earning $60 an hour back in the 1970s, but he would also be on the road for weeks at a time. He had already missed too much of his life with his two daughters, who were eleven and twelve years older than TJ, and he did not want the same thing to happen with his newborn son. Approaching fifty, he worried about his knees in a job that required a lot of kneeling, lifting, and climbing. Around his son's one-year birthday, Tom Cusumano joined his wife, his sister, and his sister's husband in opening Rossi's, an Italian market just off Main Street in Old Forge.

The early years of Rossi's were profitable ones for the two families. TJ's uncle, Larry Rossi, had trained as a master butcher after leaving the marines, and had worked in the meat departments in supermarkets around the area. Their meat counter would specialize in prosciutto, pepperoni, and capicola (also called gabagool), among other Italian delicacies, along with Uncle Larry's famous *porchetta*, a special cut of pork slow-roasted in apple juice and other flavors. Tom Cusumano had been a cook in the army. He made homemade ravioli, pizza, sauces, and other prepared dishes for the store. They sold fresh mozzarella, pepperoncini, and Italian breads, along with olive oils, dried pastas, canned tomatoes, and other imports from Italy. Toni Cusumano, TJ's mother, did the books and, along with his aunt Cathy, worked the register and more or less took care of everything else.

"Everything was going great," Toni said, "until it wasn't."

TJ was in the seventh or eighth grade when his parents and his aunt and uncle let themselves be seduced by the idea of an expansion. The family that owned the big supermarket in the center of town wanted to sell, and a group from the Philadelphia area reached out to them. "They wanted us to take over this big market and join their co-op because then all this big stuff would happen for us," Toni said.

The lawyer they retained to negotiate the deal terms asked them if they were sure they knew what they were doing. Their monthly rent would balloon to $20,000 a month. They would also be responsible for maintenance on the building, along with the insurance and property tax payments. The two families would own their new store, but, under the agreement, they were ceding much of their autonomy to the co-op. They also were required to sell the original Rossi's. "We just saw dollar signs and thought, 'We can do this,'" Toni said. "We got greedy."

They kept the Rossi name—they were now Rossi's ShurSave Supermarket. They still had their deli and meat counter, where people could buy Uncle Larry's cured meats and Tom's lasagna and baked ziti. But now they had a full grocery store's worth of products to sell. Where they didn't have $50,000 worth of inventory at the old Rossi's, they now had $400,000 sunk into the goods sitting on the shelves of their supersized market.

"Sell a can of soup and congrats, you've made nine cents," Toni said sarcastically. The registers rang up tens of thousands of dollars in receipts each week, yet they seemed to be paying bills faster than the money was coming in.

Almost from the start, they were at loggerheads with their new partners. "It came down to a bad rapport," Tom said. The two families were giving it everything they had, but their out-of-town overseers were constantly on them about their disappointing numbers. "It got to the point they wanted to get rid of us and put someone else in," Tom said. The feeling was mutual. "We just wanted out from everything," Toni said. A dozen years after they had decided to gamble on a much larger store, a shotgun deal was arranged. Rossi's ShurSave was now Ray's ShurSave, and the Cusumanos were left feeling embittered.

"The guy who bought big Rossi's," Toni said, "he knew our backs were against the wall."

"They knew we were in a position that we'd have to say yes, no matter what the amount was," Tom said.

"We got screwed," said Toni. It gave comfort that the store did not perform any better under the new owner, who gave up after a few years, yet what its closure meant for Old Forge saddened them. The store and adjoining oversized lot have sat empty ever since, leaving the town without a supermarket. People needed to travel to the Price Chopper in Taylor, Gerrity's (a local chain) in Moosic, or Weis (a much larger regional chain) in Duryea.

"Sometimes I feel maybe I shoulda stuck with the union and stayed a pipe fitter," Tom said. "But I liked that life, especially when we had the original place. I made less but I was home with the family and it's nice—people still talk about the old Rossi's."

*　*　*

Toni Cusumano never wanted a son, a fact she let her obstetrician know at TJ's birth. "I was expecting a girl like the first two," she said. "So when the doctor said, 'It's a boy,' I'm like, 'What? Oh, no. I only like girls.'" She named him in honor of her father, whom she adored. Toni had married a Tom, but she made sure everyone knew that her father, Tom Joseph, was TJ's namesake. The baby must have grown on her, because friends of TJ's growing up thought she treated him like a prince. "I forced myself to fall in love with him," Toni said.

TJ was a kid you remembered. Lou Moriano is a close friend of his dating back to kindergarten at the town's only parochial school. Their teacher that year was a hard-edged nun who Moriano described as having a mean streak. "I was terrified of her," he said. "All the kids were. But TJ wasn't afraid. He stood up to her." Moriano described TJ as "fearless," though he was no match for his teacher. She gained the upper hand, Moriano recalled, "by threatening that if TJ didn't listen, he would never see his mother again."

The third grade is the first time Moriano remembers TJ cooking a meal for him: a steak he rolled in pepper and other spices and then cooked in a skillet. TJ was all of eight years old. "It was actually delicious but it was the spiciest thing I've ever eaten," Moriano said. The meals became a regular thing. "He'd invite us over to his house and he'd cook for us. In grade school," Moriano said.

TJ had been the most adventurous of eaters as a child. On the way to a restaurant, Toni warned her kids not to order steak or lobster because money was tight. TJ ordered the rack of lamb, which was as expensive. "He was seven," Toni said. He grew up eating the cured, spiced meats they sold at the store, including soppressata, a dried salami which is made by boiling the head of a pig and then chopping up all the meat, skin, and the tongue. Pat Revello, at Revello's Pizza on Main Street in Old Forge, remembered an eight- or nine-year-old TJ. Every other kid at that age is ordering pizza or maybe pasta. Yet a pint-sized TJ ordered tripe, which is made from the stomach lining of a barnyard animal. Another friend from his parochial school days remembers TJ at ten making the tripe for St. Mary's annual fundraising picnic.

His parents were terrific cooks, yet it was his grandma Jenny (Giovanna), his mother's mother, who TJ described as his biggest influence as a cook. With his parents both working at the store, the bus dropped TJ off at his grandma Jenny's house at the end of the school day, and that's where he would stay through dinner. "She had this big old TV in a huge brown cabinet and loved watching the cooking shows," TJ said. Jenny especially loved Julia Child and a show called *Great Chefs of the World*, but also watched *Yan Can Cook*, *The Galloping Gourmet*, or whatever else was on. "It was almost on like background noise," he said.

There was a proper dinner every night. Cusumano's namesake and Grandma Jenny's husband, Tom Joseph, had died years earlier, and TJ's sisters were already in college or traveling. But his grandmother's brother, a practicing doctor in town, joined them for dinner practically every night. "She had terrible eyesight and would have me read the recipes to her," TJ said. She would quiz him as she cooked, asking him to convert cups to ounces to teaspoons, as if she needed his help.

"She was this great cook who could make something out of nothing every night," Toni said of her mother. "And there'd be TJ on a chair next to her, watching."

Jenny cooked all the old-world recipes she learned as a girl. "She was 100 percent Italian, her parents right off the boat," TJ said. She shared with him stories of killing a hog at the start of every winter and curing the meat. "They'd use bricks and pieces of wood to suppress—that's where you get soppressata—the sausages and the hams they were curing to get all the moisture and air out of them," he said. But Tom Joseph was Lebanese, and Jenny taught herself Middle Eastern cooking. From Jenny, TJ learned how to strain a yogurt for a cucumber salad and cook with spices such as za'atar and sumac.

"She had such a lovely artistry to her cooking," TJ said. His other grandmother, Grandma Annie (Anna), worked as a seamstress at a garment factory, making pants. But for forty years, she worked nights and weekends making Old Forge–style pizza at one restaurant or another in town. She was still working in the kitchen at Revello's at age ninety-two.

"My mother taught a lot of people how to make pizza," Tom Cusumano said.

TJ was fifteen or sixteen when he got a job bussing tables at Brutico's, an upscale Italian restaurant where his grandma Annie had made pizzas. A year later, TJ moved to a newer Italian restaurant opened by a brother-sister team in the next town over. The sister had worked for Michelin-star chefs in New York and took a creative approach to the menu that TJ found inspiring. "She was deconstructing Italian food and putting it back in ways that made it completely fresh and original," he said.

TJ left Old Forge for Lynn University, a small private school in Boca Raton, Florida. After a year, he transferred to Champlain College in Burlington, Vermont, another pricey private school far from home. There he studied marketing (or, as he joked when writing his bio for a Twitter account he set up while still in school, "I study marketing and skiing!") and spent a summer in New York, working for an advertising agency in Tribeca. "I really liked it there and they really liked me," TJ said. A job after graduation seemed possible—if he wanted it.

Through college, TJ worked kitchen jobs to cover his expenses. That's where his real education was taking place. In Florida, he worked at Mario's Osteria, a popular restaurant whose kitchen staff was almost entirely Haitian, including the head chef. "He was this incredible teacher and such a good guide for the restaurant," TJ said. "Everybody looked up to him and just loved him." TJ started as a dishwasher, but the high turnover in the kitchen staff that would later plague him as a restaurant owner worked to his advantage as a young man. Within a few weeks, he was cutting vegetables and trimming meats, impressing the head chef with what he was able to do with a knife. Soon he was working as the kitchen's expeditor—a kind of air traffic controller responsible for all the moving parts moving efficiently. As expeditor, TJ was stationed at the "pass" (the window where the waitstaff picks up finished dishes), placing him at the center of the chaos inside a restaurant serving one thousand meals a night. ("If I do three hundred meals [at Cusumano's], I'm having a great night," TJ said.) Mario's had fourteen cooks and two full-time pizza makers, along with a waitstaff of between twenty-five and thirty.

Every night was bedlam, TJ said, "and I absolutely loved it."

In Burlington, he worked at an Italian restaurant outside of town called La Villa. Again, he felt inspired by the chef he worked under. "He was very methodical in everything he did," TJ said. "He had a process for everything, from keeping his herbs fresh to every dish on the menu." He worked under that chef's tutelage for three years, until graduating from Champlain in 2009.

"Basically, I cooked my way through college," TJ said. "And drank."

TJ's life might have taken a different turn if not for the ordeal of making Rossi's work as a ShurSave Supermarket. He was thinking about moving to New York or some other big city and working in advertising. He contemplated law school. But while home on break near the end of his time at Champlain, Toni sat him down for a talk about Rossi's. "I'll never forget my mother telling me, 'We're broke; we might have to close the store,'" TJ said. His parents had sacrificed so that he could attend an out-of-state private college. So he would do the same for them. After graduation, he moved back home and spent the next couple of years working as a store manager at Rossi's ShurSave. His pay, he told his parents, would be room and board. He picked up shifts at restaurants in town for spending money. Mostly he worked as a bartender rather than as a cook, which TJ can't explain except to say it was a lot more fun working the bar at Cafe Rinaldi, talking and drinking with friends and regulars, than working in someone else's hot kitchen.

TJ met Nina, a fellow Old Forger a couple of years younger than him, because they seemed destined to collide with each other. Her grandfather had been friends with TJ's grandfather, and a cousin had suggested to him that he should marry her before they had even encountered each other. Nina had started working as a busser at Cafe Rinaldi when she was sixteen and continued to work as a bartender and then a waitress while going to school at a nearby Penn State campus. The two met at Cafe Rinaldi but fell in love, both agree, during late nights at GI's (as in GI Joe's), a bar that had originally been the Café Cusumano before an earlier generation of Cusumanos decided to change its name.

TJ's parents were pushing him toward law school. "My father really didn't want me getting into a small business," TJ said. By then, however, TJ had made up his mind. As long as he could remember, TJ pictured himself making his living making food. "Cooking was like the only thing I was passionate about," he said. Falling in love with a waitress seemed to cinch the deal: he had someone who could oversee the front of the house. They were engaged in 2013, and that same year they bought the building that would house Cusumano's. The restaurant had been open for nearly a year before they took time to get married.

* * *

Cusumano's regularly closed on Mondays and Tuesdays. So people were off when the governor announced he was suspending indoor dining throughout the state. Yet half the staff, it seemed, showed up that Monday or Tuesday to help. "They didn't hit the time clock, they just got to work, helping us clean out the coolers, and shut down things, whatever needed to be done," TJ said. He liked to think of the people who worked for him as family, but he was self-aware enough to know that they might not see it that way.

"It was nice to see they feel the same way about my business," TJ said. "Our employees really stepped up in a time of crisis."

TJ is on the short side, standing maybe five feet, six inches tall. Broad-chested, he has the fireplug build of an NFL fullback and what his friend Lou Moriano described as "massive hands." He has short brown hair, brown eyes, and a large nose, along with a broad, winning smile. He had no quarrel with the governor's emergency order shutting down indoor dining around the state. He felt relieved to be closed when an invisible virus was starting to infiltrate his community. A man in the neighboring county had died from COVID on the Sunday that TJ served his last indoor meal. A couple of days after that, his county, Lackawanna, confirmed its first COVID case and then, shortly after that, its first death. By the end of March, dozens had been infected across what locals call the Lackawanna Valley. The lockdown order struck him as sensible.

"This was a measure about saving lives in our community," he said. "I looked at it like doing my part."

Cash flow was TJ's big worry in the first days of the shutdown. "Flatten the curve" was the phrase on everyone's lips. That might take several weeks, but he figured that many of his customers would need more time before they felt comfortable mixing in public again. Meanwhile, like restaurant owners everywhere, TJ stared down a stack of invoices from suppliers, which sat atop his stack of bills. Fall behind in paying those and that could be the start of a restaurant's death spiral: vendors would refuse to supply the restaurant. Unless he had cash coming in, he wouldn't have enough to cover those already on his desk along with the mortgage and his other monthly bills. He needed to survive the next five or six weeks and then hope that pent-up demand delivered a strong May.

TJ had no idea what to expect when they opened that first Wednesday after the governor shut down indoor dining. He offered his full menu for takeout, but he recognized that the food he served in his restaurant generally did not travel well. A customer who spent $15 for a starter of Clams Cusumano or much more than that for a filet or salmon in a reduction of basil and fresh-squeezed orange juice expected it to arrive hot on a plate, not soggy in a bag they themselves needed to pick up and drive home. He looked into joining third-party delivery services such as DoorDash and Grub-hub but rejected the idea when he learned they siphoned off as much as 30 percent of an order, and they still didn't solve his main problem. His risottos and linguine with clam sauce, two big sell-ers at the restaurant, were prepared to be eaten immediately after they had been cooked. Being an Italian restaurant in Old Forge meant selling rectangles of Old Forge pizza, which are sold by the "cut" (slice) or "tray." Come that Wednesday, he knew he would be selling pizza, especially in Old Forge, where a couple of trays of pizza on a Friday night seemed part of the town's heritage. But he was also sure that he had way too much food on hand given the circumstances.

TJ thought a lot about Rossi's in the earliest days of the pan-demic. "That's basically where I grew up," he said. He stocked the shelves on weekends when he was old enough and remembered the exhilaration he felt the first time his parents trusted him to work the register. "So when I saw I had all this food and had nobody coming into the restaurant, my first instinct was to sell it," TJ said. People in town needed food to stock their pantries. Picking items up at his place would allow them to avoid shopping at a crowded market. He could dodge the spoilage that has been the bane of ev-ery chef-owner since the opening of the first restaurant. If nothing else, they could use the cash.

The staff that had volunteered to help bagged onions, zucchi-nis, peppers, potatoes, and carrots, and set them on a table beside breads, lettuces, and other perishables. They set out much of the dried pastas they had on hand and bagged flour and other essen-tials. Just as his father had done for all those years at Rossi's, TJ filled quart containers with his "Sunday gravy" (a basic red sauce his family ate over their Sunday-night pasta) and other sauces, along with salad dressings and grated cheeses. Nina shot a short video once everything had been laid out and, to spread the word that they had groceries for those who needed them, posted it on the restaurant's Facebook page. Barely forty-eight hours after learning of the governor's shutdown order, they had set up a pop-up market in the covered patio behind the restaurant.

They priced the produce and other staples based on what they had paid. They made a little on the sauces and other prepared foods, but the main money generator was alcohol. Perhaps for the first time ever, Pennsylvania's restaurateurs had good things to say about the sticklers at the state's liquor control board, who had agreed to relax the rules on alcohol sales. Restaurants and bars in Pennsylvania were granted permission to sell unopened bottles of beer and wine. Inside Cusumano's makeshift market, six-packs and bottles proved particularly popular given the temporary shutdown of the state's liquor stores.

* * *

The night of the governor's order shutting down indoor dining, TJ and Nina got to talking about staffing. Many of the people who worked for them may have felt like family, but the restaurant was still a business and one suddenly in crisis. They needed to lay off most of the employees they had on payroll. "What choice do we have?" TJ asked. They talked about spreading the pain: offering at least a shift or two to anyone desperate for the work.

Cusumano's has two kitchens: a large prep kitchen downstairs, where they had their pizza ovens, and a smaller kitchen upstairs off the main dining room. How much food they would need to prep was anyone's best guess, as would the staffing they might need preparing takeout orders once they opened at five p.m. TJ asked his pizza guy to work and also two line cooks. And Brenda, of course. Brenda Roscioli had been a waitress at Cusumano's since the first day they opened in 2013. Brenda had worked at the restaurant's impromptu store, as had other family and friends who showed up to help, and she would help with takeout. Nina stayed close to the phone, taking orders and credit card numbers. Brenda and Shawn Nee, the guidance counselor at Old Forge High and, in normal times, a part-time bartender at the restaurant, ran food down from the upstairs kitchen to an impromptu staging area they had set up in the Cellar, and then to the cars when customers phoned to say they were outside. The restaurant's baker and also Nina's mother, Michele Scavo, also pitched in.

TJ dreaded the conversations ahead with people he would need to lay off. To his relief, the calls did not go as he had imagined they would. His sauce chef, Angie Garzon, then thirty years old, lived with her aunts, one of whom had a pulmonary disease (COPD) that made her vulnerable to a virus that scientists already understood caused breathing problems. Ang herself was a diabetic, which also placed her in a higher-risk category. She preferred to stay home rather than work. Nina was hearing the same from the servers. One waitress was a woman in her sixties with a preexisting condition. Another lived with her mother, and a third was younger but still had concerns about her health. All three preferred to stay home. Jimmy, one of the dishwashers, was an ex-con who lived above the restaurant. He told TJ he was happy to work or happy to sit on his couch collecting unemployment from the government. The other dishwashers and the bussers were high schoolers or commuter college kids who lived with parents, who seemed to prefer they didn't bring the virus home with them after working in the restaurant.

"A lot of people basically told us they didn't want to come back until everything was all clear," TJ said. He imagined the angst other restaurant and bar owners across the country were having. There were nearly fifteen million people working at restaurants at the end of 2019, making the industry the second-largest private employer in the country (health care ranks first). It did not matter whether a cook or a waitress or a dishwasher worked for a big chain or a modest-sized Italian restaurant in Old Forge, Pennsylvania. All at once, most of them were without work. "I didn't have to go through the pain of having a meeting and saying, 'I have to lay all of you off,'" TJ said. "People sort of took that burden off me."

TJ knew the majority of his people would be okay. Most of the waiters and waitresses had another source of income. None seemed at risk of going hungry or falling behind on the rent. He also wasn't worried about the bartenders. The bartenders occupied a universe of their own inside Cusumano's and seemed chosen primarily to add character and cachet to the restaurant. "For me the job was more social," said Bob Mulkerin, the former mayor. All were part-timers and included not just a former mayor and the local guidance counselor but another teacher at the school, a lawyer who worked for the city, and TJ's cousin Anthony Cusumano, who had a day job laying concrete as a member of the Laborers' Union. Mulkerin was a tech specialist with Prudential Financial in Scranton. "I'd feel guilty if I was taking money away from anyone," Mulkerin said.

The people TJ was worried about were the people he worked next to every day preparing the food: his kitchen staff. They were the blue-collar workers who barely had any savings and probably worried about making the rent on April 1. The country's restaurants and catering halls, especially its kitchens, are a place for those who might not have the education or disposition for white-collar work, or even the front-of-the-house personality needed to deal with the guests. "I love the sheer weirdness of the kitchen life: the dreamers, the crackpots, the refugees, and the sociopaths," Anthony Bourdain famously wrote in the 1999 *New Yorker* article that launched his media career. Those who can stand it get a job at a fulfillment center or the Walmart; the nonconformists who don't want to wear that kind of corporate straitjacket often find work inside a professional kitchen. "The last refuge of the misfit," Bourdain wrote specifically about kitchens in America, "a place for people with bad pasts to find a new family." Some may dream of one day becoming a chef, but most just seek a day's pay for a day's work. Today's restaurant kitchens are like the mines and steel mills and giant manufacturing plants until most of them closed—except, unlike all those auto and steel and miner jobs of yore, the average line chef in the US working in one of these modern-day factories earns probably in the low $30,000-a-year range (Cusumano's pays slightly more than that). It was a motley crew who worked at Cusumano's, where the boss insisted that people show up on time each day but otherwise looked the other way when they snuck outside to get stoned, listened to their music too loud, or wore their hair long. "About all I really care [about] is that they do the job right," TJ said.

* * *

At the top of the hierarchy inside Cusumano's kitchen, just below TJ, stood Angie Garzon—"Ang" to her coworkers. Ang had been working at Cusumano's for just under two years at the time of the pandemic. She was initially confused by the order shutting down indoor dining. "I had no idea the government could do that," she said. Reality only hit her when Pennsylvania closed down hair salons several days after the governor ordered restaurants to shut down indoor dining. Ang was no one's idea of a fashionista. She dressed in baggy flannel shirts and loose-fitting pants and a baseball cap over her closely shorn hair.

"I don't know why," she said, "but for me, them closing down hair cutting places made it more real."

Childhood had been hard for Ang, who eventually came out as a lesbian. She had lived all over the place before settling in Scranton: south Jersey, the Jersey shore, assorted towns in Pennsylvania and Texas. "Divorced parents" was her explanation for all the moving around. She was shy and withdrawn and spoke in a clipped fashion that sometimes gave an edge to her words. If she seemed most comfortable in a hot and hectic kitchen, tending to eight or ten pans at once, that's because kitchen work was all she had known. Her first job was at a Burger King when she was in high school in New Jersey. She worked at a mom-and-pop hoagie shop in a different part of Jersey and then went to work for a place known for the twenty varieties of Buffalo chicken wings on its menu. She was living in Scranton and in her midtwenties when she decided she needed a job with health benefits. That's how she ended up working at a

Red Lobster, a job she liked until she grew tired of a corporate-run kitchen. If she had an issue, "I had to go to the shift manager, who had to go to the head manager, and then who knows who the head manager needs to talk to before something's resolved," she said.

TJ was happy to talk with Ang when she had contacted him two years earlier. "I love to hire people from chain restaurants," he said. "They have that corporate discipline. They know they have to show up when they're expected." TJ told Ang what he had told others who came from an assembly line kitchen. She had skills to build upon, but at Cusumano's she would do a different kind of cooking. The assembly line restaurants supplied their cooks with containers of premade sauces and spice packs shipped to them by corporate. "Here we make everything from scratch," TJ told her. "Sauces, our breads, all our desserts, everything." Suddenly, benefits no longer mattered. They were useless anyway, she told herself, given the deductibles and copays. She started as a pizza maker and moved her way up. "I got to be a real cook and to boot I get better pay," Ang said. She also appreciated the freedom of working in TJ's kitchen. "If I have an issue here, I talk to TJ and we resolve it." Less than six months after she arrived at Cusumano's, the kitchen's pasta cook left. The guy working salads took his place, letting Ang move to the salad station. Less than a year later, she occupied the top spot, sautéing foods to order (the chicken marsala, the shrimp risotto) and making the sauces that topped the meats she had thrown onto the grill.

Ang worked herself into knots thinking about what she would tell TJ the first time they spoke after the lockdown. He had been good on his promise and taught her a great deal about cooking. The two mixed it up occasionally, but invariably that was because the house was packed, orders were backing up, and TJ is a perfectionist. "Everyone can be a pain in the tush sometimes, but TJ's a real good guy," Ang said. She worried that, in a crisis, she was letting down someone who had been very good to her.

Yet since she was fifteen, Ang felt she had put work ahead of everything else in her life. She came in last minute because someone failed to show up for work that day and stayed late because the boss needed help. This time, though, she vowed to put herself first. She took a deep breath and phoned TJ to break the news. In a rush, she told him about her aunt's respiratory troubles and her own medical issues and explained that because both her aunts were working from home, she felt that as the third member of the household, it was best that she also stayed home.

"He was real understanding," Ang said. She quoted TJ as telling her family is family and her health is her health. "He told me there was a job waiting for me when I felt comfortable coming back and then we both kind of just hung up."

* * *

Joey Graziano, Cusumano's high-energy pizza maker, came to work on the Wednesday afternoon following the shutdown order, just as he had been doing for the prior fifteen months. Despite the pandemic, he said, "I never really stopped working." A rail-thin thirty-one-year-old, Joey lived in town with his parents, ages sixty and sixty-three. They were relatively healthy, as was he. "Honestly, I was never scared," he said. He felt grateful for the job. He had worked in the kitchen of almost every restaurant in town. "[Cusumano's] is by far the best place I've worked," he said.

TJ figured he needed help both doing prep work during the day and at the stove during the dinner hour. He turned to the cooks who had been with him the longest, Levi Kania and Brian Mariotti. Brian, from Old Forge, had started at Cusumano's as a busboy when he was fifteen. "I had no great dream of working in food," Brian said. "I was kind of just looking to get some money." Four years later, at nineteen, he was the restaurant's pasta cook, and still as uncertain about what he might do with the rest of his life. Brian was a willowy white kid with long reddish-brown hair. With a takeout-only menu, Brian handled a lot more than pasta orders.

"What I love about Brian," TJ said, "is he does whatever needs to be done."

Levi had been at Cusumano's for even longer, dating back to practically the start of the restaurant. He, too, was a son of Old Forge. Levi was fourteen when he started working there as a busboy in 2014. "His father comes to me, 'Will you straighten my fucking kid out?'" TJ said. "He tells me, 'He needs a job, he needs some kind of direction, he's fucking terrible.'" Soon Levi was working as a dishwasher, which brought him inside the kitchen. He learned pizza making from a childhood friend of TJ's named Brian who was happy to teach a kid eager to learn. Levi's promotion came when Brian died tragically from an overdose, another victim of the opioid epidemic. At fifteen, Levi was the restaurant's main pizza maker. By sixteen, he was sometimes working the salad or pasta stations in the main kitchen.

Levi, who was twenty years old at the start of the pandemic, lived at home with his parents. He took what he called a "two-week break" after the governor shut down indoor dining but then joined the restaurant's skeleton crew. He was not worried about COVID. His mother worked with the elderly, but he lived in the basement and had his own bathroom if quarantining became necessary. "I took a financial hit because the hours weren't the same but I had a little money saved up, so I was okay," Levi said.

The newest member of Cusumano's kitchen crew was Sha-Asia Johnson. Sha-Asia, who was twenty-two years old when COVID hit, had been born in Queens, New York, but her mother was what she described as a "wandering spirit." Over the years, they had lived in Charlotte and Indianapolis, among other places, before moving back to New York City. There, her mother worked as a cook for a local chain that specialized in soups, sandwiches, and salads. Sha-Asia was sixteen when she, her mother, and her younger brother moved to Scranton, and one year later, they relocated to Old Forge. This last move took some getting used to, she said. Sha-Asia is black, and Old Forge predominantly white, but for her the biggest challenge was getting used to living somewhere other than a city. "It was real, real quiet like a small town," she said. "Moving here kind of threw me off." By that point, Sha-Asia had attended six high schools. She graduated from Old Forge High, her seventh, two years later than other kids her age, she said, "because of all that moving around."

Sha-Asia enrolled in a two-year culinary program at Lackawanna College in Scranton in 2019. She credited her mother's experience as a cook in New York as her inspiration. Sha-Asia took a job at a Sonic Drive-In, where her bosses rebuffed her requests to work in the kitchen. She worked as a waitress there until that Sonic went out of business and then took a job at McDonald's, where the same thing happened. They trained her in the kitchen but then assigned her to the drive-through window. "I told them, 'I'm going to culinary school to do cooking, can I at least flip some burgers or something?'" Sha-Asia said. "But they kept me on drive-through the entire time."

One requirement of her program was a stint of at least 180 hours working in a professional kitchen. She had started at Revello's Pizza next door to Cusumano's, but barely a week into working there, the owner, Pat Revello, learned that an internship did not mean free labor, as he had thought. More as a favor to Revello than out of any great need, TJ welcomed her to his place. "I got in my hours just before COVID," Sha-Asia said.

TJ maintained that just by watching how a person holds a knife, he could get a good reading of their skill level in the kitchen. Sha-Asia, he realized, was a novice. But she impressed him as a quick learner, and she was eager to improve. "I don't care what they've been taught in the past. I can teach them kitchen skills," TJ said. "What I'm looking for is their work ethic and their desire to learn." Maybe just as important, Sha-Asia had the right disposition to work in his kitchen. TJ was no Gordon Ramsay and working at Cusumano's was not ripped from an episode of *Hell's Kitchen*—TJ, for instance, had never told someone he wished they'd jump into an oven to be rid of them—but good-natured hazing was part of the job. He would give her a big bag of onions to chop or red peppers to clean and shake his head over how long it took her to complete. "Slow-Asia," he dubbed her. Rather than take offense ("I *was* slow," Sha-Asia said), she laughed along with the others.

"TJ roasts everybody," she said. "He's always making us laugh. He's really a funny guy." Sha-Asia was partway through the internship when TJ fired his salad person, who didn't own a car and therefore couldn't reliably make it to work each day. TJ gave the job to Sha-Asia.

Sha-Asia's internship ended near the end of February. But TJ had pulled her aside just before her time at the restaurant was supposed to end. "I like what I see," Sha-Asia quoted him as saying. "You've got a job here if you want." He was paying her $9.50 an hour compared to the $10.50 an hour she had been earning at McDonald's, but to her the decision was an easy one. "They were all upset at McDonald's when I gave my two weeks' notice," Sha-Asia said. "But I'm like, 'They're actually letting me cook in a kitchen.'"

Sha-Asia understood when TJ called her to say he needed to lay her off. With no indoor dining, TJ had things covered. Like much of the country, Sha-Asia went home to wait things out.

Chapter 4

The Coronavirus Comes
to Hazleton

Jeff Cusat, the mayor of Hazleton, started his first business when he was eight years old. Cusat bought baseball cards by the crate and, with his brother, created complete sets they sold to the other kids at school. With success, they branched into Beanie Babies and other collectibles. Cusat was still in high school when they rented a small storefront to house a business called Cusat's Cards and Collectibles. He also worked at the family restaurant, Cusat's Cafe, which his great-grandparents had opened in 1936.

"I started cooking there when I was twelve and cooked there through high school and college right up to when I took office," Cusat said. The card store closed, but over the years, he had worked any number of side hustles to make money beyond the family restaurant. He bought tickets in bulk for concerts and sporting events (Phillies baseball games, Penn State football games) and then sold package deals that included transportation on the buses he booked to cart everyone back and forth. He owned a couple of self-pay parking lots and a small travel agency. In 2013, he opened

Cusat's Grill inside an off-track-betting parlor an hour away. He was a partner in a local telemarketing firm that booked time-shares and hotel rooms. Even as mayor, he still worked behind the stove on Friday and Saturday nights—at Rocco's, the restaurant he opened in 2018, in the middle of his first term.

"I love to work. That's all I do is work," Cusat said.

He had run for mayor in 2011 but dropped out once he divined that he was being used as a pawn by people out to punish the incumbent. Cusat is a heavyset, bespectacled white man who sounds like he could have grown up on the streets of South Philly. He's a clunky speaker who garbles his syntax. Yet he also had pit-bull determination. At a young age, he realized that because there were people a lot smarter than he was, he'd have to work that much harder to succeed. He ran again for mayor four years later and won, and then was reelected to a second term that began in January 2020.

The same Pennsylvania codes that dictate that Tunkhannock is a borough and not a town designates Hazleton a "third-class city." That's based on population, which has fluctuated between a high of thirty-eight thousand in 1940 and a low of twenty-three thousand in 2000, but it's still a bad joke to locals. The city had peaked in the 1960s, if not the 1930s, and the past two decades had been marked by racial tensions. The city's finances were in such bad shape Cusat had the dubious honor, barely one year into his first term, of declaring Hazleton a "distressed city." Emergency loans were arranged, its debt restructured, and at least the city could afford to pay its essential bills. A city council hostile to Cusat was replaced by a new, friendlier one. "2020 was supposed to be a fresh start," Cusat said.

* * *

Hazleton's first COVID-positive case was reported on March 21. "Citizens of Hazleton," Cusat began a press release he put out that day. He couldn't say much about the case so instead took that moment to remind everyone that they were in this together. The state's secretary of health, Rachel Levine, worked for a Democratic governor, and Cusat is a Republican. Years earlier, Levine had transitioned from a man to a woman; she ranked as one of the country's highest-profile transgender officials. Republicans who mentioned her name tended to do so with animus, a rancor that deepened with COVID. Yet Cusat's job as a public official was to echo the message put out by health officials, so he quoted her in the release: "As Dr. Levine has said, 'Pennsylvanians have an important job right now: stay calm, stay home, stay safe.'"

Cusat is not one for halfway measures. During his first term, he completed hundreds of hours of training for certificates in fire training and safety, emergency management, and code enforcement because he thought that would make him better at his job. In the earliest days of COVID, Cusat was spending every night on the phone with doctors and others in health care, learning what he could about the disease and hospitalization rates and its R-naught number, which captures how contagious an infectious disease is. "I was on the phone until eleven or twelve each night, and then waking up at six a.m. and doing it all again," he said.

One big worry was what Cusat called "dual residents." Those were people whose families lived in New York or New Jersey yet worked in Hazleton. They relied on one of a few van services that ferried people back and forth. "It says it right on the side of the vans where they go: the Bronx, Paterson [New Jersey]," Cusat said. "They're making twenty or thirty trips a day, back and forth with people in close quarters for a couple of hours, breathing the same air and then going to work in these massive factories that employ hundreds of workers." Halting the vans, he knew, was critical.

Hazleton had recorded a dozen more positives within a week of that first case. Cusat understood that his small city was looking at a crisis. With his help, a local hospital set up testing tents around the city and outside the industrial parks. They documented three hundred infections after only two days of testing. Ten days later, that number swelled to more than one thousand positives. "Almost 5 percent of our population was sick with COVID at the same time," Cusat said. Hazleton, a town once known for its coal and textile mills, was gaining attention for its alarmingly high rate of infection. "I truly believe there was a moment when we had the highest numbers in the country," he said.

A mayor, Cusat learned, does not have the power to shut down an interstate transportation company, even temporarily. Instead, he summoned the heads of the bus companies to his office, where he persuaded them to voluntarily suspend their routes. He also discovered that though his powers as mayor of a third-class city may be limited, he did have jurisdiction over the sidewalks and streets. At the end of March, Cusat issued an emergency declaration imposing a citywide curfew. Starting at eight p.m. each night and until six a.m., people were not allowed on the city's sidewalks or its streets unless traveling directly to or from work. He prohibited public gatherings of more than four people during the day and declared it temporarily the law in Hazleton that people remain at least six feet apart from non–family members.

"I don't take this power lightly," he declared, but instead cast it as "another step in a fight against the current enemy." His decree would remain in effect for five days. To extend the law beyond that, he needed the approval of the Hazleton City Council.

*   *   *

Vilma Hernandez was happy to stay locked inside and keep her distance from everyone outside of her immediate family. Still, she felt frightened. As the virus spread and more people caught it, the media coverage shifted from cases to deaths. The US had recorded two hundred deaths on the day the governor shut down Vilma's salon. Two weeks later, deaths had surpassed six thousand.

"Once they started talking about how people were dying from

it is when you begin to say, 'Wow, this is bad,'" Vilma said. Other salon owners might express envy of their counterparts in places such as Sweden, which did not shut down its hairdressers (or gyms, restaurants, bars, or cinemas), but not her. The mayor and governor were telling her to stay inside and not go to work, and she was only too happy to comply.

Remaining calm was Vilma's first challenge. "When you are in despair, you get frustrated easily," she said. "Where is everything going to come from? How am I going to pay the light bill?" She thought about disconnecting the electricity at her shop. But she wanted to leave herself the flexibility to reopen as soon as the state gave her the all clear, and she worried that turning off her utilities would result in a delay in turning them back on. "The government didn't say how long until we could open again," Vilma said. She heard rumors but nothing else.

Vilma counted herself among the fortunate. Leonardo was a maintenance worker for the local school district. He, too, was home, but he had been furloughed. That meant, unlike workers who had been laid off, his health insurance would continue unchanged, so that would be one less set of expenses to worry about. Presumably, his unemployment would kick in soon. Both knew people who were working in a warehouse or fulfillment center and only wished they had the option to stay home and collect unemployment.

She also did not feel completely isolated, like so many. She had Leonardo and also three grandchildren to look after because day care had been temporarily suspended and their parents needed to work.

Yet even with those distractions, Vilma worried constantly about the shop she had spent the prior seventeen years building. A lot of her time was spent on the phone, calling longtime customers to see how they were surviving and asking if there was anything they needed. Several, it turned out, had lost people to the virus or had caught it themselves.

"Honestly, it was a very sad time," she said.

*   *   *

Hazleton began as a resting stop along a well-traveled trail that connected the Susquehanna Valley to the Lehigh Valley, to the south and east. This dirt pathway dating back to the early 1800s and used by horse riders, stagecoaches, and carriages eventually became Broad Street, where Vilma Hernandez opened her beauty salon two centuries later. The city sits on a plateau atop Spring Mountain nearly 1,700 feet above sea level—a higher elevation than any other city in Pennsylvania. The area was thick with hazel trees, which would have given the town its name if not for a clerk's spelling error. When incorporated some fifty years after it was first settled, the name was entered as Hazleton, and the error never corrected.

Coal put Hazleton on the map—more specifically, anthracite coal. In northeastern Pennsylvania, people invariably say "anthracite coal" rather than just "coal." Plain coal is the common bituminous variety found in most other coal regions of the country. The softer bituminous coal created the sooty, acrid haze that turned the skies dark during the Industrial Revolution. Anthracite coal is a harder, more lustrous variety of coal with fewer impurities that burns more efficiently and with very little smoke. Anthracite fired the giant blast furnaces that powered the country's steel mills and helped to establish the US as a global industrial powerhouse. Anthracite also heated homes throughout the northeast. And 95 percent of it was found in this wedge of northeastern Pennsylvania, with Hazleton more or less in the middle.

The story of anthracite coal is the tale of most every industry. A tiny sliver of coal barons grew preposterously wealthy while the miners, who risked their lives working underground, struggled to provide for their families. Miners from England, Scotland, and Wales were followed by the Irish in the 1840s, who came to the US to escape famine in their own country. Economic hard times in Eastern and Central Europe spurred another wave of immigrants in the 1880s, which the mine owners worked to their advantage. New immigrants from Italy and Poland and Slovakia were desperate for work, allowing coal operators to pay what an anthropologist who studied the region called "near-starvation levels." Conditions inside the mine grew more dangerous, but the injured or dead were easily replaced by those in line behind them. In 1897, several hundred Polish, Slovak, and Lithuanian immigrants organized a protest to demand equal pay and better conditions. Holding an American flag, they marched on a mine in Lattimer, a patch town a couple of miles outside of Hazleton. The local sheriff and the posse of 150 he had deputized fired into the mass of unarmed men, killing nineteen and seriously wounding at least thirty-six others.

A downtown started to form. In 1891, Hazleton became the third city in the United States to have its own electrical grid. Textile mills opened in the area, spurring more growth. Several brick office buildings were built, reaching eight or ten or more stories. Well-known vaudevillian acts played at one of a half-dozen theaters in Hazleton, and boxing matches were held in town. At its peak, central Hazleton was home to three hotels and four department stores. Broad and Wyoming Streets were thick with restaurants and bars, along with jewelry stores and men's and women's clothing shops.

Coal production slowed down around World War I. Other fuel sources such as oil and natural gas became more popular and the coal in the region became harder to mine and therefore more expensive. Coal had a last gasp around World War II but then began its slow decline, until the area's last mine closed in 1972. Unemployment in the area hit 23 percent. "Gone to Jersey" was the expression back then when a neighbor abandoned the town for somewhere that offered more opportunities.

In the mid-1950s, local merchants and civic leaders created CAN DO (Community Area New Development Organization) to bring jobs to Hazleton. Their plan was to raise money to buy land, construct a shell building, and see if they had any takers. No one was moving to Hazleton to build on empty land, but maybe they could attract businesses to the area by offering newly built quarters, complete with utilities. CAN DO raised $14,000 through a community-wide "dime-a-week" program and several hundred thousand dollars more selling shares in their venture.

A foam rubber company was the first to move to the area. A maker of highway trailers and metal cabinets followed. The expression inside CAN DO back then was "rinse and wash." After luring a business to town, they sold the building either to the company itself or a group of investors. They then used the proceeds to buy more land, extend the roads and utilities, and build another spec building for the next manufacturer. The city began advertising in *Plants Sites & Parks* and similar publications to attract businesses to fill its properties. Continental Can moved into one of the industrial parks CAN DO built. So did the DeSoto car company and Smith Corona, the typewriter giant.

"We were going great on manufacturing, at least in the '60s and '70s," said Kevin O'Donnell, who ran CAN DO for twenty-six years, until his retirement at the end of 2020.

Competition between locales grew fiercer. That was driven home when the city lost out to Tennessee in its bid in the mid-1980s to convince General Motors to build its giant new Saturn plant in the area. Tennessee offered GM tax breaks and other incentives that Hazleton couldn't match. After Saturn, the city teamed up with Wilkes-Barre, Pittston, and other northeastern Pennsylvania towns and hired a PR firm. The world, however, was changing. Manufacturers preferred right-to-work states in the south and southwest that were less hospitable to unions. Increasingly, large businesses were moving their operations offshore in search of lower wages. Distribution centers were on the rise, however: regional warehouses that the giant retail chains, big manufacturers, and suppliers established so their product was closer to their customers.

CAN DO had an unwritten rule: no distribution centers in its industrial parks. Warehouse jobs paid significantly lower wages than manufacturing, and opportunities for advancement were limited.

The problem, Kevin O'Donnell said, "was that everything coming down the pike was distribution and none of it was manufacturing." There was Interstate 80 and also Interstate 81, an important north-south commercial route that lay seven miles north of town. A study was commissioned in the 1990s to rationalize the shift in strategy and, lo and behold, warehouse jobs were now deemed good for Hazleton. The city rebranded itself the "Crossroads of the East" and sold itself as an ideal locale for any business seeking to establish a distribution center in the Northeast. AutoZone, American Eagle Outfitters, and Michaels, the arts-and-crafts chain, were among those businesses establishing distribution hubs in one of CAN DO's industrial parks. The rise of the internet created the need for fulfillment centers on the edges of big population centers that ship products to customers in their vicinity. In 2008, Amazon opened its Hazleton logistics center, a humongous facility that employs as many as two thousand workers during the holiday season.

Hazleton's proximity to the twenty million or so people living in the New York metropolitan area was a draw for prospective businesses but also for potential employees. Starting pay for a job in the industrial parks in the 2000s was low at $10 or $12 an hour ($20,000 to $25,000 a year) but sometimes the job included benefits, and the cost of living in the area was far lower than in the city. The same rent that Vilma Hernandez and Leonardo Reyes paid for a two-bedroom apartment in the Bronx let them buy a spacious, four-bedroom house with a backyard in Hazleton. Leonardo took a job at Cargill, which moved into one of the industrial parks at the start of the 2000s, and Vilma, after helping to set up their home and get the kids settled in school, went searching for a storefront to rent.

* * *

Small business has always been central to the country's founding narrative. "From its colonial beginnings through most of the 19th century, ours was overwhelmingly a nation of farmers and small-town entrepreneurs—ambitious, mobile, optimistic, speculative, anti-authoritarian, egalitarian, and competitive," wrote Richard Hofstadter, the eminent historian. The blacksmith, apothecary, and general store proprietor embodied the self-reliance essential to the American experience. "What astonishes me in the United States, is not so much the marvelous grandeur of some undertakings, as the innumerable multitude of small ones," wrote Alexis de Tocqueville, the observant Frenchman who traveled the United States in the 1830s. Personal independence and the collective prosperity it creates seem almost as integral to our collective sense of American exceptionalism as giving birth to the world's first democracy. Indeed, starting in the latter decades of the nineteenth century, there have been those who have described a robust small business sector as not just the backbone of the US economy but essential to a functioning democracy. A political system under the control of a small cabal of corporate titans is an unhealthy one. The self-reliance (and diffused power) of the small business class is a bulwark against the state.

Yet there's a flip side to that story. The US has also given the world a long list of conglomerates that suck so much out of the economy there's little left for the small business owner. Chains dominate vast segments of the American marketplace. As a result, and despite what Americans might think about themselves, there are a lot of countries across the globe where a higher portion of the population are entrepreneurs who have started their own business. In the Dominican Republic, where Vilma Hernandez grew up, there was no Supercuts where she could find work. Unlike in the US, there was not a range of regional and urban chains where she could drop off an application. There weren't even many options for renting a chair in someone else's salon. Working as a hairdresser almost demanded that she be entrepreneurial.

Vilma's is the immigrant's story of small business in the United

States, where opening a shop or dry cleaner or small hotel is a path into the middle class for newcomers to our shores, if not also generational wealth. At the start of 2020, one of Vilma's sons worked as an administrator at Bard College. Her other son had a good job with an electronics company and was raising three kids (a fourth would be born during COVID). Vilma's daughter, after earning her master's, took a job with the federal corrections department.

But Vilma's tale also punctures this notion that the American entrepreneur is superior, or more advanced, or somehow more special than their counterparts across the globe. The Dominican Republic has a much higher per capita rate of small business operators than does the United States, as do Indonesia, Kenya, Bolivia, Nicaragua, Australia, Estonia, and Italy. "In the Dominican Republic, everybody's an entrepreneur because they have no choice," said Franklyn Nunez, who owns a three-person auto repair shop on Broad Street. He moved to Hazleton in 2006. "People open their own small shop," Nunez says of the Dominican Republic. "They sell stuff on the street, they do business out of their house, selling clothes, this and that." Small business might be the backbone of America, but then it's also the backbone of virtually every nation on Earth.

Vilma grew up in Santo Domingo, a city of three million and the capital of the Dominican Republic. Her father was a mechanic and her mother a teacher. One of seven kids, she described her circumstances as "modest." The public schools in the DR allow kids to study for a profession. At around fifteen, Vilma started taking cosmetology courses. With her family's help, she opened a one-chair salon of her own. She was eighteen years old.

She chose to leave the DR with her mother, an older sister, and her two younger brothers in 1986. She was nineteen years old and calculated that she could live a better life in the United States. She arrived with a high school diploma but spoke only Spanish. Her brothers enrolled in public school and learned English; both would graduate college. "We needed to go out and work," Vilma said of her and her sister. Her children claim she understands more English than she lets on, but she has never grown comfortable speaking the dominant language of her adopted land.

Their first year in the country was spent in Queens with Vilma's grandmother and an aunt, both of whom had moved to the States ahead of them. One year later, Vilma was in the Bronx and in a brief first marriage that led to the birth of her son Brian. Soon thereafter, she met Leonardo Reyes. The two married in 1989, when Vilma was twenty-three. (She kept her maiden name as is customary in the Dominican Republic.) The couple had two children over the next four years, Ivan and Genesis. Starting her own salon did not seem feasible when she was so new to the country and in a city as pricey as New York. Despite her prior experience running her own shop, she put in the one thousand hours of coursework that New York requires to earn a cosmetology license and took a job at a hair salon in Manhattan, thirty minutes from their home by train. Whenever there was an opportunity for her to learn a different aspect of hair care, Brian said, his mother signed up for it.

"My mom is always like, 'We've been given an opportunity here, we're doing everything right,'" Brian said. "Her attitude was, 'I'd rather prolong things than deal with the consequences.'" At some point, his by-the-book mother went through the process of becoming a naturalized citizen. The family attended church every Sunday, and the kids attended parochial school, though that decision was more about her kids getting an affordable private education than about religion.

"We were fortunate," Genesis said. "We didn't have to endure the public school system and all its problems."

Brian described the West Bronx neighborhood he grew up in as "working class." Genesis stressed its dangers, as did Ivan. "There were drugs, guns, all of it," Ivan said. "It was the wild, wild west there." They lived in an apartment building across the street from a police station, which provided a shield, but mainly the three kids had their mother watching over them. "She sniffed us a mile away if we were doing something wrong," Genesis said. "She was strict. Very strict."

Vilma gave up the job at the Manhattan salon to be closer to home to look after her kids. Even when he reached high school, Brian said, she wouldn't let him ride the train by himself. Instead, she walked him to the bus stop and then took his brother and sister to school. "I'm always telling my mom, 'You love us too much,'" Brian said. To bring in extra money, Vilma ran a small day care out of the apartment. On Saturdays, she transformed their living room into an impromptu beauty salon, complete with chair, mirror, and blow-dryer.

"It was always fun," Brian said. "My mother is this very charismatic, joyful person and people like being around her. And so by proxy people were really nice to us." What impressed Genesis was the steady stream of customers and the wad of cash her mother had earned by the end of the day. "My mother is a businesswoman," Genesis said. "She's always been all about the Benjamins."

September 11 and the attack on the World Trade Center was the inflection point that changed the course of their lives. Like a lot of New Yorkers, they were deeply unsettled by the terrorist attack. "After the Twin Towers fell, we decided to leave New York," Vilma said. "I felt afraid." There was speculation that the terrorists might attack the subway system they all rode, and there was the fear born of a contraction in the economy. "Things were getting more difficult after September 11th," Vilma said.

A neighbor down the hall had moved to Hazleton. The family made the two-and-a-half-hour drive from the Bronx for a visit and liked what they saw. They came a second time. All at once, the idea of moving to Hazleton made perfect sense. With the kids getting older, they needed more room, but they could not really afford a three-bedroom apartment in any neighborhood in New York where they wanted to live. They could find that extra bedroom in Hazleton. There was also the reputation of the local schools. "We came to Hazleton for a better education for our children," Leonardo said. The news excited Ivan, who was twelve at the time ("what twelve-year-old boy doesn't like a new adventure?" he asked), but shocked Brian, who was fifteen. "My parents were like, 'It's a cute town, great school district, we're moving,'" Brian said. "I was like, 'Wait, what?'" He had planned on attending NYU in Manhattan or Fordham University in the Bronx, not far from where they lived. Now he wondered if moving would upend his academic ambitions.

Yet Hazleton proved liberating. "It's like the leash came off," said Genesis, who was eleven when they moved. They could play on the street by themselves, and Vilma and Leonardo didn't worry any time they were outside. For the first time, each kid had their own room. "Now we had, like, more of the typical American life you see on television," Genesis said. Growing up in the Bronx, Brian never knew what to make of the Disney Channel movies he watched. "I was confused because we didn't have a white-picket fence kind of lifestyle," he said.

Vilma had never let go of the idea of opening a salon in the States. "Given the chance, we always thought we could do better," Vilma said of her and Leonardo. After several months of searching, she knew she had found the perfect spot the first time she set eyes on a two-story brick building with an inviting storefront on Broad Street, not far from the center of town. "There were banks nearby, supermarkets, other stores," Vilma said. "It was the main street. You knew that cars and people would always pass by there." They had used most of the proceeds Leonardo pocketed when selling his truck and soda route to put money down on the house. To help with the down payment on the building on Broad and the $6,000 they needed to transform the space into a salon, they borrowed from one of Vilma's brothers. Their monthly mortgage payment on the property was $1,255.

"If I had one word for my mother," Genesis said, "it's 'fearless.'" But all of Vilma's children also credit Leonardo. Another husband might have resented a wife with such lofty ambitions. Instead, Leonardo has served as what Ivan jokingly described as "chief of operations at the Vilma's Hair Salon Corporation." Leonardo paid the bills and looked after the books. He also dealt with the maintenance on the building. "They've always made a great team," Ivan said.

The early years were difficult. Vilma hung a banner for the grand opening and put up balloons—and drew only one paying customer that day. She had hired a single employee and sometimes wondered if she could afford even her. The only people who ventured in were Latino at a time when Hazleton was a predominantly white city. Hers was a well-worn path taken by generations of immigrants new to the country but also the story of most every small business owner, regardless of race or ethnicity or nationality, that earns every customer one at a time, through quality service and word of mouth.

* * *

No Italians lived in Hazleton a century and a half ago. There were no Poles or Hungarians until there were hundreds, if not thousands. Sam Lesante, an Italian American who for years ran a small music store in town, recalled the tear in his grandfather's eye when he shared with Lesante his story of trying to open an account at a local bank in the 1900s. "He puts on a suit and tie, he's proud to be an American, but he was thrown out because he couldn't speak English," Lesante said. "The guy tells him, 'Get the hell out of here, go back to where you come from.'" Longtimers criticized the smells of the foods these new arrivals ate, the unfamiliar sound of their music, the louder colors of the clothes they wore.

Yet a century later, the oppressed became the oppressor. The industrial parks on the edge of town attracted darker-skinned immigrants from Latin America, who had come in search of jobs and a better life. Just like those who had arrived before them, many did not speak English but many others did. Cesar Soriano had been born and raised in Brooklyn. He had owned a small grocery store in New York and then a restaurant before moving to Hazleton shortly after September 11. He bought a home for $40,000 and spent seven years making mattresses at the giant Simmons factory in town before opening the Hennesy Thrift Shop, just off Broad Street.

"I'm shopping in a grocery store one day and some lady, this white lady, gets all in my face. 'Learn to speak English, go back where you came from,'" Soriano said. "Because I'm brown-skinned doesn't mean I don't speak English, that I'm not an educated man. I went to college. I'm a businessperson."

The arrival of these newest immigrants put pressures on the school district, the housing market, and also the police force. The same easy access to New York City and Philadelphia that drew distribution centers to the area also attracted drug dealers, who typically carried guns and often were noncitizens. The people selling the drugs were almost always Latino and the buyers mostly white. "It was all too much for our sleepy town," said Andrea Kosko at Fellin's Jewelers, a fixture of Broad Street dating back to 1922. "We have a Mayberry police force. We have a Mayberry government. We have a Mayberry town. And suddenly we're dealing with big city problems."

Bad elements, however, had been a part of Hazleton's story dating back at least to the 1970s, when Hazleton was known as "Mob City" because of its reputation as a Mafia stronghold. The city habitually had former residents listed on the FBI's top ten most-wanted list, said Frank DeAndrea, a Hazleton native and former police chief. Merchants sold T-shirts featuring a Thompson submachine gun and the Mob City appellation. A deputy sheriff's home was firebombed and his entire family killed in 1976, while he was investigating mob activity.

Tax breaks granted to the large companies moving into the industrial parks compounded the problems created by rapid population growth. Younger families like Vilma's moved to the area, causing a spike in public school enrollments, yet there was no commensurate increase in the tax base of the schools. The cost of ESL

(English as a Second Language) increased by nearly $1 million. In a better world, the changes might have inspired a discussion about demographic change and how the community could better help these newcomers assimilate. Locals might have demanded that the corporate giants that had moved to their community hold up their end of the social contract.

"Instead," Jamie Longazel, a Hazleton native with a PhD in sociology, wrote in a 2016 book about his hometown called *Undocumented Fears*, "the focus is narrowly on how 'they' have financially burdened 'our' schools."

In 2005, gun violence erupted barely a block from the corner of Broad and Wyoming Streets, when a Latino man shot and killed his acquaintance in a dispute over a borrowed car. Six months later, a twenty-nine-year-old father of three, white, was working on his truck. He was shot dead by two undocumented immigrants. That, said Lou Barletta, the city's mayor, was "the straw that broke the camel's back."

Hazleton sits nearly two thousand miles from the country's southern border. Uniform Crime Reporting shows that crime rates in the city remained relatively stable between 1999 and 2006. But thirty-six days after the murder of a native-born white man at the hands of two undocumented immigrants from Central America, Mayor Barletta introduced the Illegal Immigration Relief Act. His aim, he declared, was to make Hazleton "the toughest place on illegal immigrants in America." Under the law, a business would lose its business license for five years if it was caught hiring an undocumented worker. A landlord faced financial ruin if they rented to one. The act expressly prohibited city employees from translating official documents, which were published only in English, into another language. An all-white city council passed the ordinance by a vote of four to one, putting tiny Hazleton in the national spotlight. Reporters from around the country came to write about this small city in Pennsylvania as the vanguard in the fight against illegal immigration. *60 Minutes* cast Barletta as an unlikely "hero" standing up to the influx of undocumented immigrants that afflicted this "all-American town."

The political fight certainly helped Barletta. He was reelected mayor by the largest landslide in Hazleton history and, in 2010, made a successful run for Congress, knocking off a popular Democratic incumbent. He raised his profile even further when in 2016 he became one of the first members of Congress to endorse Trump for president. The ordinance, however, did nothing to help this all-American town. A federal judge struck down the law as unconstitutional, a ruling the city appealed all the way to the US Supreme Court, which declined to hear the case. The city was ordered to pay $1.4 million in legal fees and court costs for a law that never took effect. The upshot of the ordinance was a cash-strapped city was in a deeper financial hole. Even costlier, however, was the damage done to white-Latino relations in town.

Amilcar Arroyo had been a banker in Peru who fled to the US after that country's economic collapse. Arroyo, who arrived in Hazleton in 1989, is a humble, smaller man who described himself on Twitter as "a person who believes in unity, cooperation, and friendship." In the early 2000s, he started a Spanish-language monthly magazine called *El Mensajero* (the messenger). "I never had any issue where there was racism or discrimination against me or any other Latino I knew," Arroyo said. Yet after the ordinance's passage, "I had people yelling at me, 'Go back to your country,' 'You're illegal,' 'You fucking Mexican.'" Other longtime Latino residents of Hazleton told a similar story, as if being cursed by a white stranger was a kind of rite of passage. "It's not like we have our immigration status stamped on our head," said Annie Mendez, a local businesswoman who had moved to Hazleton from New Jersey a few years before the ordinance passed. Anyone with darker skin was viewed as an invader, regardless of legal status. "The whole community becomes the target," Mendez said.

Vilma and family felt shielded from the worst of the discrimination. Living in a largely white neighborhood not far from downtown, they had good luck with their neighbors. Brian described them as welcoming and polite. "I mean, they were curious, and they asked a lot of questions and stuff, but they were always super friendly," he said. Ivan felt some discrimination at school. "I got looked at differently in school, like I was from outer space," he said. It was especially bad around the time of the debate over Barletta's ordinance. "I had kids telling me, 'Go back to where you came from,' 'Learn English,'" Ivan said. Brian was enthusiastic in his praise for his teachers and the high school's guidance counselor, but he, too, felt like an outsider. It was not until he started working at Burger King, he said, that he started hanging around with white kids his age.

Genesis also had an easier time of it. It helped, she said, that she was in the honors class and later took AP courses in high school. "Not that I'm bragging about it," Genesis said. "But I was more upscale, education-wise, and the people that were dealing with bias were at a different level." The kids that had it the worst, both Genesis and Ivan said, were those who only spoke broken English. "We weren't treated like outsiders like the kids dealing with a whole language barrier," he said.

For Vilma, the ordinance's passage felt personal. "We're all immigrants," Vilma said. "So when you attack one part, I feel you're attacking all of us." Certainly she felt its economic sting. She recalled one family—a husband and wife with four girls and a boy—who came as a group to her shop one or two times a month. "They'd all come to have their hair done," she said. After the passage of Barletta's law, she never saw them again. "I lost a lot of families at that time," she said.

By that time, Leonardo had left Cargill ("*muy frío*," he explained, hugging his body and pretending to shiver) and taken a job at a plastics factory in the same industrial park. Vilma's was barely breaking even, and the family lived on his paycheck. "That was a very difficult time," Vilma said. Not for the first time, she wondered if her shop would survive.

More businesses relocated to Hazleton's industrial parks, and more Latinos moved to the area. Before the ordinance's passage, most newcomers to Hazleton were from Mexico or countries to the south. Now, almost all were like Vilma, a Dominican via New York or New Jersey. Hazleton is in Luzerne County. In 2009, Luzerne ranked first in the country in Latino population growth. The 2010 census revealed that 37 percent of the city's population was Latino, a number that continued to climb.

The rapid demographic change left many whites resentful of the changes to their small city. The opening of the Laurel Mall outside of town in the 1970s helped accelerate the city's decline, as did the opening of a Walmart Supercenter, a Lowe's, and other big-box stores just beyond the city line. The shift of the economy from good-paying coal and manufacturing jobs to lower-wage warehouse work predated the arrival of Latinos and in fact was what drew them to Hazleton in great numbers. Yet many of the town's long-time residents blamed their Latino neighbors for all of Hazleton's ills. Longtime white residents fled to the patch towns scattered around the area, causing the city's population to tilt further Latino.

Rival Latina-owned salons opened, but there were enough customers for everyone to make a good living. "For me it wasn't really competition," Vilma said. "Everyone has their own customers." She hired more people to keep up with demand. She even started working on the hair of the occasional white client. A deeply religious woman, she said, "God gives everyone the clients they receive."

Baseball's Joe Maddon, who had grown up in Hazleton, in the apartment above his father's plumbing and heating shop, was among those white Hazletonians who worked to repair the city's relationship with its newest immigrants. Maddon, who in 2016 managed the Chicago Cubs to their first World Series in 108 years, had helped start the Hazleton Integration Project, or HIP. Founded in 2013, HIP's aim has been to unite the city through after-school programs for kids and with free English-language classes. That same year, Krista Schneider, who had grown up in one of the patch towns, created a nonprofit called the Downtown Hazleton Alliance for Progress. A former army officer who earned a master's in urban design at Harvard, Schneider treated the town's mix of old and new as a positive rather than as a problem to be solved. The rest of Luzerne County, like similar communities around the country, was getting older. Yet in Hazleton, the portion of the city's population under eighteen grew by 30 percent between 2000 and 2010. Roughly half the city's population would be under the age of thirty in 2020.

Slowly, people came to recognize that the city's newest residents didn't spell its doom but its rescue. Latino entrepreneurs followed Vilma into abandoned storefronts on Broad and Wyoming Streets. Amilcar Arroyo, the publisher, kept a running list of Latino-owned businesses in town on a large whiteboard in *El Mensajero*'s offices on Broad Street. By 2016, he had listed more than one hundred, including hair salons, restaurants, bars, furniture stores, clothing stores, and food markets. Even Joseph Yannuzzi, a city councilman who had voted in favor of Barletta's immigration legislation and served as mayor, acknowledged that the city's Latinos had saved the local economy. They "started to open every little store," Yannuzzi conceded in a 2016 interview with the *Philadelphia Inquirer*, which "was a real positive." The new businesses added to the city's tax base and contributed to the vibrancy of its downtown.

Community building is a slow process. Latinos were finally added to the board of the local chamber of commerce. An annual Festival Latino de Hazleton was launched, but even with its food booths and musical acts, it took time to draw whites in any kind of numbers. Construction began on a new arts center near the corner of Broad and Wyoming. Someone Dominican was put in charge of a new downtown incubator created to give rise to more small businesses. Then COVID hit, and it seemed that a lot of the progress of the prior half-dozen years would be undone.

* * *

During his two runs for mayor, Jeff Cusat printed his campaign materials in both English and Spanish. He would do the same for every public health message related to COVID (which would have been forbidden under the 2006 immigration ordinance, without a special vote by the city council). He enlisted allies of his in the Latino community to spread the message that people needed to be vigilant. He was not the world's most progressive mayor, but he was squarely on the side of a single, unified Hazleton. Joe Maddon enlisted baseball great Albert Pujols, among other players, to videotape messages on Spanish-language TV. They warned: don't be cavalier about this virus spreading throughout the community.

There was a coronavirus outbreak at the Cargill plant, where roughly three-quarters of the workers were Latino. More than one-fifth of the plant's work force—nearly two hundred people—had tested positive by the time the company shut down operations for two weeks. There was an outbreak at Amazon's giant AVP1 complex in the same industrial park, which the *New York Times* declared had more known COVID-19 cases than any other Amazon facility. That outbreak, too, disproportionately affected Latino workers, many of whom needed to work or risk losing their job. Most labored shoulder to shoulder without a mask or any other protective equipment. Yet rather than feeling sympathy for their Latino neighbors who were forced to work, some whites blamed them—for spreading the plague around their city. When Hazleton City Council extended Cusat's emergency curfew, whites resented them for the loss of freedom.

Latinos who were aware of what was going on grew alarmed by the statements they were reading on Facebook, Instagram, and other social media. It felt like a replay of the Barletta era. A respiratory therapist at the city's hospital posted on social media, "I know of no Hispanics that are good. . . . They hate us like we hate them." Another hospital staffer posted, "The Latino Community does not care and . . . they do not follow the rules and advice of our government. And it has been that way since they flocked to Hazleton."

The difference this time was that the city's elected officials and business leaders defended the Latinos rather than siding with aggrieved longtime residents. "Everybody's out there working hard," said Jimmy Grohol, the third-generation owner of Jimmy's Quick Lunch on Broad. "I think it's empathy we have for the people who work there. It doesn't matter if they're Latino or white or whatever. We're all Hazleton now."

Chapter 5

Washington

B ig business, as always, seemed Washington's first priority. That's the way it was in 2008, when the federal government bailed out the Wall Street giants and other firms that played a central role in the subprime meltdown, but never really got around to helping the homeowners who were innocent bystanders in the disaster yet still lost their houses to foreclosure. With COVID, the airlines received their bailout. Airlines for America, the industry's lobbying group, spent $6.5 million on forty-four lobbyists in 2020, and there were all those lobbyists on the payroll of the individual carriers (United employed thirty-one and American Airlines forty-six). The pandemic was only a few weeks old when the ten airlines split the $25 billion the government had set aside for them. Hospitals may have deserved the $70-plus billion in federal aid they received in the first couple of months of the pandemic, but much of it enriched the coffers of huge hospital chains that were sitting on deep financial reserves, according to a *New York Times* investigative piece, while the smaller hospitals that desperately needed the cash saw little of it.

No pot of money was reserved for the country's restaurants.

They would need to vie with everyone else for money. So, too, would the country's retailers, movie theaters, hotels, and a long list of sectors decimated by COVID. Each had its own small battalion of lobbyists (the National Restaurant Association, for instance, the lobbying group for the giant chains such as McDonald's, Taco Bell, KFC, and Olive Garden, employed twenty-seven lobbyists in 2020). Each sector was a mix of large chains and smaller independents. The eternal question, as it has been since there were bigger enterprises for small businesses to tussle with, was whether there would be money left to help the country's mom-and-pops, or if the chains and other giants would grab most of it before it trickled down to them.

* * *

There was no small business sector on whose behalf to fight until there were business goliaths to organize against. Before the mid to late nineteenth century, *every* business was a small business, at least by today's standards. The second half of the nineteenth century saw the rise of monopolies and oligopolies and industrialists who used structural complexity and economies of scale to dominate the competition. The steel and oil and railroad barons of the late nineteenth century gave rise, in 1890, to the Sherman Antitrust Act, and then twenty-four years later, the Clayton Antitrust Act. "What most of us are fighting for is to break up this very partnership between big business and the government," Woodrow Wilson said in making the case for a ban on predatory pricing, among other misdeeds common among the big trusts, "and make men in a small way of business as free to succeed as men in a big way."

F. W. Woolworth and Sears might have been the Walmart and Amazon of that time, but the real colossus in the early twentieth century was the A&P, the first retailer to sell more than $1 billion in merchandise in a year. Chain stores started taking over in the 1920s, and none were mightier than the Great Atlantic & Pacific

Tea Company, which at its peak owned nearly sixteen thousand stores scattered across the country, along with seventy factories and one hundred warehouses. The two brothers behind the stores, wrote Marc Levinson, the author of *The Great A&P and the Struggle for Small Business in America*, stood as the "most reviled American businessmen of the first half of the twentieth century." The complaint against the A&P would be the lament voiced by small business owners ever since: the grocery store chain's market power allowed them to demand lower prices from their suppliers, if not massproduce the goods themselves, causing countless mom-and-pop stores to shutter their doors.

Small business seemed to score a major victory during the Depression. Legislation championed by Texas congressman Wright Patman, the son of tenant farmers and a Democrat, dictated that suppliers could not favor large retailers with lower prices. Small businesses across the country celebrated the Robinson-Patman Act of 1936, but the compromise to win its passage granted manufacturers the right to offer "reasonable" price discounts—a loophole so expansive as to render the legislation ineffectual in the battle against chains.

"It's largely for that reason," said historian Benjamin C. Waterhouse, who teaches at the University of North Carolina, "that most historians consider [passage] of the Robinson-Patman Act not as the beginning of a sort of sustained anti-chain movement, but really as the end."

Dwight Eisenhower and a Republican Congress created the Small Business Administration in 1953. The GOP sought to counter the view that it was the party of big business, yet, in creating the SBA, its architects demonstrated that they had a distorted view of what constituted a small one. Polling at the time showed that a majority of the public saw a small business as one with fewer than ten employees. One survey showed that only 3 percent thought that a business with more than one hundred employees qualified as a small business. Yet the enabling legislation defined small business as one with up to five hundred employees, if not thousands, depending on the industry.

On paper, the SBA was an independent agency whose people would "aid, counsel, assist, and protect the interests of small business concerns." Its most important function, though, was financing. Local banks, not the SBA, would make the loans, but the agency would cover up to 85 percent of any loss in case of a default, freeing lenders to take a risk on new businesses. The money could be used to start a business or to grow a larger small business that had had some success. In 2019, the SBA guaranteed more than $28 billion in loans to start or expand a small business.

From the start, the SBA has been a work in progress. For years, it worked with banks that discriminated against borrowers of color, despite a push by civil rights groups to drop them as lenders. Only under pressure did offices in the South start hiring black lending officers in the 1960s. Lyndon Johnson, as part of his War on Poverty, created a microloan program to help black-owned businesses, sparking conservative criticism. Richard Nixon, whose father owned a grocery store, pledged a commitment to what he called "black capitalism," and promised an "equal chance" for everyone. Critics, however, charged that under his administration, "SBA" stood for "Stop Black Advancement."

Controversy continued to dog the SBA. The American Motors Corporation, a Detroit-based car maker created in the 1950s, was a publicly traded outfit that employed more than twenty thousand people. Yet it never captured more than a few percentage points of the US auto market with cars such as the Gremlin and Pacer. So when the company ran into financial troubles in the 1960s, the SBA, run by the Democrats, expanded its definition of what constituted a small business in the automotive industry to free up bailout funds to help AMC. During the Watergate era, in the early 1970s, some in Washington redubbed the SBA the Small Scandal Association. A district director approved his brother-in-law's request for $1.1 million in loans. A regional director was investigated for accepting kickbacks on loans. The SBA director removed both from office. Ronald Reagan had declared that deeming small business "vital" to the US economy was not enough. "Small business *is* America," Reagan proclaimed—and then tried to eliminate the SBA. The vote in Congress was not even close. Few politicians wanted to shutter the one agency in Washington helping small businesses, along with the not-so-small ones with hundreds of employees that contributed to their campaigns.

Presidents continued to extoll the virtues of small business. Bill Clinton called small businesses the "engine" of the US economy. George W. Bush in 2006 said they were a cornerstone of his administration's "pro-growth economic policy." The same year, a milestone was reached: for the first time in the country's history, more people worked for a business with more than five hundred employees than one with fewer than that. For Barack Obama, small businesses were "the cornerstone of America's promise." Meanwhile, the US was steadily becoming less entrepreneurial. Where in the late 1970s, new businesses represented 16 percent of all businesses in the US, by 2011 that number had decreased to 8 percent. Donald Trump vowed, "We're going to create an environment for small business like we haven't had in many, many decades." Yet heading into 2020, entrepreneurship was still in decline—in large part, wrote Stacy Mitchell of the Institute for Local Self-Reliance, due to "anticompetitive behavior by dominant corporations which routinely use their size and market power to undermine and exclude their smaller rivals." The increasing power of large businesses was stifling new business starts.

The SBA morphed over the years through different administrations and in different times. Women-owned businesses were deemed a priority in the 1970s, under Jimmy Carter. Within the year, loans to female-owned businesses doubled. A venture capital arm was added, and what the agency dubbed its Small Business Investment Corporation provided early funding to Apple, Hewlett-Packard, and Intel. "I had $4 billion a year to invest in small business," said Mark Walsh, who served as the SBA's chief of innovation and investment under Barack Obama. "I was like the venture capitalist for the entire United States government."

Its 7(a) program ("the SBA isn't exactly Coke or Nike when it comes to branding," Walsh said) is what people turn to when they want to start a dry cleaner, a wedding dress business, or an Italian restaurant in Old Forge, Pennsylvania. The 7(a) program is how TJ and Nina Cusumano successfully secured the funding to buy their place in 2013. A second program matched small businesses with government agencies requiring goods and services, and disbursed grants for those needing help building capacity if they were too small to fulfill a demonstrated need. The SBA includes an advocacy arm that, among other things, is supposed to ensure that the US government, which spends roughly $4 trillion a year, gives small businesses a chance to compete for a share of it.

"The SBA actually does incredible stuff," Mark Walsh said, "but has no talent for describing what they do."

From the start, the SBA has had as its core mission "assisting in the economic recovery of communities after disasters." Toward that end, the SBA disburses Economic Injury Disaster Loans, which are called EIDL (pronounced "idol") loans. Historically, these had been loans of up to $150,000 to help small businesses (and also small farms and nonprofits) in declared disaster zones, to be paid back with 3.5 percent interest. The EIDL disaster loans helped businesses in New Orleans after Hurricane Katrina and have been issued countless times after floods, tornadoes, wildfires, and other calamities. The problem in 2020 was the scope of the crisis. Katrina had hit a vast expanse of the Gulf Coast, but it still represented only a small patch of the country. A record 155,000 disaster loans from Louisiana overwhelmed the SBA back in 2005. Yet, with COVID, the roughly six million small businesses in the country with at least one employee could be said to be operating in a disaster zone. If the federal government was going to help small businesses survive COVID, another way needed to be found.

* * *

The job of saving small business, along with the rest of the US economy in the wake of COVID, fell to a man whose most salient skill seemed an ability to suck up to his boss. As secretary of the treasury, Steven Mnuchin had lauded Donald Trump's "perfect genes" and described him as "unbelievably healthy," despite the president's lack of exercise and preference for junk food. Mnuchin, who is Jewish, defended Trump after violence broke out in Charlottesville, where marchers chanted, "Jews will not replace us," prompting the president's "fine people" comment about the anti-Semitic protesters. Mnuchin also blocked congressional Democrats seeking Trump's tax returns. According to press accounts, Trump routinely cursed out his Treasury secretary, but Mnuchin's loyalty never flagged. He jumped to defend the president with every outlandish statement Trump uttered and in the face of every unflattering tell-all by a former aide. Perhaps "the greatest sycophant in cabinet history," said Lawrence Summers, Bill Clinton's Treasury secretary. But Mnuchin was also a survivor. Trump had gone through four chiefs of staff, four national security advisors, and six communications directors. Mnuchin was one of the few original cabinet members left when COVID caused the economy to lurch to a stop.

Treasury secretaries invariably have some prior government experience. Mnuchin, by contrast, was a former Goldman Sachs executive and hedge-fund manager who had invested in a pair of Trump's real estate projects in the early 2000s. In 2008, Mnuchin assembled a group of billionaire investors that included George Soros and Michael Dell to buy the remains of a fallen mortgage lender and create a new bank called OneWest. OneWest foreclosed on more than thirty-six thousand homeowners in California alone, earning Mnuchin the moniker of "Foreclosure King." Mnuchin made hundreds of millions of dollars when he sold the bank in 2015 and then served as Trump's national finance chair for the 2016 campaign.

Mnuchin moved into the Trump International Hotel in Washington while awaiting his confirmation as Treasury secretary, a process delayed because he neglected to list $95 million in assets (including homes in New York, Los Angeles, and the Hamptons) on his Senate disclosure forms. Until COVID, his signature accomplishment as Treasury secretary had been the 40 percent cut in the corporate income tax he championed at the end of 2017, along with tax cuts that disproportionately benefited the richest 1 percent. A profile in the *New York Times Magazine* described Mnuchin as maintaining a "demeanor of such perpetual awkwardness that he sometimes calls to mind an alien in a science-fiction movie trying to impersonate a human." Yet Mnuchin, as Treasury secretary, would be Trump's liaison with congressional leaders as they sought ways to help those waylaid by the coronavirus.

There seemed no shortage of those in need. The third week of March saw new unemployment claims rise by 2.9 million, shattering the previous record of 695,000 in 1982. First-time claims spiked another six million the following week while lawmakers in Washington were still hammering away at a compromise. Any rescue package would need to target the unemployed. Testing was another area of need, as were the faltering budgets of state and local governments looking at plummeting revenues in the wake of widespread shutdowns. Small businesses needed help, but so did larger corporations. The giant restaurant and hotel chains were negotiating the same unchartered territory as the small independents. Nearly 1,600 groups reported lobbying Congress as officials debated a massive relief package.

Deliberations stretched for two and a half weeks, with Mnuchin as the man in the middle. Control of the House had flipped to the Democrats in 2018, but, by all accounts, Mnuchin had a good working relationship with House Speaker Nancy Pelosi. In a town thick with partisan warriors and ideologues, he was a creature of Wall Street, where positions are fluid and everything negotiable. He may have come across as android-like, but by all accounts, he was courteous and competent and professional in an administration in which those qualities were generally lacking. Mnuchin and Pelosi had negotiated a budget deal in 2019 and reportedly developed a mutual respect—no easy task when his boss had called the Speaker a "sick woman" with "mental problems." The *Times* reported that Pelosi and Mnuchin spoke as many as eighteen times a day by phone during negotiations. There were dozens of more calls with Chuck Schumer, the top Democrat in the Senate, along with countless conversations with trade groups and lobbyists representing a long list of industries kneecapped by the virus.

The Republicans, who controlled the Senate, proved a tougher negotiating partner. Mnuchin had sold Trump on a massive bailout package that included cash payments for most Americans. Yet a subgroup of Republican senators was adamant about holding the line at $1 trillion. A lunch was arranged with Senate Republicans, where Mnuchin gave a presentation showing that without a bigger bailout, unemployment was likely to hit 25 percent. Perhaps more persuasive was the argument that Trump needed passage of as large a package as possible if he stood any chance of reelection.

There were any number of ideas for helping small business survive COVID. Some Democrats wanted the IRS to send businesses tax rebates. Others on the left looked to Europe, where countries avoided widespread layoffs by paying a large portion of every business's payroll—a freeze-the-economy-in-place measure. Marco Rubio, a Republican senator from Florida and chairman of the Senate's Committee on Small Business & Entrepreneurship, first looked to the SBA as the vehicle for getting money into the hands of all those restaurants, retailers, and others shuttered by the pandemic. But he changed his mind after getting in touch with people there. Congress had just allocated the extra $50 billion for EIDL that Trump had requested, and already the deluge of applications was overwhelming the staff. The SBA did not have the capacity to handle anything more.

The Senate created a bipartisan small business task force. The two

Republicans on the task force were Rubio and Maine's Susan Collins, who was facing a tough reelection campaign that fall. Maryland's Ben Cardin, the ranking Democrat on the Small Business Committee, and New Hampshire's Jeanne Shaheen were the Democrats. In the House, the key negotiators were Nydia Velázquez, a Democrat from New York and chair of the House Small Business Committee, and Steve Chabot, a Republican from Ohio. Together, they came up with the Paycheck Protection Program (PPP) to get government-backed, forgivable loans in the hands of small businesses with fewer than five hundred employees. At the insistence of the Republicans, the private sector and not the SBA would administer the program. A bank (or any approved lender) would file a completed application on behalf of a business requesting cash assistance. That institution would then be reimbursed by the government for any money it loaned out.

There were last-minute hitches in passing the overall bill. Recognizing how desperately the Trump side needed a massive bailout, the Democrats held firm on a plan that gave an extra $600 a week to any American on unemployment. The delay in a final plan caused another drop in the country's stock markets, which were down one-third from their February highs. The two sides compromised on a $600 weekly supplement that expired in four months. The Senate unanimously passed what was dubbed the Coronavirus Aid, Relief, and Economic Security Act, or CARES, and the House quickly followed suit. Trump signed the bill into law on March 27. At $2.2 trillion, it was the largest economic rescue package in US history.

The single biggest program part of the CARES Act benefited bigger corporations. Congress set aside $454 billion—one-quarter of the total dollar amount—for a rescue fund targeting medium- and large-sized businesses. (The initiative created for medium-sized businesses was oddly named the "Main Street Lending Program.") It also earmarked additional dollars for specific industries: the airlines and hospitals but also hotels and cruise ship operators.

Another $135 billion was set aside as a tax break for wealthy real estate developers. The cost of giving most of the country's adults $1,200, plus an extra $500 for each dependent, was estimated at $300 billion. The extra money the unemployed would receive from the US Treasury, in addition to whatever state benefits they collected was expected to cost another several hundred billion dollars. State and local governments received $340 billion, not including the $40 billion or so set aside to help schools reopen.

Small businesses' share was $349 billion and came with strings attached. Any business with fewer than five hundred employees could apply for a loan equal to 2.5 times their average monthly payroll up to $10 million. A business was free to keep its PPP allotment—so long as it spent at least three-quarters of the money it received paying its employees. Those spending more than that on rent, utilities, or other outlays approved under the program would need to pay the money back, plus 1 percent interest. Congress also required that businesses spend the money within eight weeks of receiving it.

PPP included another provision added shortly before its passage. As originally conceived, PPP was strictly for businesses that qualified under the already inflated five-hundred-employee threshold. Yet three words were inserted after spelling out the five-hundred-employee limit: "per physical location." The head of the country's hotel and lodging association, which earlier in the year had donated $7,500 to her reelection campaign, praised Susan Collins for her help adding those words to the bill, and Collins acknowledged the role she played. So, too, did Marco Rubio, who partially apologized for it. It had been his intention to help the country's franchise owners, most of whom were small business operators even if they were running a McDonald's or a Subway. Yet as phrased, he confessed in a tweet, those three words opened the program to publicly traded restaurants and hotels with thousands of employees, but no more than five hundred in any one locale.

Chapter 6

Preexisting Conditions

In Tunkhannock, Glenda Shoemaker stayed away from her store, J.R.'s Hallmark, and then wondered if she should have her head examined. The earliest days of lockdown were largely a blank, she said, as the miasma that took over much of the population in those disorienting first days of the pandemic enveloped her. It had been years since she had taken any time off from the store. Her vacations in recent years had been an overnight trip to Syracuse, two hours to the north, or to the town of King of Prussia, just outside of Philadelphia, for a gift expo or traveling clothing show in search of new product. "I was burned out," Glenda said. She almost welcomed the pandemic as a forced vacation.

One day, however, she woke up, and she needed to get herself to her store. She barely had enough money in the bank to cover the bills already on her desk. The last things she needed were new bills for product that would sit in cartons until she could reopen.

"A mad dash of ridiculousness"—that's how Glenda described her first days back inside J.R.'s. "I'm at the computer, checking 'hold,' 'hold,' 'hold,' 'cancel,' 'cancel,' 'cancel,' on everything I had on order," Glenda said. And if it was too late to stop an order by clicking a box, she phoned. "Some of these people I've worked with forever," Glenda said. "I was not above begging." Of course, many were also small business owners who, not unlike Glenda, were themselves in dire straits.

Glenda could not say what kept her going to the store each day once she had stopped suppliers from shipping her more product. In that regard, she had plenty of company. Over in Hazleton, a trio of women—Celeste Kosko and her daughters, Mary Celeste and Andrea Kosko—owned Fellin's Jewelers, a few blocks from Vilma Hernandez's salon. Their shop, too, had been deemed a non-life-sustaining business and forced to keep its distinctive red door shut to customers. Yet every day, the three women traveled to the store, dressed properly in blouses and skirts and nice shoes as if they would be greeting customers. As they always had done, they unlocked the store's vault, where its merchandise was placed at the close of business for safekeeping. "Someone turned these tumblers every day since 1922," Mary Celeste said. "Through World Wars, on 9/11, Armistice Day. Every day. It's the first thing we do when we open. So, pandemic or no pandemic, we turned those tumblers." Similarly, Jennifer Donald-Barnasevitch at Smith Floral, also on Broad, never stopped going to her store, though she was also closed to customers. "I just didn't want to stay home," Donald-Barnasevitch said. There never seemed a loss of things to do at her combination flower shop and greenhouse. "I cleaned up, I painted, I reorganized, I worked on the books," she said. The phone didn't ring much, but when it did, she was happy she was there to pick it up.

In Tunkhannock, Glenda left the house more or less at the same time she always did. But she felt no great desire to dress as if preparing for a regular workday. Normally, her wrists rattled with bangly bracelets, and she wore rings, pins, earrings, and layers of necklaces. But what was the point when she'd be by herself? Each morning, she brushed back her mane of blondish hair and pulled on jeans and a sweatshirt. "I would sometimes have the same clothes on for days," she said.

The strip mall that had been J.R.'s home for the prior thirty-two years, the Towne Plaza, is only a few blocks from Glenda's home. From the outside, J.R.'s was not much to look at. The Towne Plaza is a one-story, redbrick stretch of worn-out storefronts capped by an aquamarine metal awning faded by too many years exposed to the sun. The thick wood strip below the awning used to hang a store's sign might once have been white but now was marred by water stains. Wood had chipped away under one of J.R.'s GOLD CROWN signs.

Inside, though, J.R.'s stood as something of an oasis. It was a handsome store with wooden display racks, glass cabinets, and a carpeted floor. Roughly half the store was devoted to greeting cards. The other was half was filled with trinkets, collectibles, clothes, and jewelry. J.R.'s sold baskets in a wide variety of sizes and colors and shapes, fuzzy slippers in pink and baby blue, inspirational sayings quilted on pillows, and framed posters of uplifting words written out in beautiful longhand, accompanied by majestic images of sunrises and rainbows. There were also food items she sold as gifts, including small-batch jellies, barbecue sauces, and popcorns flavored to taste like champagne, peanuts, or margaritas.

Glenda parked wherever she wanted in the Towne Plaza's ample parking lot. For once she didn't have to think about making it easier for her customers to find a spot in front of her store. She unlocked the door and every day went through the same ritual. Among the Hallmark items she was featuring was a Disney Princess Dreams Go Round Carousel, a music box shaped like a carousel that retailed for $119 and let the customer choose to hear the signature song of one of its four princesses. "I'm not a princess girl," Glenda said. Yet day after day, she went from the front door straight to the Princess Dreams Go Round Carousel. She always chose Belle from *Beauty and the Beast*, and a calliope-sounding version of her song played while the princesses rode their horse or seahorse or tiger around the merry-go-round.

"I'm going to the store every day, I'm an absolute wreck, and then that song," Glenda said. It drove her mad and yet she could not help herself. "Oh my God. Every day for weeks and weeks."

Glenda had a small desk for herself at the back of the store, in a storage area overstuffed with paraphernalia for seasonal promotions and backup stock. She knew she should work on a website for the store. She had a Facebook page that she used to advertise the occasional sale. But in March 2020, customers still could not shop her store online. There were companies such as Shopify that helped small retail businesses like J.R.'s sell their goods online. But as much as Glenda knew about the tastes of her Endless Mountain clientele, she knew little about technology and e-commerce platforms. She had grown accustomed to ordering and reordering online and tracking the Hallmark products she bought through the company's portal. Otherwise, the machine on her desk was something she generally sought to avoid. She was already feeling overwhelmed without adding to her to-do list.

The ringing phone was a constant. For Glenda, the calls were her saving grace. The loneliness of lockdown seemed for her the hardest part of her ordeal. Longtime customers called to check in, as did employees phoning with questions. Occasionally, it was a fellow business owner in town in the same predicament. Glenda was always glad when Gina Suydam from the local chamber of commerce phoned. "Gina was my lifeline," Glenda said. A couple of weeks into the pandemic, the chamber began hosting Zoom webinars for any local businesses needing help. Logging on to those at least made her feel like she wasn't so alone.

A few times each day, Glenda drifted to the front door and stared out at the street. Tioga, the main artery through town, was normally busy with traffic. But during those first couple of weeks of the pandemic, Glenda could stand there for several minutes before she saw a car pass by. She felt as if she were a bit player in *Day of the Dead* or trapped in some other dystopian horror film. After a while, Glenda didn't bother turning on the lights before locking the door behind her, adding to the surreal nature of those days.

"Sitting in a dark store, all by myself, it was freaky," she said. "I'm a strong girl but it's just me."

* * *

The original J.R.'s opened in 1988. It had been a narrow storefront with little room to sell much beyond greeting cards and a few other trinkets. Yet from almost the start, the shop proved a moneymaker. "Back then, a card shop was a very good business," Glenda said. When the storefront next door became available, J.R.'s took over the space. That doubled the shop's footprint, allowing her mother, Janet Shoemaker, to sell an expanded product line that included candles, soaps, and other gift items. Hallmark had its dictums and decrees, but the company didn't have nearly as much product to peddle as it does today. "Hallmark wasn't as pushy back then," Glenda said.

Glenda had been pitching in at her mother's store since it opened. The McDonald's where she worked all those years was only one block away. Often she showed up wearing her fast-food uniform. It wasn't until around 2004, when Janet Shoemaker was pushing seventy, that Glenda went to work full-time at J.R.'s. At some point, the "R" in "J.R." retired to Florida and a new J (Janet) and G (Glenda) LLC was formed. The grocery store next door closed, providing another opportunity to expand. Mother and daughter spent thousands of dollars on construction costs to nearly double the size of the store, and spilled thousands more on racks, cabinets, and other displays. With 4,200 square feet of space, the store had enough room for six long rows of Hallmark cards along with clothes, jewelry, and anything else they thought they could sell. "We were having the best years we ever had," Glenda said. J.R.'s, she said, had become a "destination store" that drew people from as far away as the towns lining the Pennsylvania–New York border an hour or more away.

"We were women really doing it," Glenda said. "Things were going great. And then the economy went terrible." The Great

Recession of 2008 hit, sales plummeted, "and we've never really recovered," Glenda said. Except now they were stuck paying nearly twice as much rent each month.

When Glenda's mother had moved in, the Towne Plaza was anchored by the town's CVS. Its departure proved the next big blow. In 2014, CVS built a new building for themselves in the center of town, on Bridge Street, half a block from Tioga, and the giant thirteen-thousand-square-foot space the chain formerly occupied has sat empty ever since. The closing of the grocery store next door allowed J.R.'s to expand, but it also represented one less reason for locals to drive west from downtown. A jewelry store that had been a long-standing tenant of the mall also closed. Aside from J.R.'s, there was little left beyond a cheap Chinese buffet, a pregnancy clinic, a Verizon store, and a small FedEx outpost.

"There's no traffic coming this way anymore," Glenda said. The center of gravity had shifted to the other side of the river and the Walmart, Weis, and other chains that had set up shop in Eaton Township. Janet Shoemaker started coming into the store less often. The two jointly owned the store, but its daily operations became Glenda's responsibility.

There are moments, Glenda confessed, when she missed McDonald's. Her problems as a manager there were simpler: flaky employees who failed to show up for work, those rare occasions when the mothership added items to its menu. At McDonald's, she never had to worry about making next week's payroll or if there would be enough money to pay suppliers. At J.R.'s, by contrast, she seemed to be fighting sweeping forces over which she had no control. Nearly half her store was devoted to greeting cards, yet technological changes and a generational shift meant younger people were less likely than their parents to buy a paper card. The internet seemed to siphon off an ever-greater share of her business with each passing year, and there were her daily battles against the market giants that had come to dominate the retail sector.

The Walmart just outside of town was a constant irritant. For years, scented candles made by a company called Yankee Candle were one of J.R.'s bestsellers. "There were some days we sold more Yankee Candles than we did cards," Glenda said. But in 2015, Yankee Candle was purchased by Newell Brands, a publicly traded giant that owns Rubbermaid, Mr. Coffee, Sunbeam, and Elmer's. "All of a sudden," Glenda said, "Yankee Candles show up in Walmart." Shoemaker felt something like the shock that Judy Mead had experienced when she visited Walmart's underwear aisle. Glenda's wholesale price for a Yankee Candle was $14.99—the same price that Walmart charged its customers. J.R.'s charged $29.99, but, unlike Mead, Glenda did not have to imagine that people secretly thought they were being cheated.

"People are telling me, 'I can get the Yankee Candle for $14.99, you're ripping me off,'" Glenda said. Yet she had to cover her monthly rent, and insurance and utilities and labor costs, and hoped to make a little money for herself. She considered charging barely more than her price for a candle but, she said, "unlike Walmart, I can't afford to charge a dollar more than I pay."

Hallmark was another source of aggravation. Carrying the gold crown, Glenda said, used to mean something. "Ours was the only place [in town] that you could buy their cards, and nobody makes nicer cards than Hallmark," she said. But now it seemed anyone willing to sell its cards was considered royalty. CVS, Walmart, the Dollar Tree, and Weis were among the places in town that carried their cards. Even the local post office had a spinner stocked with Hallmark greeting cards. Anyone with a computer could buy Hallmark goods—at Hallmark.com but also on Walmart's website or Amazon's. Glenda is contractually obligated to buy Hallmark-sanctioned racks from the company to display its greeting cards. "Guess who doesn't have to pay for them?" Glenda asked, and then immediately answered her own question: Walmart. (Hallmark declined comment, saying through a spokesperson that the company was "unable to disclose details of agreements with any of our business partners.")

"Hallmark for years was one of the best companies to work with, but the world has changed," Glenda said. In the mid-1990s, there were five thousand Gold Crown Hallmark stores in the US. Fifteen years later, that figure had fallen under 1,400. Just prior to the pandemic, Hallmark laid off several hundred people, including Glenda's last human contact at the company. "We used to have a rep that came out to the store to check on things," she said. "Now we don't even have somebody that calls us on the phone." Hallmark lists her store on its website but improperly refers to it as "Jr.'s" rather than J.R.'s.

"My mom always says to me, 'Glenda, I worked hard but not like you,'" she said. Her mother worked five days a week for most of the year and added a sixth day in the weeks leading up to Christmas. So long as she put in her hours, Janet Shoemaker never had to worry about paying the bills. "Me, I work seven days a week," Glenda said, "and there's points where I'm working from morning till night every day. And it's not like I make near the money she did." For Janet, starting a small business had entailed risks but large rewards. For Glenda, it's demonstrated how heartbreaking owning your own business can be. As in many family-owned businesses, she suffered the additional burden of knowing that if she was forced to shut her doors, she would be not just disappointing herself, her employees, and her customers but extinguishing her mother's legacy.

Glenda had thought about giving up long before the pandemic. But she continued to run J.R.'s because the alternative was so grim. She imagined herself in a minimum-wage job that paid $15,000 a year. "If I shut down, I'd have to get a crappy job somewhere except there's a lot physically I can't do and nobody would probably hire me," she said. Health insurance also kept her tied to the store. "I stay here and make sure I have the Taj Mahal of insurance," Glenda said. "Even if I cut what I pay myself in half, I'm still better off than if I shut everything down."

Even before the word "coronavirus" was on the lips of people around the world, Glenda had been talking about selling her home.

It was a handsome two-story place on a corner lot, built in the nineteenth century on what Glenda described as "one of the most beautiful streets in town." But the house needed work, and her mother owned a perfectly nice house barely one block away. Eventually, she would inherit her mother's home, and selling her own meant one less bill to fret about. So when she wasn't at the store or looking after her mother, she was at home painting, getting her house ready to sell.

"That's what happens when COVID hits and you're looking at using your personal savings to pay your bills," Glenda said.

* * *

Two weeks of shutdown became three and then four. The news reported on COVID-19's rising death toll, but all of it seemed far away from Tunkhannock. Glenda was still in painting mode when the full weight of her predicament hit her. "I'm up there on a ladder when I realized, like, he's not going to open this back up," she said.

She worried that Tom Wolf, the pinch-faced technocrat who seemed to have near-total control over her life, might not let her open in time to save J.R.'s Hallmark.

Glenda was not the only one in town stewing over the governor's order locking down stores around the state. Across the street from the Dietrich movie theater, inside Greenwood's Furniture Store, Mark Monsey had the same worry. Mark, a crusty, outspoken figure in town, was never quiet about his opinions. One month into the pandemic, he wrote a letter to the editor of the *Wyoming County Press Examiner*. "I am ready to give up the family business after 59 years," he wrote. "Government has failed us." He phoned a television station in Scranton, which sent out a camera crew to let him vent. The governor needed to end the lockdown, he told them, or Tunkhannock was facing the prospect of a large, abandoned storefront in the center of town. Mark and his eighty-eight-year-old mother, with whom he co-owned the store, could hang on for maybe another few weeks, but then they faced an impossible choice. He had some money in the bank, as did his mother, but depleting his savings to cover his costs, he told the visiting TV reporter, "might mean that I'm looking at being broke *and* out of a job."

Mark made no effort to hide his disapproval of Wolf. A self-described "ultra-conservative Republican," he had disliked Wolf from the moment he saw his first ads introducing himself to the state, driving his Jeep, wearing his fleece vest. Now this same government was threatening his business. "I understand in the big cities where this thing was running around like crazy," Mark said. But Wyoming County, which only registered its first positive case in early April, didn't cross a dozen cases until the middle of the month. An epidemiologist would point out that it was the young and mobile who tended to spread the virus, but to Mark, the answer was to focus on those most at risk of dying from it. "You protect the people living in the nursing homes and the sick," Mark said, "and not lock up the entire state."

Yet Wolf wasn't heeding the advice of anyone outside his small team of department heads and bureaucrats. "With him, it's just, 'This is the way it's going to be and we're not going to listen to anyone else,'" Mark said. Wolf reminded him of every know-it-all on TV or in government who thought he or she knew better about his life, except now rather than merely being annoyed, he was worried about his livelihood and that of his mother and other family members (his wife, an uncle, a brother-in-law) who worked for the store. Greenwood's occupied a cavernous fourteen-thousand-square-feet storefront segmented by furniture categories. A person looking at bedroom sets would be standing at least twenty feet from someone browsing dining room tables, or appliances, or floor coverings.

"I could've made appointments with people," Mark said. "'You come at two, you come at three.' I could have limited the store to a few people at a time." Glenda would have been able to do the same thing at J.R.'s, where it was easy to stay far from others. Yet, like Glenda had done, Mark laid off everyone, which in the case of

Greenwood's meant his family and the two delivery people he kept on staff.

Mark was a talker. Normally, he'd be at the Second Wind, the bar next to Greenwood's, "yakking about this or that we don't like." Now it was the phone. He asked anyone who would listen to imagine the size of his store. You've been to my place, he told people. If he had four or five people browsing at once, that would signify a busy day. "We'll sanitize after [you're] gone, we'll wipe every surface someone might have touched," he said. He'd even agree to a mask requirement if that's what it took.

It was near the end of April that Mark stopped at the Walmart to pick up a few things. Seeing the size of the crowd there on a Sunday morning, he pulled out his phone and took some pictures. "They probably had five hundred people inside," Mark said. "But this governor says it's okay to shop there but not at my store." He printed a few of the photos he had taken of Walmart's parking lot, taped them to a sheet of poster board, and scrawled a message about the governor's hypocrisy. The poster, which he hung in his store window, was crude, but the point was clear: it was okay for hundreds to mingle in the same store, many of them without masks, but not okay for him to have one or two people at a time.

Mark was not without his connections. He headed Tunkhannock's downtown business association and had always stayed involved in local politics. "I know the county commissioners, we're good friends, we're all local yokels around here," he said. The commissioners were talking to the state legislators and others they knew in Harrisburg. Those who reached out to the governor's office reported silence in response.

"If Wolf would have tried to blow some smoke up my skirt and said, 'Small business owners, I know we're killing you, I know this is gonna hurt, but we need you to take one for the team,'" Mark said. "Instead, it was, 'This is the way it's going to be and we're not going to even listen to what anyone else has to say.'" The Great Oz makes his pronouncement from up high, and the expectation is that all of Pennsylvania comply with his directives. "This governor doesn't care about small business," Mark said.

* * *

Even Tom Wolf's allies criticized him for handling COVID as if trapped inside a bunker. Yet they also recognized that he was largely operating alone. There was no coordinated federal plan, and Trump and his team seemed to have no interest in creating one. In mid-March, the White House Coronavirus Task Force had urged people to work from home and recommended they stop traveling and limit social gatherings to no more than ten people. The Trump administration directed billions to vaccine development. But that was about the beginning and end of the federal response to the pandemic. Hospitals and other facilities in Pennsylvania and throughout the country were clamoring for surgical masks, gloves, and other protective equipment, but Trump disabused anyone of the idea that the federal government might be there to help. "We're not a shipping clerk," he had said. Asked about a nationwide testing rate lagging much of the world's, Trump had said, "I don't take responsibility at all."

There was no order, say, to shut down every bar and live entertainment venue in the US with the promise of aid to make them whole for their business losses. There was no decisive moment where Trump implemented a countrywide stay-at-home order, or a clear directive for Americans to wear a mask when inside. ("You can wear 'em. You don't have to wear 'em.") Facing criticism for failing to create a national system for distributing desperately needed items, from ventilators to nose swabs for testing, Trump put his son-in-law, a novice administrator, in charge of crisis measures. Largely what emanated from Washington were distractions. Trump suggested that ingesting bleach might be a useful way of defeating COVID, and then it was a random malaria drug that he had seen touted on Fox. At five p.m., there was the nightly Trump show, featuring a rambling, incoherent president who contradicted himself, publicly squabbled with his medical advisors, and made time to boast that the briefings made him number one on Facebook. The country was in the midst of both a health and economic crisis, and even allies complained that Trump's daily briefings were creating chaos.

Primary responsibility, then, for containing the virus would fall to Wolf and the country's other governors. Most governors, regardless of party or region, had implemented a lockdown order near the start of the pandemic. Stay-at-home orders were handed down in states both red and blue. Nonessential businesses were forced to close: retail, restaurants, bars, barbershops. The difference generally reduced down to the duration of the initial lockdown and life after it had been lifted.

The burden of responsibilities that fell on Wolf was immense. Hospitals around the state were overwhelmed, as were Pennsylvania's eight-hundred-plus assisted living facilities. Monitoring the virus's spread and keeping pace with the science were full-time jobs in and of themselves. Wolf extended his order shutting down all in-person K–12 through the end of the school year and, as governor, was responsible for the agency that administers unemployment to state residents. Almost 1.5 million of the more than 20 million Americans who were newly unemployed lived in Pennsylvania. New claims had deluged the state's unemployment system, causing severe delays for people who were counting on that money to pay the rent and buy food. Small business had already gotten a bailout from the federal government with the PPP program. Its advocates would need to get in line.

Like Trump and Wolf's fellow governors, Wolf communicated with the public through regular coronavirus briefings. Wolf's briefings, however, could never compete with Trump's theatrics in Washington or Andrew Cuomo's one-man show in neighboring New York. Unlike Cuomo, Wolf never wore a baseball cap or a windbreaker embossed with the state seal or cracked jokes about his daughters. Wolf frequently spoke from home, sitting at a desk backed by a bookcase. As Health secretary, Rachel Levine could be said to be his Anthony Fauci, except Wolf often let his top infectious disease expert do most of the talking at the briefings. Whoever was speaking shared a split screen with a signer who translated for the deaf.

With fifty states, there were fifty sets of rules. Florida was on one end of the spectrum. Florida's Ron DeSantis was a little-known congressman until he impressed Trump with his full-throated defenses of the controversial president on Fox. In 2018, the forty-one-year-old DeSantis was elected governor. One in four residents of Florida was older than sixty, but DeSantis only agreed to issue a stay-at-home order after Trump publicly pressured him to do so. Even then, Florida's directive expired in less than thirty days. In Georgia, Governor Brian Kemp invalidated mask orders in more than a dozen jurisdictions, including Atlanta, Savannah, and Augusta.

Wolf could be lumped in with the governors who tended to follow their public health experts, even when that meant sometimes imposing drastic measures to slow the spread of the virus. If nothing else, Wolf never wavered over the seemingly straightforward question of wearing a mask. The prevailing science, and also logic, dictated that people were far less likely to spread an airborne disease if they wore a face covering. On the same day in early April that the CDC recommended that every American wear a mask, Wolf, speaking from the podium in the state's emergency operations center, asked all Pennsylvanians to don face coverings when in public. In mid-April, that request became an order: businesses were instructed to deny entry to any customer not wearing a mask.

States when temporarily shutting down businesses relied on a detailed, seventeen-page list of essential businesses produced by the Department of Homeland Security in mid-March. Pennsylvania was one of the few that created its own criteria. Pennsylvania's Department of Community and Economic Development, working with deputies in the governor's office, spent three days assembling a list of "life-sustaining businesses." A waiver process was added for those businesses that believed they were improperly classified.

"The mantra from the start was always, 'We're basing our decisions here on the science,'" said Gordon Denlinger, the National Federation of Independent Business's Pennsylvania director. "Yet somehow the science in all the other states was different on a whole range of issues." Denlinger offered the example of real estate. Open houses around the country were generally on hold, but agents were permitted to arrange walk-throughs for prospective buyers in other states and meet face-to-face if they maintained a reasonable distance.

"Pennsylvania was the only state to shut down real estate," said Denlinger, a former Republican legislator. "What's the scientific basis of that? Did the governor talk to any Realtors? Did he have any Realtors at his table as he was considering this? The answer is no, he did not." Pennsylvania shuttered auto dealers, unlike other states, as well as liquor stores, golf courses, private campgrounds, and construction projects.

More than forty-two thousand business owners around the state applied for waivers from the state's shutdown order. The state granted fewer than one in seven. Among the disappointed was Jennifer Donald-Barnasevitch at Smith Floral in Hazleton. Donald-Barnasevitch was sixteen and still in high school when she started working for the Smith family at Smith Floral, a store that has been operating continuously since 1896. She was in her forties and still working there when in 2014 she bought the shop from the founder's grandson. Under Homeland Security's guidelines, she could remain open ("workers supporting the growth and distribution of plants and associated products for home gardens") but not in Pennsylvania. A form email informed her a couple of weeks after she had applied that her application had been rejected. Hers was a joint garden center/florist, but a day or two later, watching the news, she saw a feature about a florist an hour west that was open and delivering flowers to customers. "Clear as mud," the head of a chamber of commerce in central Pennsylvania told a pair of reporters with Spotlight PA, an investigative unit funded by news outlets across the state. An investigation by the state auditor general described the program as "a subjective process built on shifting sands of changing guidance, which led to significant confusion among business owners."

In mid-April, Wolf joined the governors of New York, New Jersey, Connecticut, Massachusetts, Rhode Island, and Delaware on a video call. Together, they announced a multistate council of advisors that would share and coordinate ideas for safely dropping restrictions each had put in place. Wolf described his as "a measured, careful approach to prepare for the future while ensuring that we don't undo all of our efforts." Nine days later, Wolf unveiled a color-coded plan his staff had created to oversee a phased-in reopening. "We will not just be flipping a switch to go from closed to open," he said. Wolf reminded people that COVID was a confounding, highly infectious virus that scientists were struggling to understand. "The virus will set the timeline, not us," he said.

All of Pennsylvania's sixty-seven counties started in the red phase. The state's 12.8 million residents would remain under strict stay-at-home orders. Under red, all non-life-sustaining businesses in a county must remain shut. Restaurants and bars were still limited to carryout and delivery. Moving to yellow meant lifting stay-at-home directives. All retail would open, but only once a county was designated green could those in "personal care services" (hair salons, barbershops, massage parlors) reopen, and then only at 50 percent of capacity and by appointment only. "Health and wellness facilities" (gyms and spas), along with movie theaters, casinos, and shopping malls, could also reopen in green, but they, too, needed to abide by a 50 percent occupancy rule, as would any restaurant wanting to resume indoor dining. Moving from red to yellow to green would be determined by a range of factors, the governor and his people said, including the fourteen-day average of new cases, hospitalization rates, testing capacity, and other metrics the general public could monitor via an online dashboard the state had created. People in each county needed to await word from the governor, who had the final say on when a county could move to a new phase.

"Ultimately," Wolf warned, "there's going to be a measure of subjectivity to this whole thing."

* * *

In Tunkhannock, Glenda watched too much cable. She watched a good cross-section of networks: Fox, CNN, ABC. "The news was ridiculous. I would just sob and sob and sob, all the while trying to figure out if I should be applying for PPP and seeing what else was out there," she said.

In a different time, Glenda might have phoned someone at Hallmark for guidance, or at least for a sympathetic shoulder. But who would she even talk with? "They're just another big corporation now," she offered.

Glenda had her mother, who obviously understood the business. But she was eighty-five years old when the pandemic hit, and Glenda sought to shield her from additional stresses beyond the daily news. Even living in Wyoming County, a rural county with fewer than thirty thousand people, it was hard not to feel like the virus was lurking just outside the door. The *Wyoming County Press Examiner* arrived every Wednesday, bringing more bad news about creeping case counts and the fallout. The county laid off a third of its staff. The schools, the library, and the county courthouse were closed. There were more cancellations every week: the Kiwanis's annual Easter egg hunt, the Assembly of God's Good Friday fish fry, bingo at the local firehouse. Glenda and her mom talked regularly about the pandemic. But on the topic of J.R.'s, the answer was always the same: we're fine.

"I didn't want her to see all that I was going through," Glenda said. "I didn't want to push her over the deep end."

Privately, though, Glenda was convinced she was doomed. Wasting time on the internet, she came across surveys of small business owners imagining their future. More than half did not think they would survive the pandemic. If that was the case, she did imagine herself among the survivors. Public health officials warned that those with select comorbidities—preexisting medical conditions—faced much greater risks should they catch the virus. Her shop suffered structural impairments that were the equivalent of a bad heart and compromised immune system. That, Glenda recognized, greatly diminished its chances of survival.

Chapter 7

The Old Forge

TJ's brief return to the grocery business proved a success. Just the very act of bagging flour and onions and other basics gave him a sense of purpose. It felt good to know they were helping to feed the town, though in a different way, and there was the extra pleasure that again a Cusumano was in the grocery business. The one thing their open-air market wasn't was lucrative. In two weeks, they brought in maybe a few thousand dollars, and almost all of that went to pay the restaurant's suppliers.

Browsing industry blogs and other sites he visited, TJ read about restaurants around the country similarly selling groceries to the public: in Los Angeles, in New York, in Atlanta. The reports put a smile on his face. "I was like, 'Hey, maybe our little town can be ahead of everyone on something,'" TJ said. If anything, Cafe Rinaldi next door had opened even faster than they did. "The morning after the governor shut us down, we had the toilet paper and hand sanitizers and anything else we thought people might need laid out on a table," said Russell Rinaldi, in a robust Old Forge accent that made it sound as if he had grown up a street urchin who survived turf wars in South Philly or Bayonne or Canarsie. Rinaldi, who has a shaved head and the bulging muscles of an action hero, described COVID as a "sucker punch." They gave away the toilet paper and other basics. He and his siblings, with whom he co-owned the restaurant, priced most everything else at cost. Every Monday, the Rinaldis boxed up dinners they gave out at no charge to anyone who had lost a job or could use a hot meal.

Takeout at Cusumano's picked up after the first couple of weeks of the pandemic. But people in town still seemed skittish about interacting with another human when picking up their food, or even touching the bags and containers that were handed to them. Cusumano's was selling about as much pizza as they normally would, but they were lucky if they got a dozen dinner orders on some nights. (In Scranton, at a bar and grill called Andy Gavin's, owner Don Surace had a day in April where he was open for eight hours and sold a single pretzel.) The orders that did come in couldn't compare to the sales they racked up when people were sitting around the table enjoying a meal. People weren't ordering the restaurant's specialty drinks or $12 bourbons, let alone refills. There were no appetizers or main courses being run down from the kitchen to feed those who felt hungry while drinking at the Cellar. At some point, he had learned the magic of what his friends teased him was "drug money"—dinners of twelve or fourteen or twenty when one pharmaceutical giant or another organized a roundtable discussion, or however they rationalized eating and drinking on the dime of the company. Before COVID, that could mean an extra couple thousand dollars in a good month.

The mortgage was $4,000 a month. But before April's payment became due, their banker phoned to tell them they could suspend their mortgage payments for six months and tack any missed payments at the end of the fifteen-year term of the loan. The Cusumanos chose to miss their April payment. At that point, the restaurant was barely bringing in $1,000 a week. Labor costs were down, but they weren't zero, and there was always another bill coming in:

from an insurance company, from a utility, from the liquor control board. Cusumano's needed to bring in more cash.

TJ brought up the idea of meal kits with Nina one night. People were at home cooking more. The Blue Aprons and HelloFreshes of the world had proven there was a market for satisfying, easy-to-make home-cooked meals. Why don't we post a limited menu on Facebook each day and let people order what they want to make at home that night? Nina thought of people buying food from them and still needing to clean the pots and pans they had dirtied cooking it up themselves. Unlike the big meal-delivery companies, Cusumano's wasn't offering to deliver a box to their door. But who knew what might work? If nothing else, it gave TJ a way of feeling he was doing something when there were no orders coming in.

Taco Tuesdays were an easier sell. The first cook TJ had hired after opening Cusumano's had been an undocumented worker from Mexico. "He was one of the best chefs I've ever seen," TJ said, but he was lured to a higher-paying job as the head chef in a kitchen in nearby Pittston. Before then, TJ taught him how to prepare Italian classics and he taught TJ traditional Mexican cooking. In the past, they had been closed on Tuesdays, but a few weeks into the pandemic, TJ went in early every Tuesday to make the salsa from scratch, stew the meats, and cook up his version of Mexican rice. Cusumano's posted the new Tuesday menu on Facebook and counted on word of mouth. They charged $12 for those wanting premade margarita mix or $25 for those who wanted the tequila to make four margaritas.

Just prior to COVID, TJ had cleared out a spot behind his restaurant that had been choked with weeds. The plan was to install large garden boxes and grow tomatoes, peppers, and herbs that spring. TJ's uncle Larry was the one who suggested that instead he use the space to create a barbecue pit. TJ had never particularly cared for the taste of barbecue. To him, ribs were slow-cooked in balsamic or red sauce. Chicken, if it wasn't pounded into a cutlet, was a full bird roasted in the oven, Italian-style. Yet his uncle's suggestion propelled him to search on YouTube for instructional videos and look for recipes that might provide inspiration. TJ canceled the truckload of soil he had on order and bought a used barbecue rig he found online.

"I'm like, 'We have no money and you spend it on this? Really?'" Nina said. "I was ready to kill him." Not far from town, TJ found a sawmill happy to sell him their scraps of cherry, hickory, and other woods for smoking. "The idea was good old Southern barbecue here in northern Pennsylvania," TJ said. The question was whether anyone would want to buy their barbecue brisket or ribs from an Italian restaurant.

TJ started looking into tents and was relieved to find they were plentiful. "With all those concerts and festivals and weddings that had to be canceled, the tent rental places had this big surplus," he said. The only thing that wasn't clear was whether the governor would allow outdoor dining once the weather warmed up and what rules might apply. There was no mention of outdoor dining in the state's red-yellow-green plan, and those trying to reach the governor's office for a clarification came up empty. TJ put down a deposit on a tent and hoped for the best.

"The truth was no one knew what the fuck was going on at that point," TJ said. "So you do the best you can do." Theirs was a town of coal miners who knew about hard work and hard times. TJ got up every morning, heated up his ovens, and looked over the "prep list" he and his cooks maintained on a whiteboard hanging at the back of the kitchen. And he got to work, chopping and searing and sautéing and thinking up other ways he might save his restaurant. "The Old Forge way," people in town like to say.

* * *

There needed to be a new forge before there could be an old one. The original was built shortly after the Revolutionary War, by an army surgeon who was among the first to recognize the value of the

Lackawanna Valley's rich deposits of both coal and iron ore. Coal, carted by oxen, could provide the heat needed to melt the iron ore in a furnace. A half-dozen years after the Continental Army had defeated the British, Dr. William Smith, working with his two sons-in-law, built a forge near a bend in the Lackawanna River. There, in a rickety wooden building, they converted ore into iron, and played their small part in sparking the Industrial Revolution in the US. Dr. Smith's operation shut down after a new, more durable forge was built upriver toward Scranton, and the area that was home to the old forge had its name.

Like Tunkhannock, Old Forge is technically a borough. (And Pennsylvania a commonwealth rather than a state, but never mind.) Old Forge might be described as a suburb of Scranton, but that does not seem right. People living in Old Forge drive the ten or fifteen minutes to Scranton for a job, but Scranton, a city of seventy-five thousand, doesn't quite have the gravitational pull of a bigger metropolis. Besides, Old Forge seems insulated from most outside influences. Years ago, when Taylor, Moosic, Pittston, and other surrounding towns, as a cost-savings measure, started merging school districts, Old Forge declined to join them. Instead, the townspeople decided to maintain its own single-building school district, even though it meant paying more in property taxes. "You start on the ground floor in kindergarten and basically work your way to the top until you graduate," explained former Old Forge mayor Bob Mulkerin. Mulkerin's kids attended school there, just as he and his wife and his in-laws had. The coal mines closed, as did the textile mills. Yet people chose to stay.

"Not too big, not too small," TJ said. "Kind of Goldilocks in being just right."

There's a small-town feel to Old Forge. On the main road into town, a parade of banners hang from the lampposts, each featuring "Hometown Heroes" who serve, or have served, in the military. In 2020, there were also plenty of Trump placards along that drive in what had been a Democratic stronghold, but there were more signs proclaiming support for the local police (and virtually no BLM signboards in sight). American flags line the front of the town's American Legion outpost. It's a tight-knit community where the guy coaching a Little League team had been teammates with half the people in the bleachers watching their kids play, if not their future boss. Mulkerin was TJ's coach before he was his bartender and friend.

There's a scrappiness to Old Forge, along with a brawling spirt. "Growing up, if you were out on a Friday night, you had a fifty-fifty chance someone was getting punched in the face," TJ said. "There was a fist fight like every ten minutes." The kids from Taylor or Moosic or West Scranton would come to town looking for trouble, or the Old Forge boys would go to them. And the combat would begin. Joe Lech, a seemingly mild-mannered pharmacist plying his trade in the Endless Mountains, grew up in Old Forge. He remembered a car full of kids from a rival town driving Main Street on a Friday night, taunting the locals after their school's football team beat Old Forge's. Joe mentioned the name of a short, stout kid. That kid busted the driver's window at a stoplight, pulled him out of the car, and threw him through a storefront's plateglass window. "When the cops came, they were pissed at the out-of-town guys for instigating a fight," Joe said.

"We've always been this tiny place with a little tiny school that's stood up to bigger towns like Scranton and [Clarks] Summit," said Anthony Parisi, a childhood friend of TJ's. "We don't back down."

Food, rather than coal or iron ore, is now the reason people in the area travel to Old Forge. The draw, specifically, is its unique pizza. Years back Old Forge declared itself "Pizza Capital of the World," and if that seems presumptuous, consider that in 2017 *USA Today* published an article about the town under the headline, "The American Pizza Capital You've Never Heard Of." Picture pizza that is Sicilian-style in shape and cooked in the same kind of shallow, rectangular pan but with an airier crust than Sicilian. Each place selling Old Forge pizza has its own recipe, but the sauce is sweeter than the typical sauce and more flavorful. TJ uses a blend of American cheese and mozzarella on his pizza, but some use only American, and Cafe Rinaldi next door uses cheddar. The initiated know to order a "cut" rather than a slice, or a tray or half tray. When someone asks for a "pie" rather than a tray, the joke inside Arcaro & Genell, which has been serving Old Forge pizza since 1962, is to ask, "Apple or blueberry?"

The provenance of Old Forge pizza isn't exactly clear, but the siblings who own Cafe Rinaldi credit three women, including their great-grandmother Louisa, who served what she called *lupitze* (pronounced more like "lu-pits") to hungry miners at the Main Street speakeasy she ran in the 1900s. TJ serves his version of Old Forge pizza as he learned it from his grandma Annie, who taught it to several generations of pizza makers. Revello's Pizza, next door to Cusumano's, over the years has included Ozzy Osbourne and Hillary Clinton among its diners. Across the street from Cusumano's sits Arcaro & Genell. This pizzeria, which *USA Today* once declared among the top ten best in the US, has a following so loyal that people pay $50 to ship their pizzas long distance. There was also the pizza at Anthony's, Mary Lou's, Salerno's, Popsy's, and Augustine's Club 17.

Old Forge, like virtually every last town of any size in the United States, has been infiltrated by chains. Across the street from Cafe Rinaldi on Main Street is a McDonald's. The old Cafe Rinaldi, which started in a small strip mall a couple of blocks away, houses a Domino's Pizza. There's a Burger King and a Dunkin'. Old-timers still complain that the bookstore, electronics shop, and other Main Street establishments were bulldozed a couple of decades earlier to make room for a giant CVS. But it's Old Forge's unique pizza and the family-owned restaurants that are the main source of commerce in town and that keep people's lives intertwined. Old Forgers socialized at the Cellar or at Arcaro & Genell or while waiting to pick up a couple of trays at Revello's. The restaurants were the town's meeting place and a large part of what tied people there.

TJ was the exception in leaving Old Forge for college. In this community where the median income barely breaks $33,000, roughly 80 percent of those who continue their education after high school stick close to home and commute to classes, said Shawn Nee, Old Forge High's guidance counselor. People tend to return to Old Forge even if they left for college. That's what TJ did and also Anthony Parisi and Lou Moriano. The place, Moriano said, has a way of imprinting itself on the brain.

"Old Forge is a Friday night in the fall, the windows rolled down, and all you can smell is the terrific smell of pizza for blocks," Moriano said. In his mind, it's a Friday night, and the school's old science teacher is doing the play-by-play over a PA system so loud his voice carries to Main Street.

"This whole pizza-capital-of-the-world thing has become our identifying marker and really helps," Anthony Parisi said. He knows Old Forge as a tight-knit community where people know one another. "But the pizza and the restaurants is what really identifies us."

* * *

TJ traced his Old Forge roots to great-great-grandparents on both sides of his family. One great-grandfather, along with his two brothers, opened Café Cusumano in 1916. The place was a bar that served homemade wine they made in the basement and Italian specialties, including a local delicacy called "sofrito" (calf hearts and pork shoulder simmered in white wine). That same great-grandfather also started a cemetery in town so Italians had a place to bury their own. By birthright, TJ has a spot on the cemetery's board "into perpetuity, or something like that," he said. Toni Cusumano's father and TJ's namesake, Tom Joseph, ran a beer distributorship out of a Main Street storefront three blocks from where his grandson's restaurant now stands.

The list of people thinking it was lunacy for TJ to buy a restaurant was long and included, he said, "at least half my family." Age was a factor. TJ was only twenty-seven and Nina twenty-six. If nothing else, his parents' life offered a case study on the perils of owning a small business. "I tried to tell him, but TJ knows his own mind," Tom Cusumano said. TJ's closest friends, however, were not surprised by the decision. "He talked about doing these other things," Lou Moriano said. "But we always thought he would be a restaurant guy. A chef. Always."

Cusumano's took the place of Brutico's, a traditional red-sauce Italian restaurant that had anchored Main Street for decades. Dominica Brutico, a local legend, reigned for decades over her white-tablecloth restaurant where smartly dressed waiters and waitresses served Italian classics. Dominica turned away potential diners whom she did not believe were dressed appropriately and slighted those patrons she deemed unworthy of her food—working people in town, for instance, there for a special splurge, rather than her regulars, who tended to be the lawyers, doctors, and others with money and status. Strangers who stumbled on Brutico's were banished downstairs to what back then was called the pizza room—unless, of course, that night Dominica was feeding special guests who wanted to gather out of view. Members of the Bufalino crime family were Brutico's regulars, including Russell Bufalino, whom Joe Pesci played in the Martin Scorsese film *The Irishman*. Local legend is that it's from Brutico's that Russell Bufalino called in the hit on Jimmy Hoffa, but Russell Rinaldi, who was named in Bufalino's honor and whose father was a bookmaker and loan shark for the family, said he heard from people who presumably would know that the order to kill the teamster leader came from a restaurant in the Poconos.

A Brutico's regular who owned a group of Sunoco gas stations in the area bought the restaurant from Dominica while TJ was still in college. He wasn't a chef, but he thought the Brutico name, along with Dominica's recipes and the restaurant's reputation for well-prepared Italian classics, would be enough. It was not. His name was added to the long list of people who learn the hard way how difficult it is to make money in the restaurant business. The man had been at it for maybe a half-dozen years when he approached TJ: Was he interested in buying the restaurant from him? TJ did not need to ask for a tour to see the property up close. "I was a busboy there, a dishwasher, a pizza maker," he said. He had bartended upstairs in the main restaurant and had even picked up extra shifts as a waiter. "Me working there, my grandmother working there, my sisters—it felt like fate," TJ said.

Nina was on board. She was made of the same Old Forge steel, practical and up for the challenge. She had been working as a waitress at Cafe Rinaldi when TJ broached the idea. "What's the worst that could happen?" she asked. "It doesn't work out and I end up a waitress?"

Money to buy the place was the last stumbling block. Neither had a degree in hospitality or experience running a restaurant. It helped in securing a loan that they were white. A study by the Federal Reserve showed that black- and Latino-owned enterprises were less than half as likely as white-owned ones to be approved for business loans. According to that same survey, which looked at fourteen thousand small businesses across the country, black and Latino applicants with high credit ratings were approved for loans at roughly the same rate as white applicants with lower credit scores. The Cusumanos went to a local branch of the Fidelity Bank, which had been making loans in northeastern Pennsylvania since 1902. There, they spoke to the head of commercial lending, who was a Cusumano family friend. TJ and Nina had some money saved up and were fortunate that both sets of parents had money to chip in on the 10 percent down payment that the SBA required to receive one of its 7(a) loans. That left them with a fifteen-year loan that would have them paying nearly $750,000 by the time it was paid off in 2028. TJ, however, did not flinch.

"I had lived with the idea of a restaurant for so long it's like I had no fear about it," he said.

A common assumption holds that opening a restaurant is riskier than other ventures. Data from the SBA demonstrates that that's not true—eating establishments don't fail at any higher a rate than other businesses—but that underscores the gamble that anyone takes when starting a new enterprise. The odds were better than fifty-fifty that Cusumano's would be closed within five years. Arguably, the Cusumanos had a leg up when they bought an existing restaurant with a loyal clientele, but then both TJ and Nina did everything to set themselves apart from Brutico's.

The man who sold them the restaurant thought TJ was a fool to drop the Brutico name. "He's like, 'That's what you're buying, are you crazy?'" TJ said. Maybe he was. But his last name was not Brutico, and he had in mind a very different restaurant. He loved what he called the "1980s-style Italian restaurant with red sauce and veal parm," but his people were from Southern Italy: Sicily, at the toe of Italy's boot, and Felitto, a small town at around the ankle, 150 miles south of Naples. His style of cooking, to the extent it could be categorized, was Southern Italian, though he described it as "new age Italian cooking" on the restaurant's website. "Our menu is not like your typical Italian restaurant," it continued, but "a fresh twist on classic Italian dishes" that could please "even the biggest of foodies."

The first changes they made in the restaurant were cosmetic and more pragmatic. Despite its upscale food, the place looked dingy on the outside. It was a freestanding, two-story Art Deco–style building more or less at the center of Main Street in Old Forge. The designer seemed to be going for classy, but the façade read more funeral parlor than restaurant. They painted the outside white and gray and replaced the old black awning with a snazzy new sign that spelled out C-U-S-U-M-A-N-O in silver letters.

They also gave the main dining room a makeover. They ripped out the drop-down ceiling, exposing the original tin ceiling, and put in new lighting, including a spectacular central fixture that was like a tree shooting out metal branches tipped with lights. They

painted the walls a muted gray and installed a dark-patterned car-
pet, and then hung brightly colored posters to give the room some
life. To keep expenses down, they kept the three-sided granite bar
they inherited, though TJ described it as "the color of an infant's
shit and a glass breaker."

The upstairs kitchen proved the biggest project. The floor had
to be replaced, which is how they learned the restaurant had a
pest problem. That added to their unanticipated expenses. After
installing a new kitchen floor, TJ outfitted the room with three
used stoves he had found online. He pushed them together so he
had twenty-two burners. The restaurant opened in December of
2013 on Friday the thirteenth, which was also his namesake's birthday. "People begged me not to do it on Friday the thirteenth but
my mom was like, 'It was your grandfather's birthday, I think you
should do it,'" TJ said.

Some restaurants are birthed fully formed. Cusumano's fell into
that other category of places that are a work in progress. "It was
touch and go early on," said Brenda Roscioli. Roscioli had become
friends with Nina at Cafe Rinaldi, and then Roscioli moved next
door when Cusumano's opened its doors. Cusumano's problem was
TJ. He was Primo, Tony Shalhoub's character in the movie *Big
Night*, who sought to serve dishes that set him apart, like a grilled
octopus over a white bean puree with pistachio pesto—a classic
Sicilian dish.

Jessica Barletta had waitressed on Fridays, Saturdays, and Sundays when the restaurant was called Brutico's, and she worked
those same shifts at the new Cusumano's. Barletta, who was also
in her twenties (and no relation to the Hazleton mayor with the
same last name), loved the energy this young couple brought to the
restaurant, but their longtime regulars did not necessarily share
that enthusiasm. "The food was amazing. It was gorgeous," Barletta said. "But people would say, 'Yeah, but where's the manigot
[manicotti]?'" There were complaints as well about their prices.
"TJ was buying the highest quality meats and fish but they didn't

care," Barletta said. Regulars saw prices higher than they had been paying. Worse, an entrée no longer came with a side dish of pasta or vegetables.

Barletta, Roscioli, and others gave TJ credit for his ability to listen and willingness to change. TJ shaved his prices by a dollar or two and offered a house salad with a main course. When people still complained, he changed his menu again so that every entrée came with at least one complimentary side dish. He would cook people their chicken or veal any way they wanted it: piccata, parmigiana, marsala, Milanese, or calabrese. He expanded his pasta offering so that someone could try his wild boar ragu or stick with reliable standbys like cheese or meat ravioli or fettuccine Alfredo. He also added pizza to the menu, which pleased Cindi Heyen, a Brutico's regular who eventually attained the same status at Cusumano's. She had loved his father's pizza at the old Rossi's and was pleased that she could order it at Cusumano's. "They've really adapted over the years," Heyen said.

The early years were as hard as people had warned TJ and Nina they would be. He remembered his parents complaining about their old accountant, but it was only once he started complaining about his that he understood. They had survived their first year but then learned they owed tens of thousands of dollars in back taxes. That almost did them in. "We had a ton of customers," TJ said. "We had a slamming business. What we didn't have was any money."

Nina wasn't bubbly and all smiles. She didn't have the personality of the typical host or hostess. TJ had the personality, except with a razor's edge. He described his philosophy of customer service by talking about the restaurant where he worked when he was sixteen. As busboy, it was his responsibility to ask if the guests wanted water and, if so, whether they preferred still or sparkling. TJ turned the question into a conversation. "The dad pulls me aside and tells me, 'Go up to the next table and ask them, 'Do you want some fucking water?'" TJ said. He did not take the father literally, but the lesson stuck with him.

"That's sort of how I train the staff to interact with our customers," TJ said. "Don't fluff them. Don't talk to them beyond what you need to say. People are here for dinner. They didn't come to talk to the waitress or the bus kid. Just give them their fucking water."

Originally, they decided to open six days a week and take Mondays off. But Mondays were merely a shorter workday for TJ, not a free day: he would be at Cusumano's for six or eight hours rather than twelve or fourteen. "I'm not going to lie to you, our marriage was really strained," TJ confided. "We had some rough patches, the two of us." They decided to remain dark not only on Mondays but also Tuesdays, which at least gave TJ something like a single day off. "We needed more time," he said. "Our relationship had become nothing but the restaurant."

They were in year four of the restaurant when TJ began thinking more seriously about doing something with Brutico's old pizza room, where Russell Bufalino and his crew met. TJ proposed turning the room into a bar, and the blowback was instant. "I hated the idea," Nina said. They finally had a bit of money saved up. Yet now her husband wanted to build a second bar and another set of bathrooms downstairs?

"I think we all thought it was a bad idea," said Jessica Barletta, who became one of Nina's closest friends. "He'd sit upstairs with his little diagrams and then run downstairs and we'd be like, 'Here he goes again.'" For TJ, though, the Cellar was an important final step in distancing themselves from the lingering legacy of Brutico's, where some were deemed unworthy of her cooking. "There was still a fanciness to upstairs which meant people wouldn't come unless they had a chance to put on a nicer shirt and do up their hair," he said. Both he and Nina saw it in people they had known their whole life. "Our friends weren't coming to the restaurant like maybe it was too fancy for them and that started to really upset me," TJ said. The Cellar meant a back door through which people could enter the restaurant after an outing with the kids or come straight there from work, regardless of how they were dressed.

TJ enlisted friends and family to keep expenses down. His father-in-law, a mason, built a wood-burning fireplace with TJ's help, and TJ served as an assistant to his cousin "Chunky," a plumber. They added a bar made of walnut and put down new carpeting but kept the walls, which were knotty pine. They scattered old black-and-white photos around the room, including one of TJ's great-grandfather, sporting a bushy mustache, and another of his grandfather pictured with Nina's. A mounted deer head graced one wall, along with a mounted fish, a neon sign for Genesee Cream Ale, and a banged-up metal Royal Crown Cola thermometer sign. Being there felt like hanging out in a friend's living room. "The idea was this little hidden speakeasy under the restaurant that only insiders knew about," TJ said.

The Cellar opened at the end of 2017. Soon Nina was among those admitting she had been wrong. "The place would be packed every weekend," Cindi Heyen said. "Wall-to-wall people. One of us would have to go early to claim a big high-top so we could have our little group there on Friday nights." The Cellar doubled the restaurant's alcohol sales and boosted its food revenues. People who came for drinks would grow hungry and ask for the food menu. The Cellar goosed appetizer sales in a restaurant where starters are on the pricey side (calamari fried and tossed in a spicy arrabbiata sauce, for instance, costs $16) and also sales of Cusumano's Old Forge pizza, which came a dozen different ways. TJ expanded his menu to include a filet mignon French dip sandwich (caramelized onions and Gruyère cheese on a crusty bread) that cost $18, and different varieties of stromboli (similar to a calzone but rolled rather than folded and crimped at the seam) for $13.

"He's always right," Nina said. "That's the annoying part." That's not to say TJ was immune to the risks they were taking on with the Cellar. He pounded so many Long Trail Double IPAs on the night they opened that he christened the new room by throwing up on the expensive walnut bar they had splurged on. The endeavor had been expensive but probably paid for itself inside of six months.

"We had smiles on our faces every night," TJ said, "because not only were we bringing in a little more money, but we saw people really, really enjoying themselves."

TJ's next big idea was an outdoor patio. He imagined a space with a solid roof and open sides. It felt like reruns inside Cusumano's. Nina worried about the cost, the staff teased him about his obsession with schematics and architectural plans, yet TJ bulled ahead. This time the naysayers included some of his neighbors. "A lot of the restaurants around us said, 'Why is he doing this, it's not worth the money, it's too risky,'" TJ said. "But we had a gut feeling this was the right move so we put our necks on the line." Once again, he relied on Nina's father to build a giant fireplace that would both warm people in cooler weather and add a homey feeling to a space that could seat sixty people. The patio opened in mid-summer 2019 and seemed an immediate hit. Inside Cusumano's, they looked forward to 2020 and their first full season with covered outdoor seating.

* * *

The town's restaurant owners were all close friends. When the mixer broke at Salerno's, Angelo Genell at Arcaro & Genell made their dough until it was fixed. Pizza boxes, cheese, a bottle of alcohol: the other restaurants in town were there if someone ran out. "The borrowing between restaurants has been going on for fifty years," Pat Revello at Revello's Pizza said. They took trips together—hunting, or to Florida, or to the Super Bowl the year the Eagles won it all. "A day or two doesn't go by where I don't speak to at least one of them," Revello said of his fellow Old Forge restaurant owners.

In the hierarchy of restaurants in Old Forge, Cusumano's sat at or near the top of the heap by virtue of the food he served. Yet that also meant that TJ and Nina ranked high in the ordering of establishments most hurt by the shutdown of indoor dining. "Doing pizza takeout is a lot easier than doing filet mignon," Pat Revello said. Even before COVID, takeout accounted for half of Revello's business.

In the middle spot between the upper-tier (and pricier) dining rooms and the pizza restaurants that dotted Main Street was Cafe Rinaldi. People ate there for heavy platters of Italian mainstays such as veal parmigiana, linguine with clam sauce, and gnocchi. (Its motto: "We promise you'll leave happy—and with leftovers.") To survive COVID, Russell Rinaldi said, they turned their restaurant into a takeout machine. Rinaldi had the phone company install a couple of new phone lines and ordered two additional computer setups for entering orders. The waitstaff (including his sister-in-law and her sister) chopped ingredients for salads and made dressings. The bussers (assorted nieces and nephews) and the restaurant's hostess (Rinaldi's mother-in-law) pitched in as well, making pizza boxes, taking orders, and swiping credit cards. A lot of the orders were for their *lupitze* and also their spaghetti and meatballs, fettucine Alfredo, and other pasta dishes. But, Rinaldi said, their chicken, veal, and steak also sold. Customers wanted the familiar tastes, and many wanted to do what they could to support the Rinaldis. They paid restaurant prices for the bottled wine that the liquor board was temporarily allowing them to sell and splurged on desserts.

"The first couple 'tree weeks," said Rinaldi in a thick Old Forge accent, "things were real slow, but then it got super-busy"—so much so that they set up a second staging area for pickup so people could more easily distance themselves from one another.

Until shortly before the pandemic, there were two fine-dining establishments in Old Forge: Cusumano's and Anthony's, though TJ would list the restaurants in reverse order. "Her food is unbelievable," TJ said of Phyllis Mischello, the chef-owner of Anthony's. Mischello had started there as a waitress with five children at home, until adding a sixth to her brood when cancer took her sister. She kept the restaurant name when she took over in 1999 but threw out the menu and cooked the recipes she had learned from her mother and her mother's mother before that. In her early sixties, she was still behind the stove every Friday and Saturday night. "Phyllis is like my hero," TJ said. He was confident that Mischello would survive, he said, "because that's Phyllis. She's tough." Rather than give up on the ten-ounce filet mignons ($45.95) or twenty-ounce New York strip ($44.95) that ranked among her bestsellers, she found a higher-quality takeout container that kept meats hotter for longer. "I was amazed at how many people were getting full steak dinners for pickup," said Rose Harding, a hostess at Anthony's.

Billy Genovese was not feeling as fortunate. Genovese, a well-regarded local chef, had rented a storefront directly across from Anthony's on Main Street nine months before COVID. There he opened Billy G's, which Genovese described as "American fine dining." The waitstaff did not put a basket of bread on a table but offered what he called a "bread service" of breads baked in-house and served with a high-end olive oil, a balsamic glaze, roasted garlic, and roasted peppers. The meal ended with a "coffee service" featuring raw sugar and fresh whipped cream.

"Cusumano's and these other guys," Genovese said, "they sell pizza, they sell pasta, they're selling their veal marsala and veal Milanese for $18, $19 a pop." (Actually, $21 at Cusumano's, where the veal they serve was raised on a farm about an hour from the restaurant.) "I had the pasta bowl tableside," Genovese said. "The raw bar, my craft cocktails, dessert for twelve or fourteen a pop.

"My dining was an experience," Genovese said—one he didn't imagine traveling well in takeout containers. "No one's ordering my duck with blood orange glaze," Genovese said. "No one's buying my osso buco. No one's buying my prime steaks." He laid off his entire staff and remained closed through April. After that, he would reevaluate.

* * *

Ang Garzon, Cusumano's sauté cook, was sitting home doing nothing, making more than she would working all night in front of a hot stove. That's the way it was for most laid-off food workers with the weekly $600 supplement to unemployment Congress added so people didn't have to choose money over their health. "It wasn't astronomically more, maybe $200 more a month, but it meant I could maintain my way of living and still have extra left over," Ang said. She fished a lot (her Facebook profile picture showed her happily holding up a trout she had just caught) and spent a lot of time on social media. She posted on a range of topics, from the awfulness of Trump to memes supporting LGBTQ rights. The rapper Lil Nas X came out as gay shortly into the pandemic, and she shared a quote from him that began, "I spent my entire teenage years hating myself because of all the shit y'all preached." She shared joke posts (the proper way to fold a sheet? Roll it into a ball and toss in the back of a closet) and self-revealing ones, like the quote from someone who described herself as "probably the most friendly unfriendly person ever." She ogled over a stove chef Daniel Boulud had custom-built for $270,000.

Ang was among the fortunate. Around the country, people filed for unemployment and waited weeks, if not months, for a first unemployment check. Ang remembered receiving her first check maybe ten days into the pandemic. Sha-Asia Johnson, who had been laid off at the same time as Ang, waited more than a month for unemployment to kick in. For her the lockdown was not about indulging favorite hobbies or laughing over memes. She is a black woman in a country where black Americans were nearly three times as likely to test positive for the coronavirus as whites. (Latinos were more than three times as likely.) The death rates were similarly disproportionate. Two of Sha-Asia's uncles died that spring. Both were in their forties. "It was a very sad time for our family," she said.

Still in school, Sha-Asia lived in an apartment with her mother and younger brother. Her mother was a manager at a local Dollar

Tree and therefore considered an essential worker. That proved a mixed blessing for the family. The expectation that her mother go to work each day added to the stress of their household but also helped keep them financially stable. Sha-Asia also experienced the disappointments of attending remote classes. Watching a cooking demonstration via a laptop was not the same as sitting in a class-room. Half the time the angles weren't right to fully see what an instructor was demonstrating. Cooking along with the class when everyone was in his or her own kitchen also seemed useless without hands-on guidance. "It was all very frustrating," she said. On the upside, Sha-Asia felt almost rich when unemployment kicked in. With the $600 supplement, she was banking nearly twice as much as she earned at the restaurant—and more than she had earned in her life by a lot.

Chapter 8

Governor Dictator

One month into the pandemic, when Governor Wolf announced his color-coded reopening plan, he declared May 8, a Friday, as the start date for Pennsylvania's partial reopening. That would be the first day that counties in the state could be moved out of the red phase and into yellow. The governor and his people stressed that the state's Department of Health would use a range of metrics and employ a data analytics tool developed by Carnegie Mellon University, in Pittsburgh, to make its decisions. But people around the state fixated on a single stat: a per capita infection rate of fewer than fifty COVID-19 cases per one hundred thousand over a fourteen-day period. In Tunkhannock, Glenda Shoemaker, Mark Monsey, and other small business owners circled May 8 on their calendar.

Theirs was a rural county with few coronavirus cases. Surely, Tunkhannock and the rest of Wyoming County would be among the first the state would allow to reopen.

* * *

April had been a grim month for Pennsylvania and the rest of the United States. On April 1, the US surpassed one thousand deaths from COVID-19. Less than one week later, that number had doubled to two thousand total deaths. By month's end, the country had registered sixty thousand COVID-related deaths, exceeding the number of US soldiers who had died during the Vietnam War. At that point, the US accounted for one in every four COVID-related deaths around the world, though the US represented only around 4 percent of the globe's population. The US Bureau of Labor Statistics reported the greatest month-over-month increase in the unemployment rate since they started tracking it in 1948. An unemployment rate that had been under 5 percent at the start of the pandemic tripled to nearly 15 percent.

May proved less deadly, though only slightly. The month started the way April ended, with daily COVID death counts that sometimes topped two thousand. But there were days near the end of May when the recorded death toll fell under one thousand. Restrictions were lifted in parts of the country, and businesses reenlisted their people. More than two million Americans went back to work in May, nudging down the unemployment rate to 13.3 percent. On *Fox & Friends*, Jared Kushner, Trump's son-in-law and a senior White House advisor, took a victory lap on behalf of the president. "The federal government rose to the challenge," he said. "This is a great success story."

COVID hit the restaurant sector particularly hard. An estimated two-thirds of restaurant workers were laid off or furloughed, according to the National Restaurant Association. Forecasters warned that one in four restaurants might not survive the pandemic. The numbers were bleaker still if only looking at the country's independently owned eateries. A new group called the Independent Restaurant Coalition formed to advocate on behalf of those that were not part of a chain. They warned that the country risked the permanent closure of as many as 85 percent of its independent restaurants without a dedicated rescue fund like lawmakers in Washington had created for the airlines and hospitals. The Cu-sumanos had their own meager savings, but, like most every other independently owned restaurant in the country, they were largely on their own.

Headlines in April declared a one-month drop of 8.3 percent in consumer spending—the steepest collapse in sales since the gov-ernment started keeping track. In May, consumer spending fell by 16.4 percent. JCPenney, J.Crew, and Neiman Marcus were among the big-name brands that filed for bankruptcy that spring. Pier 1 went out of business (subsequently the brand name was purchased by an investment firm and Pier 1 relaunched as an online-only en-deavor) and Papyrus announced it was closing all 254 of its stores. News reports listed Macy's and Nordstrom among the venerated stalwarts teetering on extinction. "I'm looking at the news," Glenda said, "and I'm thinking, 'What chance do I have?'"

Sales at furniture stores declined by two-thirds in the first two months of the pandemic. Sales at clothing stores plummeted 89 per-cent. By comparison, Glenda noted, hers were down 100 percent. TJ in Old Forge and Vilma in Hazleton might be thinking the same thing. Data from the Department of Commerce showed that restaurant and bar revenues were down 54 percent in the first two months of the pandemic. TJ only wished he was still making nearly half the revenue they were before the pandemic. His revenues had fallen around 80 percent, or even more if fac-toring in lost pharmaceutical bacchanals, wedding showers, and bereavement luncheons that Cusumano's had been hosting before the pandemic. A data analytics firm called Safegraph that uses anonymized cell phone data reported that foot traffic to barber-shops and beauty salons fell 60 percent. The traffic to Vilma's place was down 100 percent, leaving her to wonder why it wasn't at or near 100 percent everywhere else. "I was glad to stay closed," Vilma said.

* * *

The renegades of the business world tend to be its smaller players. The property managers at the big hotel chains are listening to corporate. All those Foot Lockers and GAPs and Williams Sonomas and restaurant chains scattered across the land have legal departments and public relations people, who invariably told their people to abide by whatever rules the local authorities had adopted to tamp down the spread of the virus.

For a small business—a true small business—the owners might be answerable to their spouse or a silent partner, but there wasn't much to stop them from bending the rules, if not defying the authorities, when they saw a restriction as an infringement of their constitutional freedoms.

Around the state, businesses challenged Wolf's shutdown order in the courts. The general manager of a public golf course in western Pennsylvania sued in federal court, claiming the governor had overstepped his authority when he shut down large segments of the state's economy. A Laundromat owner joined that suit, as did a Realtor and the owner of a small logging company, among others. A bell manufacturer near Philadelphia charged that the governor's orders violated the Fifth Amendment right to due process. A gun shop said it violated the Second Amendment right to bear arms. In Harrisburg, a group of attorneys defended small businesses of a different kind. They said by shuttering law offices around the state, Wolf was meddling with the judicial branch.

Other small businesses around Pennsylvania were more defiant. They simply opened their doors to customers in violation of the governor's decrees. Just outside of Wilkes-Barre and not far from Cusumano's, Lawrence Danko, the owner of Danko's All American Fitness, had grown fed up waiting for permission from the governor to open his own business. In May, Danko bought a bunch of hand sanitizer bottles and put them by the entrance and elsewhere around the gym, which was housed in a barnlike structure made of corrugated steel. With the county still in red, the fifty-four-year-old Danko opened his doors each day to any customer willing to defy the local rules with him. And every day, someone with the county drove out to inform him that he was in violation of the state's Disease Prevention and Control Act and issued him a citation.

A new Facebook page called "Screw Tom Wolf" was created to bring attention to the governor's "unconstitutional, Orwellian" response to the pandemic. A second Facebook page was set up to document the "tragedies Governor Wolf ignores." Those that dominated the page—those that saw themselves as "collateral damage" of Wolf's policies—were small business owners. On Twitter, a spoof account abused Wolf practically every time the governor opened his mouth. They mocked him for the patrician background and ivory tower posture and dubbed him the "Czar of the Commiewealth" after that beat out "Nerd King of Pennsylvania" in an online contest to award this fake Wolf a title. A congressman, three state legislators, and four rural counties in the western part of the state sued Wolf and Rachel Levine, charging they had overstepped their authority in shutting down small businesses. They were joined by a hair salon and a drive-in movie theater.

A rally was held in Harrisburg that April to protest what demonstrators were inclined to call the governor's "edicts" or "decrees," as if issued by a king in feudal times. The state had recorded more than thirty-three thousand confirmed cases and twelve hundred deaths when several hundred people stood shoulder to shoulder to hear from a group of speakers that included several Republican legislators. "I was there because it was clear to me that the governor was trampling on the individual liberties that are guaranteed by the constitution of Pennsylvania," said Russ Diamond, a conservative state legislator from central Pennsylvania who spoke to the crowd. In mid-April, Republican majorities in both the House and Senate passed legislation that gave the governor seven days to spell out the steps for a business to reopen safely. The governor had settled on a measured, deliberate plan that reopened the state in phases. Yet as written, any business that complied could reopen immediately, putting "more lives at risk," Secretary of Health Rachel Levine said. Unsurprisingly, the governor vetoed the bill.

Trump, of course, openly sided with protesters, if not egged them on. He had abdicated responsibility for containing the virus to the country's governors, and then took to Twitter to undermine the efforts of those he had left in charge. "LIBERATE MICHIGAN!" he tweeted. "LIBERATE MINNESOTA!" The president had staked his reelection on a robust economy. "We have met the moment and we have prevailed," Trump declared the first week of May. A week later, the Wisconsin state Supreme Court ruled in favor of a Republican challenge to the stay-at-home orders that the governor, a Democrat, had imposed. On May 13, every shuttered business in Wisconsin, including restaurants, bars, and salons, was permitted to reopen without any special restrictions.

Polling was on the side of the cautious. By a ratio of more than two to one, Americans in early May told the Pew Research Center that they were more worried their state would lift coronavirus-related restrictions too quickly rather than too slowly. A *Washington Post*/Ipsos poll found that 74 percent agreed that government should slow the spread of COVID, even if that meant keeping businesses closed. The numbers in Pennsylvania told the same story. A Fox News poll found that 64 percent of the state's residents agreed that Pennsylvania needed to wait before reopening the economy, even if it prolonged the economic crisis. Only 25 percent agreed with the statement that the governor should lift restrictions, even if that prolonged the public health crisis. That same Fox poll found that 69 percent of Pennsylvania's residents approved of Wolf's handling of the coronavirus, compared to just 44 percent for the job Trump was doing.

At that point, it wasn't clear that there was an upside to reopening a business. Near the end of April, Georgia lifted restrictions on restaurants, gyms, salons, and other businesses around the state. Yet enterprises that tracked credit card transactions, payroll payments, and other data found that the reopening had far less impact on the Georgia economy than elected officials had hoped. Roughly three in ten businesses were still closed weeks after restrictions were dropped, and customers stayed away from many of those that had reopened. OpenTable, the restaurant reservation service, found that one month after their liberation from restrictions, sales at their member restaurants still were down 85 percent from prepandemic levels. Businesses ranging from movie theaters to tattoo parlors also reported dismal numbers. Closer to home, Danko's gym did okay but only because it drew so many people from outside the area interested in demonstrating their support rather than locals showing up for a regular workout.

* * *

Almost immediately after passage of the CARES Act, TJ was on the phone with his banker. He was eager to fill out an application for PPP—if anyone could figure out how to do that. It wasn't until the night before the program went live in early April that the Treasury Department released its guidelines for applying, and even then, the rules were ambiguous. Vilma had read about the program and wanted to learn more before applying. In Tunkhannock, Glenda reached out to a part-timer at the store who also worked for an accounting firm. "We kind of went back and forth but the rules were so vague," Glenda said. She decided to wait and see.

Right away, TJ saw a major flaw in PPP: its requirement that a small business spend at least 75 percent of the money on payroll or be forced to pay it back with interest. CARES took care of the unemployed with a $600 weekly supplement paid by the federal treasury. Yet the main aim of PPP, as its name implied, was as a paycheck protection program. Vilma didn't need help paying her employees, who would have nothing to do at a closed salon except increase the chances of spreading the virus to one another. She was worried about her mortgage and other expenses. Similarly, J.R.'s Hallmark in Tunkhannock would not be helped by a payroll protection program. Glenda's people didn't want to come to work, and she didn't need them there. Yet under the rules, both Glenda and Vilma would need to spend at least 75 percent of any money they received paying their workers, and do so during an eight-week window, or they would owe the money plus interest. PPP was advertised as a program that would help small businesses. In reality, it had been designed to keep employees working, and presumably that would help the business owner.

"I don't know why they didn't just give us the money and let us document that we spent it on legitimate business expenses," TJ said. "As long as it was injected into the American economy, what difference did it make?"

The speed with which the government launched the PPP program was impressive. Less than two weeks after the passage of CARES, the SBA had created a portal that banks could use to submit applications on behalf of its customers. The Trump administration touted what it called the most sweeping small business rescue program in US history. But then after just thirteen days, the SBA announced that the program was out of money. Only a small fraction of those small businesses seeking help had received it.

Putting the banks in charge of doling out the funds seemed unavoidable. The SBA could not process what the agency itself calculated would be the equivalent of fourteen years' worth of SBA loans in maybe a few weeks' time. Yet entrusting the private sector to run the program created its own messes. Democrats and some Republicans insisted that smaller lenders and nontraditional financial institutions be included to ensure broader access to the funding Congress had set aside for small businesses, but the program opened before the government had completed a process for certification. The Treasury Department did not release its guidelines for applying for a loan until the night before PPP went live, leaving the banks confused over the parameters of the program and the ground rules for applying. Some banks forged ahead anyway, submitting applications on behalf of customers, while others waited for their questions to be answered. Bank of America required its customers to have not only a commercial checking account with them but an outstanding loan with the bank. Other banks announced that they would only help small businesses that were also credit card customers. JPMorgan Chase and Wells Fargo were among the financial institutions that declared that they would only work with existing customers.

A natural assumption was that the money had drained so quickly because the demand was that great. But then came the regulatory filings from publicly traded companies, which by statute have a responsibility to share news that might have an impact on their share prices. Shake Shack, with more than 6,000 employees and nearly 200 locations around the country, reported that it had taken $10 million in PPP dollars. Ruth's Chris, with 5,700 employees at its 150 locations (and $86 million in cash on hand at the start of 2020) took $20 million. That was twice the $10 million limit, but the high-end restaurant chain had applied through two subsidiaries. Potbelly, a sandwich chain that employed 6,000 in 470 locations, also received a pair of $10 million loans. Each of the companies had qualified for a program designed specifically for firms with fewer than five hundred employees because of the "per physical location" exemption. A Ruth's Chris might have thirty or forty employees per locale. A hotel might employ tens of thousands of people but have no more than one or two hundred people at any given property.

Larger enterprises had innate advantages competing in a system that creates winners and losers. Some of that was practical. Bigger business had lawyers and accountants on staff. Restaurant Brands International, which owns Burger King and Popeyes, set up "franchisee liquidity teams" to help its franchisees fill out the paperwork required to secure a loan. Most truly small businesses had no one but themselves to negotiate what Josh Gotbaum, a former Treasury official who had worked for five previous administrations, called a "ridiculously complicated system." Glenda, who described herself as computer-challenged, was at a disadvantage negotiating a program that was administered electronically. Some of her records were digitized but not all of them, which caused its own mini-crisis. Every small business owner was up against technology, relying on hastily created websites that constantly crashed while at a bank's site to work on an application.

An unspoken assumption of PPP was that the banks would handle things in a fair and equitable fashion. Instead, many used an ability to turn around a business's PPP application as another concierge service it provided to its best customers. PPP was advertised as first come, first served, but the banks had great leeway in how they administered the program. The *New York Times* outed JPMorgan Chase, Citibank, and US Bank for prioritizing the applications of its richest clients. Chase branch employees were instructed not to help even long-standing commercial customers. Instead, the customers were told to go to the Chase portal, fill out a form, and wait in line. Meanwhile, the bank's deeper-pocketed business customers who might qualify for PPP had their own private banker to guide them, if not fill out the forms for them. There was another financial incentive for banks to prioritize larger customers over smaller ones. Under PPP's fee structure, a bank helping a client secure $10 million through PPP collected $100,000 (plus the 1 percent interest if the loan was not forgiven). By contrast, assisting a hair salon owner in securing the $25,000 she would be owed under the program generated a fee of $1,250.

Among the 8,500 commercial and private banking clients that JPMorgan helped apply for PPP, the *Times* found, nearly all of them received the government money they requested. By comparison, only one in fifteen of the roughly three hundred thousand small businesses applying for the PPP loan through Chase were able to secure one. Ultimately, more than four hundred public companies disclosed that they received PPP dollars, as had countless privately held businesses with far more than five hundred employees. That ensured that PPP was tapped out before most small business owners even had a chance to decide if this was something they wanted. TJ had gotten his application in early. So did Mark Monsey at Greenwood's Furniture in Tunkhannock. Both learned from their bankers that the government had run out of money.

"The entire program was set up to benefit well-connected, well-banked businesses," said Amanda Ballantyne, then executive director of the Main Street Alliance. The worry among Ballantyne and other small business advocates in the spring of 2020 was that the postpandemic landscape would be dominated even more by chains and other giants. And here was a government-backed program helping to accelerate the process.

The backlash had been almost instant once the news spread PPP had run out of money. Shake Shack had a stock market worth of $4 billion. Ruth's Hospitality Group, which owned Ruth's Chris, had a market cap of $700 million. Shake Shack, Ruth's Chris, and Potbelly returned all the money they received, but each also had had the misfortune of being singled out in the early media accounts. At the end of April, Elizabeth Warren posted a tweet accusing the banks of "playing favorites" and "serving the wealthy & well-connected first & leaving mom-and-pops behind." Lawmakers on both sides of the aisle threatened congressional hearings.

The EIDL disaster loan program proved another disappointment to many. This program that had been around for decades to help small businesses endure disasters was quickly overwhelmed by applications. By early May, the SBA had received applications numbering in the millions but had processed fewer than fifty thousand. The government had advertised emergency loans of up to $2 million for businesses with under five hundred employees that needed a cash infusion because of COVID. The agency announced a cap of $150,000 on loans, which made sense given limited funding, and then abruptly lowered it to $15,000, which didn't. Key Republican senators, the *Washington Post* reported, pushed so that farmers could tap into the program. A message was posted on the SBA website declaring that it was only accepting applications for disaster loans from those in agriculture "due to limitations in funding availability and the unprecedented submission of applications already received." Democrats in both the House and Senate wrote to SBA administrator Jovita Carranza demanding the agency immediately lift its $15,000 cap and reopen the program to non-farm applications.

Mitch McConnell, then the Senate majority leader, was the first to offer small businesses a lifeline. Shortly after learning that the Paycheck Protection Program's funds had been depleted so fast, he introduced legislation that would chip in an additional $250 billion. Democrats, however, balked at a bill that did nothing except replenish a program rigged in favor of larger players. Democrats demanded new rules to ensure that more money reached the microbusinesses most Americans thought the government was supporting through PPP, including those owned by people of color, women, and others traditionally locked out of the lending market. McConnell pushed what Republicans described as a clean one-page bill, but Democrats used the moment to seek additional funding also for COVID testing and to bail out struggling state and local governments. Charging that Democrats were playing politics with America's small businesses, McConnell refused to negotiate. The onus again fell to Mnuchin to broker a deal.

Even as the parties in Washington sought a compromise, the anger directed at PPP was mounting. As originally conceived, a business did not have to demonstrate need to secure PPP funding, only attest that the "current economic uncertainty" justified a loan. That opened up the program to those who didn't necessarily need help but saw an opportunity for government to cover their payroll for a couple of months—those, not incidentally, that generally had the capacity to handle a complicated application process precisely because they were not in crisis. "We sort of erred on the side of expediency," Marco Rubio confessed. The fix would be an addition to the Treasury's "Frequently Asked Questions" page. Larger companies, it now read, must vouch that taking money was "necessary to support ongoing operations" and demonstrate that they took the loan because they had no other financing option.

Mnuchin joined the chorus of those expressing their outrage on a day the media was reporting that the Los Angeles Lakers, a franchise worth nearly $5 billion, had taken $4.6 million from the program. Appearing on CNBC, Mnuchin said that when hammering out the details of PPP, he "never expected in a million years" that a basketball team worth in the billions would think it might qualify for a small business bailout fund. Playing the role of the aggrieved Treasury secretary, he used some of his time on CNBC to warn that any company taking $2 million or more in PPP funding would be audited and could be held "criminally liable" if it was determined that they didn't need government money. Mnuchin gave publicly traded companies until May 7 to return the money, and then, when he had too few takers, extended the deadline again to May 14 and May 18. Many did, but more large recipients kept the money than gave it back.

A compromise was reached on a $484 billion bill called the Paycheck Protection Program and Health Care Enforcement Act. Twenty-five billion dollars was designated for testing (and a mandate that the Trump administration develop a national testing plan), and $75 billion to help struggling hospitals, but no money for local governments. The rest was earmarked for businesses covered by the SBA. Sixty billion dollars was set aside to replenish EIDL along with an additional $310 billion in PPP funding: McConnell's $250 billion plus another $60 billion exclusively for businesses whose applications came through smaller community lenders.

Elected officials from both parties patted themselves on the back for a job well done. Expanding the pool of lenders would help get the money into the hands of a broader pool of business owners. The additional cash would help countless businesses. But PPP was a program conceived when officials were measuring the pandemic in weeks, not months or perhaps years. What happened after eight weeks, when the funds were depleted and customers still had not returned? Then it wouldn't be just those suffering preexisting economic conditions that were threatened but fundamentally healthy businesses—healthy unless they were denied 80 percent of their weekly revenue, if not 100 percent because they were shut down indefinitely.

* * *

By May 8, J.R.'s Hallmark and Greenwood's Furniture had been shuttered for seven weeks. Glenda, Mark, and other small business owners in town felt like they had done their part. It was time to reopen. The Creekside Gardens, a beautiful shop that Kevin and Sherri Kukuchka had opened two decades earlier, was practically next to the Walmart. Yet its doors were locked while down the street, the aisles at the retail giant's garden center were crowded.

"There were literally lines out the door at the Walmart," said Gina Suydam, president of the Wyoming County Chamber of Commerce, "while their garden store was closed."

The county's COVID numbers remained low. Wyoming County had registered all of twenty-seven positives in those first seven weeks of COVID. There had been ten in the prior two weeks—well below Wolf's stated threshold of a fourteen-day average of fewer than fifty new confirmed cases per hundred thousand residents. The local hospital was empty.

The state, however, chose not to sift through data from all sixty-seven Pennsylvania counties in anticipation of that first week of openings. The Wolf administration announced it would only focus on the north-central and northwest segments of the state. Wyoming County was lumped in with the counties in the northeastern corner of the state, which included Lackawanna and Luzerne Counties, where the numbers were still high. Business owners in twenty-four counties were told they could reopen on May 8 but not those operating in Wyoming County.

A rally was held in Tunkhannock at the county courthouse, a lovely, Italianate-style building with arched windows, overhanging eaves, and an ornate clock tower. The *Wyoming County Press Examiner* estimated the crowd at 150 people. There, each of Wyoming's three county commissioners spoke about the importance of reopening area businesses. Mark Monsey from Greenwood's Furniture was there, as was the owner of a hair salon ten minutes north of Tunkhannock. She held up a sign that read, SMALL BUSINESSES CAN CLEAN, CAN COUNT, CAN CUSTOMIZE, AND ARE CAPABLE. The virus is real, she told the *Press Examiner*, but she was also confident she could keep people safe.

Mark Monsey started talking about an "outlaw opening." That was what a group in Lancaster County, partway between Philadelphia and Harrisburg, were openly plotting. "We've all helped flatten the curve," the owner of a diner called Round the Clock told his local newspaper. "I think it's time that people get back to work." A group of 150, most of them business owners, held a meeting, in defiance of the governor's prohibition against large indoor gatherings. The local sheriff there announced he would not cite businesses that operated in defiance of Wolf's shutdown order, and county officials sent a letter to Wolf laying out the plan to transition the county from red to yellow. We "prefer to act with your cooperation," they wrote, "but we intend to move forward with a plan to restore Lancaster County."

Mark reached out to other business owners in Tunkhannock. He pointed to the county's low numbers and the empty hospital—if the others did not bring those up themselves ("the people I was talking to were pretty steamed up about what was going on," Mark said). He mentioned Lancaster and other counties where small businesses and local officials were openly talking about defying the governor's orders. He took aim at Wolf. "We don't produce enough tax money for them to care about us," Mark said.

But Wyoming was not Lancaster County, which had helped give rise to the Tea Party in Pennsylvania. "I had enough to worry about without worrying about lawyers and law enforcement knocking on my door," Glenda said. No one was up for joining Mark for his outlaw opening. Instead, he worked the phone and thought up angry letters to the editor. "It'll be a ghost town," he said of Tunkhannock.

* * *

Wolf felt obliged to respond to the small business owners of Lancaster and their call for mutiny. Defy his orders, he warned, and there could be consequences. The state could revoke a liquor license, he reminded them. A store or restaurant needs a certificate of occupancy to operate. A defiant business might face problems with their insurance carriers. "Insurance does not cover things that happen to businesses breaking the law," he said. He aimed his most pointed comments at his fellow elected officials. "Those politicians who decide to cave into this coronavirus, they need to understand the consequences of their cowardly act," Wolf said. He also called them "selfish" and threatened to withhold CARES Act relief dollars from any county that violated his orders.

Donald Trump traveled to Pennsylvania in mid-May, a few days after Wolf issued his warning. Hundreds of supporters lined the road from the airport to the medical supply warehouse outside of Allentown, one hour south of Hazleton, where Trump was appearing. Speaking in front of around one hundred workers, Trump again insinuated himself into a local debate over the lockdown. "You have areas of Pennsylvania that are barely affected and they want to keep them closed, you can't do that," Trump said. "We have to get your governor of Pennsylvania to start opening up a little bit." It wasn't just Wolf. "The Democrats are moving slowly, all over the USA, for political purposes. They would wait until November 3," Trump said, referring to Election Day.

The day after Trump's visit, around one thousand people gathered outside the statehouse in Harrisburg for an antilockdown rally—a protest, a state senator from the area said, against "seventy days of dictatorial rule." The crowd wanted a governor more like those in charge of Georgia or Texas or Florida, all of whom flipped a switch reopening the economy more or less at once rather than poring over health data. Yet much of the crowd's ire was directed at Rachel Levine, one of the country's few openly transgender public officials. "Lock her up" was one popular chant. Another was directed at the governor: "Impeach Wolf."

Business trade organizations stayed away from the protests, including the National Federation of Independent Business, the most conservative of the country's mainstream small business advocates. Gordon Denlinger, the director of the NFIB's Pennsylvania chapter, was a graduate of Bob Jones University, an evangelical Christian institution in South Carolina. He was a reliably conservative vote during his six terms as a state legislator. Yet the group behind the rally, Pennsylvanians Against Excessive Quarantine, was started by a gun rights group in Ohio, and there were media reports of ties to the Proud Boys and other white supremacy groups.

"There was a lot going on at these things beyond just reopening the economy," Denlinger said. "We decided to take a pretty guarded approach."

Two weeks into the pandemic, Russ Diamond, the conservative state rep who had led the lock-her-up cheers, had introduced legislation to strip Wolf of many of his powers to manage the pandemic. Diamond himself had been a small-business person before becoming a legislator. He ran his own small music recording studio and then a tiny company that stamped out CDs at cut-rate prices for anyone finding them on the internet. "I saw the way he [Wolf] shut down all the restaurants with almost no notice and I realized I don't trust this governor's judgment," Diamond said. Diamond had gotten almost no support from his fellow legislators but, after Trump's visit, "I was suddenly Mr. Popularity," Diamond said. "More and more people were like, 'Wait, this guy [Wolf] is going too far, we need to rein him in.' And I was like, 'Well, okay, I have this bill.'" The House and Senate passed the legislation Diamond had introduced six weeks earlier, and of course Wolf vetoed it. The state Supreme Court would have to decide this question of what role, if any, the Pennsylvania constitution grants the legislature in an emergency—and how they might exert that power if a governor can simply veto legislation approved by a coequal branch of government.

* * *

John Longstreet, the CEO of the Pennsylvania Restaurant & Lodging Association, finally was able to secure thirty minutes with Wolf and his people that May. He was joined on the phone call by several restaurant owners who sat on his board. "Governor, there's two things we want to talk about today," Longstreet began once they were beyond pleasantries and introductions.

The first item they discussed was outdoor dining, which had not been included in the state's reopening plan. "The shock for us is that they hadn't even thought of that before," Longstreet said.

The other was dining inside a restaurant once a county went green. Rather than impose a restriction based on seating capacity, as the governor's people were suggesting, Longstreet's group recommended that the state focus on the CDC's social distancing guidelines. Dictating that a restaurant could operate at 50 percent or 25 percent of capacity seemed arbitrary. Instead, why not make sure a restaurant is putting at least six feet between tables? Just over half the states would use social distancing rules rather than capacity.

The governor assigned one of his deputies to work out the ground rules for outdoor dining. Longstreet and the restaurant owners, however, lost their other argument. Pennsylvania would stick with capacity limits for indoor dining. On the upside, the governor agreed to sign legislation that, temporarily, allowed restaurants to sell cocktails to go.

* * *

The governor's office had more disappointing news for Tunkhannock. Wolf announced that another thirteen counties would move to yellow on May 15. Again, Wyoming County was not on that list. Driving from Tunkhannock, you can be in downtown Scranton inside of an hour—and that proximity, apparently, was the holdup. Rates in both Lackawanna and Luzerne Counties were well above the governor's fifty-per-hundred-thousand threshold. Local officials made noise about reopening anyway, but the governor repeated his threat to withhold recovery dollars from the county. "Our hands are tied," the chair of the county commission said. One week later, Wyoming County was included among the dozen counties permitted to move to the yellow phase on May 22.

Yellow meant J.R.'s could again open its doors. Glenda reached out to her people and felt relieved that most seemed eager to return to work. Greenwood's also reopened on May 22. "All my people came back," Mark said. "The question then was if we'd get any customers."

Hairstylists in Wyoming County, however, were among those who needed to wait until green to reopen. A frustrated Christine Robinson at the Shabby Shek Salon & Boutique in Tunkhannock told the local paper she was convinced she could reopen safely. She could stagger appointments, she said, and wipe down between customers—if only the state trusted her.

* * *

Hazleton and the rest of Luzerne County were moved to yellow on May 29, one week after Wyoming. Lackawanna County, however, remained red. That meant Cusumano's still could not offer outdoor dining.

TJ Cusumano, however, did not feel singled out. Unlike other small business owners, TJ harbored no ill will toward Wolf or his people. "I mean, are restaurants really life-essential businesses?" TJ asked. "Shouldn't it just be pharmacies and grocery stores?"

TJ estimated that takeout orders that May accounted for a small fraction of their regular business—not even 10 percent. TJ's meal kits idea—his attempt at being a small-time Blue Apron or HelloFresh—proved a bust. He and his people made the sauces, portioned the ingredients, and wrote out straightforward instructions for cooking the pasta or piece of meat. Yet as Nina had predicted, people who bothered to drive to his place and pay restaurant prices for their food did not also want the work of finishing a dish at home and then dealing with the cleanup. "That was one that didn't work," TJ said.

More popular, though, were the restaurant's departures from its set menu. Taco Tuesdays continued to be a success, and the special menu TJ put together for Mother's Day—pan-seared sea scallops over lemon-herbed risotto ($25), crab cakes ($32), or a broiled lobster tail ($35), including a twice-baked potato and vegetables—drove more sales. Over the Memorial Day weekend, TJ debuted what he called the Devil's Pit—his attempt at southern barbecue in northern Pennsylvania. He offered a takeout menu that included beef brisket sandwiches or half a barbecue chicken for $10, or a full rack of ribs for $21. Over three days, the restaurant sold in excess of one hundred orders of ribs and more than one hundred fire-roasted chickens, plus hundreds of dollars' worth of baked beans, corn bread, and other side dishes. "That was like the first decent weekend since it all started," TJ said. He barbecued again that final weekend in May. Again, he sold out everything.

"Whatever they let me do, I'll do," TJ said. "I'll make it work."

Chapter 9

Bikini Season

A t the end of another long and depressing day, three brothers gathered in their Bronx living room to talk through
their options. They had devoted all of themselves to Sol
Cacao, the chocolate bar business they had founded five years earlier. But on this night in May, two months into the pandemic, they
were at a loss. They went around the room, but none of them had
anything positive to report.

"No one was reordering," said Dominic Maloney. The oldest of
the three brothers, he has a round face, a shaved head, and the most
growly New York City accent of the three. He was thirty at the
time of COVID.

"No one was paying any invoices," said Daniel Maloney. "Because they weren't sure if their own businesses were going to make
it." Daniel, the youngest, was twenty-seven and wore his hair in
twists. He was the most talkative of the three and took on company
communications as one of his responsibilities.

Invoices from suppliers needed to be paid. There was also the
rent. "The landlord gave us no relief," said Nicholas Maloney, the
middle brother. Like both his older and younger brother, he had an

open, friendly face and a quick smile. He sometimes leaned back and closed his eyes when talking or held his hands together as if in prayer to say thank you. "The spiritual one," his brothers said teasingly.

The Maloneys shared an apartment in a part of New York City that had been hard-hit by COVID-19. The wail of ambulances in the background was a constant. "We're watching our savings just dwindle," Daniel said. They couldn't even count on PPP money for temporary relief. The Maloney brothers did everything themselves, from roasting the cacao beans to hand wrapping the bars and packing the boxes for shipping. PPP had been built entirely on helping owners keep their people employed, and Sol Cacao did not have any employees.

They talked about giving up. Their cash reserves were gone, and their store of beans had been depleted. And even if they received a shipment of cacao the next day, they had booked barely any orders in two months. June's rent was due in a couple of weeks. They were three young black men raised by immigrant parents. They didn't have much in the way of resources to fall back on, and sympathy in the US wasn't exactly high for three men of color who had been born somewhere else.

"We had to face reality," Daniel said. "And the realities of what the numbers were telling us was not good." The high-quality chocolate market was expanding, much like coffee and wine before it, and since 2015, the Maloneys had been fighting for their share. Yet now it was not a global giant like a Nestlé or Hershey that was doing them in, or one of the white-owned chocolate bar companies that seemed to have the connections and access to resources that they did not. Instead, it was a microscopic virus that a writer for the *Atlantic* described as "a thousand times smaller than a dust mote."

* * *

Chocolate, the Maloneys say, is in their blood. Their great-grandfather had been born in Ireland but moved to the country of

Trinidad and Tobago in the 1940s, drawn by the quality of cacao beans grown there. He married a local woman, and together they ran a cacao farm on this island nation, just off the coast of Venezuela and at the southeastern edge of the Caribbean. Cacao beans from Trinidad fetched some of the highest prices on the planet. Their great-grandparents and grandparents on their father's side made a good living selling them to people to make chocolate.

Dominic, Nicholas, and Daniel were all born in Trinidad. They grew up on a farm, where their parents grew mangoes, cashews, and hibiscus—but not cacao. Life was largely lived outdoors, at least when not at school, roaming the countryside, staring at a giant anthill for hours or digging in the soil for earthworms. "The three musketeers," an aunt described them—inseparable. For the three of them, it seemed just another adventure when, in 1996, they joined the great migration of Caribbeans to New York City and the neighborhoods of Brooklyn and Queens. "It was always our great-grandmother's dream for us that we get an education in the United States," Dominic said.

The Maloneys settled in Bedford-Stuyvesant, the iconic Brooklyn neighborhood where Spike Lee set *Do the Right Thing*, released in 1989. Their father found a job as a janitor at a big hospital in Manhattan, and their mother, Daniel said, "just like most Caribbean immigrants, worked as a nanny," watching other people's children. The three brothers were born three years apart, with Nicholas arriving almost precisely at the midpoint between Dominic and Daniel's birth dates. Daniel, the youngest, started kindergarten at the local public school. His older brothers entered the New York City school system in the second and third grades.

Gentrification has transformed Bed-Stuy. By the pandemic, it had become a more transitory, mixed-race, mixed-income community than it was when the Maloneys lived there. "Bed-Stuy back then was basically just another Caribbean Island except a lot colder," Daniel said. Its residents were black and working-class. There were block parties, fairs, and festivals, and an annual green block competition to see which street could plant the most trees. There were the "little rough patches" as first Dominic said, and then Nicholas repeated. "We all got in one or two fights growing up," Nicholas said. They rode the train and buses by themselves to get back and forth to school, where they learned to deal with classmates from a wide range of cultures and backgrounds. "All in all, it was a good experience," Nicholas said of growing up in Bed-Stuy.

The brothers were teenagers when their parents bought a home in Bridgeport, Connecticut, a city of almost 150,000. Their mother and father both sought someplace quieter and slower than Bed-Stuy and also a place that offered more room than their apartment in Bed-Stuy. "When my dad figured out that we could live close to a real downtown area and hop on a highway to get into New York, it just made a lot of sense to move to Bridgeport," Nicholas said.

A backyard seemed to revive a dormant agriculture gene inside the Maloney family. Their parents grew tomatoes of all kinds, along with string beans, peppers, and anything else they could find that grew in the northern climate. "That's when our dad started telling us stories about our great-grandparents and grandparents and how Trinidad is known as the country to produce the best chocolate in the world," Daniel said. Growing up, they all loved a cacao tea spiced with cinnamon, nutmeg, and a bay leaf that their parents made for them. Only once they heard their father's stories about growing up on the cacao farm did they understand their own relationship to chocolate. Chocolate was part of their heritage. Sol Cacao seemed inevitable.

Since they had arrived in the US, the brothers had been watching nature shows on PBS. "Our dad was talking about organic long before it became a mainstream thing," Daniel said. But it was tales of growing cacao beans, he said, "that really awakened something in all of us." That's when they learned that their great-grandmother had spoken about the possibility that they would return home after getting their education and making their mark in America. "She had this idea we would make it full circle," Dominic said. "She wanted land in the Maloney name." That became their goal as teen-agers: to save enough money to buy land in Trinidad and get the Maloneys back in the cacao business. In time, they added a second component: once they were producing a healthy yield of beans, producing bars that they would sell in the United States.

Dominic was still in high school when he started poring over maps and downloading two-hundred-page PDFs to learn every-thing he could about growing cacao beans and Trinidad. That's when he learned that the island's richest treasure was not the raw material for making chocolate but natural gas, petroleum, and am-monia. Doing more research, Dominic learned that a cacao tree can take as long as five years before it starts bearing fruit. That would mean years of making no money or spending tens of thousands, if not hundreds of thousands, of dollars they did not have to buy an operating cacao farm.

"That was a very anxious time for us," Nicholas said. "We each had our own goals but we all just loved the idea of the three of us doing something together." Dominic, the oldest, went to the Borough of Manhattan Community College, where he studied bio-technology, but he grew disillusioned. "Most of the time in Amer-ica, biotech is extracting oil from corn to make ethanol and things like that," he said. "That's not really the form of agriculture I was interested in." Nicholas, the middle brother, started at Southern Connecticut State University but decided to become an RN, and transferred to a nursing school affiliated with Mount Sinai and Beth Israel Hospitals in Manhattan. Daniel, the youngest, studied en-gineering at Fairfield University in Connecticut, a fifteen-minute drive from their home. By the time Daniel started college, they had turned their original idea on its head. They would start by making chocolate bars. Then, when they had made enough money, they would buy that farm in Trinidad.

Daniel was a junior at Fairfield when he won a business plan com-petition based on their idea of starting a chocolate bar company. He used the $500 prize to buy their first piece of equipment—a small coffee roaster to cook the cacao beans. Daniel graduated the next year with a degree in electrical engineering and took a job with a group helping to modernize New York City's 911 system. Dominic worked as a manager at a Vitamin Shoppe in Manhattan. Nicholas, who was still working toward his RN degree, took a part-time job as a technician at the same hospital where his father stripped and waxed the floors. All three saw their jobs as a temporary way station.

* * *

The Maloneys devoted themselves to the art and science of making chocolate bars from scratch. They were three single men in their twenties who managed to have some fun. But life was mainly about chocolate when they weren't working or sleeping.

They taught themselves the proper technique for drum-roasting fermented cacao beans and then cracking and winnowing the beans (separating the nibs from the husk) before grinding them. The most difficult task to master proved tempering. That's the finely calibrated heating and cooling process that gives a bar its sheen and that satisfying snap when breaking off a piece. Fail to properly temper a bar, and it can look mottled, and crumble and melt in the hand. "We went through a lot of beans before we got that down," Dominic said. One formative experience was attending a chocolate festival held in the city, where they met other chocolatiers and sampled dark chocolate by other makers.

"We spent a good two to three years just eating through every bar we could find," Daniel said. The three had grown up American kids who spent their dollars on Hershey's and M&M's and other sugary milk chocolates. Despite being Trinidadian by birth, each needed to train his palate to appreciate the richer, more complex tastes of dark chocolate.

Mass-produced bars stamped out by Big Chocolate use palm oils, emulsifiers, lecithin, and sometimes even wax. The Maloneys decided they would produce bars using only two ingredients: cacao beans (and the cacao butter they produce) and cane sugar. The big makers rely on what in the trade is called "bulk" cacao beans: cheaper, lower-quality beans typically grown on industrial farms in West Africa. Sol Cacao would specialize in "origin" bars, made using beans from a single locale. Just like wine producers, the Maloneys spoke of terroir, and regional distinctions.

The Maloneys started with a Madagascar bar. Its beans have a fruity, berry-cherry taste. The three agreed that Madagascar beans would let them produce the perfect gateway dark chocolate for an American palate generally less accustomed to rich, dark chocolates. That was followed by an Ecuador bar (earthy, nutty) and one from Peru that starts off with a taste something like champagne, Daniel said, but then hits with hints of strawberry and peach. "Peru is known for bringing your mouth on a roller coaster ride," he said. (They experimented with a bar in honor of their heritage, but beans from Trinidad proved prohibitively expensive. Where they could purchase cacao beans from a farm in Madagascar, Ecuador, or Peru for between $4,000 and $5,000 per ton, those from Trinidad cost closer to $10,000.)

Chocolate had started as a way for the Maloneys to connect to their heritage. Steeped in the craft, they became evangelists for the curative properties of high-quality dark chocolates. Chocolate as a daily ritual was a healthy pleasure, they argued, if not a way of being. Chocolate making for all three became a calling. Even the decision all three made to become vegetarians was rooted in their desire to connect to the land. "Cooking more with raw ingredients, we realized that the tastes go back to the soil and the weather and how things grow," Nicholas said. "That was very interesting to us." They embraced social entrepreneurship and this idea that a business can create positive change and not just extract resources from the earth. "There would be no destructive externalities of what we did," Daniel said. "We would be contributing to the cause and not harming it."

The name Sol Cacao was a happy accident. One of the brothers said it aloud, and it rolled off the tongue. Dominic did not appreciate that "*sol*" was Spanish for "sun" when he first heard the name but he liked it anyway because it made him think of the word "soul" and conjured up a sense of the essence of something. "The more we thought about it," Nicholas said, "the more we realized how perfect it was." The sun brought cacao beans to life. Their effort would shed light on the unique flavors of beans grown in different parts of the world.

Thinking about the packaging for their bars got the brothers thinking about the term "luxury." It had come to imply exclusivity and something out of reach for most of the population. "The word 'luxury' leaves a bad tase in the mouth in modern-day life," Dominic said.

"There's a connation of snobbery," Daniel continued. Yet they were three sons of Brooklyn with the same bespoke attitude and dedication to the art and science of their craft just like all those makers who had set up workshops and small production facilities in that same borough in the years since the brothers had moved away. "Luxury for us is more about craftsmanship," Daniel said. "It's the idea that a person pays attention to every detail of the product they're making." They looked at how other specialty foods marketed themselves, along with a couple of small-batch bourbon brands and even a company that sold individually crafted leather handbags.

"We realized there was a storytelling aspect in the marketing [of] all of them," Dominic said. They spoke about the quality of the raw materials used and a maker's passion for the craft. The Maloneys had the extra element of their grandparents and great-grandparents having grown cacao in a nation once renowned for the quality of its beans.

"For us it's about the journey," Dominic said.

"Of doing things the right way," Nicholas said.

"And no shortcuts," said Daniel, finishing the thought. That, too, would be part of their story. In a world where most of the cacao beans were raised in an industrial fashion, they were celebrating food grown in more organic, biodiverse environments. They would be part of the broader farm-to-table movement, where traceability, and a respect for those growing the food, is central. They had an artisan's respect for craft.

The Maloneys chose a heavy-stock matted paper for its outer packaging. An artist friend painted a beautiful, colorful image for each country so that each bar looked something like an individually packaged piece of art. The artist painted a trio of Madagascar's stark baobab trees, three of Peru's distinctive cock-of-the-rock birds perched on a branch, and three blue-masked goldfinches from Ecuador to represent the three brothers.

The biggest challenge would be the price tag: $7 for a single bar. That was in the middle of the price range for higher-priced, hand-crafted bars but also nearly twice as expensive as a bar by Green & Black's, a once-small-batch chocolate maker bought by Mondelēz International, a $26 billion food giant that owns Oreo, Cadbury, Toblerone, and Chips Ahoy!, among other brands. It, too, was a premium bar sold in similarly handsome packaging.

* * *

Sol Cacao debuted their chocolate bars in 2016, at a pop-up market in Sugar Hill, a Manhattan neighborhood just north of Harlem. This venue, which the *New York Daily News* dubbed an "artisanal flea market," was short-lived, but in the year that the Maloneys participated, they built a small following. They had their start.

The brothers moved in together in an apartment they found in Harlem. Daniel went to work as a project manager for a construction company, a job that offered more flexibility than his previous position. Nicholas, who had earned a BS in nursing, got a job at Harlem Hospital. Working at this storied public hospital that had been serving the community since 1887 had been a goal. "I just felt like I wanted 'Harlem Hospital' on my résumé," Nicholas said. Dominic left the Vitamin Shoppe. He was the only one of the three without a day job, though even he picked up work doing cyber-security to earn living expenses.

Producing high-quality chocolate proved easy compared to the fight for shelf space inside a store. They had focused on smaller specialty shops in the early days of the company but caught a break when Whole Foods, in anticipation of opening a supermarket in Harlem, in 2017, sought out locals with products they could sell inside their store. That opened the door to the other Whole Foods stores scattered around New York City.

The brothers had gotten lucky early on when a church in Brook-lyn allowed them to use its kitchen at no cost. But when it was time to move on, they learned how pricey it was to rent space in New York City. At the southeastern tip of the Bronx, in an industrial neighborhood called Port Morris, they found a good price for a handsome, six-hundred-square-foot work space with exposed pipes and hardwood floors.

"When we moved to the Bronx," Daniel said, "that's when all of us would say the business really got started."

The Maloneys had their setbacks, as they'd known they would. As teens and into their twenties, the three brothers watched a tele-vision show called *How I Made My Millions*. A common theme was that bad news was inevitable; what counted was how an en-trepreneur overcame that adversity. "Every year since 2017, some nonsense has happened," Daniel said. Prime time in the chocolate industry was December through early May. They were in the mid-dle of the chocolate season that first year in the Bronx when they learned that the business that had subleased the space to them had done so illegally. The complex's landlord found them a place in the same complex, but the mishap cost them thousands of dollars. "Ev-ery cent I had managed to save through my twenties, gone," Daniel said. They had not been in the new production space for more than a few months when, at the peak of the next season, the pipes burst.

Whole Foods proved its own Rubicon. Getting inside that first store was only the first step in a long, arduous journey. They were grateful for the chance to reach customers inclined to shop at a Whole Foods but disappointed when they saw that their bars were placed in a small specialty section tucked at the back of the store, next to the cheese. The three took turns handing out samples at the few Whole Foods that carried their bars, talking up the uniqueness of their product and sharing their personal story, which drove sales. They did the same at cheese shops and other places that sold their product. "That's how we got reorders," Daniel said. They showed up at fairs and farmers' markets and manned tables at special events (which is how one of their bars first showed up in our home in 2018).

"Traditionally, most of our money came from demos and in-store effort," Dominic said. "Any place we got to tell our story in person." That had been the one constant of Sol Cacao from the start: face-to-face encounters that let them connect to potential customers.

* * *

It's never a good time for a pandemic. But from the perspective of a modest-sized chocolate maker, this one could hardly have come at a worse time. The lockdown killed their Easter and Mother's Day, which are two prime holidays in the industry. "Once you're past Mother's Day, the bikini effect takes over," Daniel explained. "May comes and everyone's like, 'Oh, chocolate's bad, it's gonna make me gain weight.'" There was also the more practical issue that bars melt in the heat and can make a mess.

"In our world," Dominic explained, "you might as well just close down for three months. No one is buying chocolate."

The first weeks after COVID hit were less about Sol Cacao for the Maloneys and more about processing what was happening around the globe. Since the founding of Sol Cacao, the Maloneys had given short shrift to most of the rest of their lives. Now they felt something like the opposite. In the early days of COVID, with so much heartache and hardship around them, it proved difficult to focus on chocolate. "It was hard to find the same energy," Nicholas said. Normally, Nicholas worked the psychiatric unit, but Harlem Hospital had been overwhelmed by COVID. The hospital had even made the national news when a lack of beds meant gurney-filled corridors filled by patients struggling to breathe. Nicholas worked as a floater assigned to wherever he was needed. "That added to everyone's worries," Daniel said.

Sol Cacao was one of more than 350,000 manufacturing companies in the US in 2020 that had no employees, according to the Small Business Administration. Another 188,000 small manufacturers—defined as any business that creates a product from a raw material, including cacao beans, or assembles components produced by someone else—employed between one and twenty employees. Manufacturers represented a huge portion of the country's micro-businesses. Most remained open through the pandemic.

There was never any question Sol Cacao could operate through COVID. They were classified as food producers and therefore deemed essential. Slowly, the three brothers made their way back to their one-room workshop to start planning. In-store demos and in-person events would be discontinued indefinitely. A broken supply chain added to their woes. Normally, it took around two weeks to receive a shipment of the raw cacao beans they needed to roast to make their bars. Yet in early May, they were still waiting on hundreds of pounds of beans they had ordered more than a month earlier. "We were literally melting down our last block of chocolate," Daniel said.

The lockdown in New York meant Daniel was working his engineer management job from home and had more free time than in the past. "I'm posting on social media more than I've ever posted," he said. "I'm reaching out to people, calling people I had always wanted to talk to but now had the bandwidth," he said. Yet that made it even more frustrating when he didn't hear back from anyone. Daniel set a target of at least $100 in sales a day. There were many days they did not come close to even this modest goal.

"I'm working harder than ever to get the word out," Daniel said, "and that would translate into three bars sold that day." Figuring people were strapped for cash, they temporarily lowered the price of a bar to $5.99. That just meant earning less money on the few orders that came in.

Their late-night session in May, at the apartment they rented ten minutes from Sol Cacao's workspace, had them considering the unthinkable: giving up. They were exhausted. They had no answers. The brothers went round and round before Nicholas posed the gut-check question. "Are we totally running on E [for empty] or do we have enough in the tank to floor it?" he asked. "Is this as hard as we can push or can we push a little harder—"

"And our answer was—" Daniel interrupted.

"We can push a little harder," Nicholas finished. They saw themselves as building Sol Cacao not just for themselves but for their adopted borough, if not black entrepreneurship itself. "We didn't want to be a statistic, another black-owned business that closed down," Daniel said. They posted a message on their Instagram account that reaffirmed their commitment to Sol Cacao. *We're still here in the Bronx*, it proclaimed, three black men committed to the craft of chocolate making, still operating through COVID and eager to share their bars with the world.

"Whatever it takes to get through the summer," the brothers repeated to one another. Orders would pick up once the weather cooled. In the waning days of May, even that seemed an overly ambitious goal.

Then, on May 25, George Floyd was arrested in Minneapolis on suspicion of passing a counterfeit $20 bill. Two members of the Minneapolis police force pinned down the forty-six-year-old Floyd's back and legs, while a third officer, Derek Chauvin, kneeled on Floyd's neck for eight minutes and forty-six seconds. Floyd repeated, "I can't breathe," at least sixteen times before he lost consciousness and died. Floyd's murder sparked protests around the country, along with a racial reckoning and a push for racial justice that would help a small black-owned chocolate maker struggling to make it in an industry dominated by whites.

The "George Floyd effect," as Daniel called it, saved Sol Cacao. They had posted the Instagram message reaffirming their commitment to the business—"And then like a week or two later," Daniel said, "it was nonstop."

Chapter 10

Family Reunion

The Paycheck Protection Program had been created to aid small businesses keep their lights on through the pandemic. It did that—as well as assisting a long list of outfits that hardly needed government help. A lawsuit filed by several media outlets, including the *Washington Post*, the *New York Times*, and ProPublica, forced the SBA to release the names of every applicant that received at least $150,000 in PPP funding (later the government posted a database that included every PPP recipient). That sparked more outrages beyond the publicly traded giants outed earlier, starting with businesses backed by private equity's deep pools of money.

P.F. Chang's, with more than two hundred outlets scattered around the US, received millions in PPP dollars. So, too, did TGI Fridays, a chain with nine-hundred-plus locations in sixty countries, and also Five Guys, with more than 1,500 locations, and Bojangles, with more than 750 outlets. All told, businesses backed by private-equity firms received at least $1.2 billion through the PPP and EIDL programs, according to a 2021 study by Americans for Financial Reform, the Anti-Corruption Data Collective, and Public Citizen.

The Riviera Country Club, which included Steven Mnuchin as a member, received millions. Lobbying firms were on the recipients list, as were the Church of Scientology and Kanye West's multibillion-dollar apparel and sneaker company. The prestigious Aspen Institute took $8 million from PPP, despite a $115 million endowment. Tom Brady has a net worth in the hundreds of millions, but his nutrition company, TB12, Inc., scored $961,000 in PPP dollars. A mining company with more than 750 employees also received PPP dollars because, an SBA spokesperson explained, "under SBA's small business size standards, mining operations allow for more than 500 employees."

The antigovernment Ayn Rand Institute might passionately oppose bailouts, but that did not stop them from taking hundreds of thousands of dollars from PPP (as "partial restitution for government-inflicted losses," the organization wrote in its application). The Americans for Tax Reform Foundation, the research arm of Grover Norquist's antitax group by that same name, took money from the program. Normally, members of Congress were not permitted to receive money through the SBA, but the agency waived that ethics rule. At least seven members of Congress or their spouses received PPP loans, including Oklahoma Republican Kevin Hern, who owned so many McDonald's franchises (eighteen at one point) scattered around his state that he had been dubbed "the McCongressman." Hern had pushed for the "per physical location" exemption to PPP so that franchises were eligible and then accepted at least $1 million in PPP dollars.

The records show that Cusumano's Restaurant, Inc., in Old Forge received a PPP loan of $44,800. The money had arrived at the end of April, almost immediately after the government replenished PPP funding. The requirement that he spend 75 percent of the money on payroll was irritating. "I was hating on PPP in the beginning," he said, citing the strict terms that had been imposed. But it also let him survive until June 5, when Lackawanna County went yellow and Cusumano's could offer outdoor dining on its back porch. "PPP was really a big help," TJ said.

Mark Monsey in Tunkhannock was also pleased. He, too, received his money shortly after Congress approved additional funding—$18,500 from the federal government, ostensibly to cover the cost of five employees. He, too, resented the requirement he spend most of it on employees. Just like government, Mark cracked. "They help you but they make it unnecessarily hard on you to take it," he said.

Vilma Hernandez benefited from her patience. In early June, the House and Senate passed legislation loosening the rules for spending PPP dollars. Two days later, Trump signed the bill into law. That let a business spend as much as 40 percent of its allocation on non-payroll expenses, rather than 25 percent, and still have the loan forgiven. A business also had twenty-four weeks to spend that money—until December—rather than the original eight weeks. Vilma received $22,800 later that month to cover eight employees. The new conditions gave her breathing room. She didn't need to bring back everyone right away, and she could stagger hours through December if need be.

With the rule changes, Glenda also decided to apply for PPP—a process she described as a kind of torture. "I'm not a QuickBooks person," she confessed. In mid-June, she received $27,745 and immediately regretted it. The more she thought about it, the more she grew uncomfortable keeping the money. "It didn't make sense," Glenda said of the program. "The way they originally did the program, I would owe the money back but now they're telling me they've come up with another set of rules." She imagined officials in Washington changing their minds again. "The last thing I needed was taking on debt," she said. She gave back the money, even though the US government would have picked up a large portion of her payroll expenses and provided money toward the rent and utilities. (Glenda was hardly alone: thousands of businesses returned their PPP allotment unspent.)

Ultimately, 5.2 million businesses received funding help in this first round of PPP. Yet more than one-third of the dollars approved were allocations of $1 million or more, and well over half were for more than $350,000. Some microbusinesses with only one or two employees had no commercial relationship with a bank and therefore no ready-made way to apply. Many mom-and-pop operations were doing all they could do to survive and did not have the wherewithal to wrestle with a complicated online application. The tiny proportion of small businesses owned by people of color and women that received PPP money was scandalous. "If you want to do something at large scale that helps the economy, it can't be perfect in every micro fashion," Steven Mnuchin said. They could have spent weeks fine-tuning the program, Mnuchin argued, but then the money would not have gotten out there as quickly.

"We expected things to be much worse for small business," said Christopher Stanton, a Harvard professor who was part of a small research team that surveyed 5,800 small businesses only a few weeks into the pandemic. PPP served as a "sort of backstop for a lot of businesses," Stanton said, an infusion of cash when they needed it, no matter how inefficiently it was delivered. "Those worst fears were probably not realized because of the injection of aid like PPP."

* * *

"As of one minute after midnight this morning," Tom Wolf announced at a press conference held on Friday, June 5, "every county had moved out of the red phase." Old Forge and the rest of Lackawanna had been lumped in with Philadelphia and Allegheny (Pittsburgh) Counties. Finally, all of them would be shifted to yellow. That night, Cusumano's offered outdoor dining. It would be the first time in nearly three months they had served people at a table.

A tent had been pitched behind the restaurant, though one far more modest in size than erected by its neighbors on either side of them. Revello's had two tents, including one that could seat around one hundred people. The Rinaldis were similarly blessed with empty space behind their restaurant. They erected a tent more capacious than even Revello's. To put up a tent of that size, TJ would have first needed to knock down a cinder-block bunker they used for storage. Even with a smaller tent, they lost nearly half their parking lot in a town where customers who parked even two or three storefronts away might decide to eat at Cafe Rinaldi instead of TJ's place. Cusumano's could fit maybe twenty in their tent and still abide by social distancing rules. The sixty people they had the room to seat on the patio became a maximum of forty because of distancing guidelines. Together, that represented less than half of Cusumano's normal capacity of 130 to 140.

Reopening for outdoor dining meant bringing back more staff. Nina and Brenda Roscioli could wait tables, and also Jessica Barletta, who had been working at the restaurant since before it was called Cusumano's. Barletta opened her own dance studio, 5 Star Dance Academy, in Scranton in 2017. The studio had been shut down until the county entered the green phase; Barletta was eager for the hours. Others who worked a front-of-the-house job either were not ready to work or they gave a version of a speech that Cousin Anthony delivered when TJ called to check in. "I let him know, 'Don't worry about me,'" Anthony said. "If you need me, I'm there. But take care of people who need the shifts."

The kitchen people sitting at home had no financial incentive to return to work. Economics 101 dictated that while the government was still paying an extra $600 a week to the unemployed, TJ had no chance of luring them back to work without a bump in salary. Yet working the phone, TJ did not hear a single no. "Fuck yeah," Ang Garzon, his sauté chef, told him when he called to ask her about coming back. Despite the extra $200 a month she was making on unemployment, she was bored and missed the clatter and comradery of the kitchen. "We're kind of like a family here," Ang said. "I missed all my coworkers." She felt useless sitting at home collecting unemployment and also missed the good feelings she experienced when she was behind the stove. "It's the only thing I really know how to do well," she said.

Sha-Asia Johnson was collecting nearly twice the pay she earned at the restaurant. Yet she also did not hesitate when TJ asked if she was ready to come back to work. "I was done being stuck in the house," Johnson said. "TJ tells me, 'We need you back next week and you'll get your first check the week after that,' and I was like, 'Yes, thank God.'"

* * *

The day before Cusumano's reopened for outdoor dining had been a busy one. TJ arrived early, as did all his line cooks. TJ began by cooking a vat of his Sunday gravy in a $20,000 contraption called a tilt pan that he refers to as a "magic skillet." Prepandemic, the restaurant went through as much as fifteen gallons of his signature red sauce on a busy Saturday night and sometimes more than fifty gallons a week. He also mass-produced trays of focaccia. Every table was served a few complimentary wedges along with a small dish of ground-up olives in olive oil. ("A nice, little herby, salty snack to get you drinking," TJ said.) There were other sauces to be made (a veal Bolognese; his wild boar ragu) and several gallons of risotto that they would rehydrate and finish to order in the upstairs kitchen.

"It was insanity," TJ said. "Total, total insanity." He figured there would be pent-up demand but was shocked how keen people were to be around others. Cusumano's was one of the few restaurants in town that opened that first weekend. They ended up seating people as late as ten p.m., by which time the kitchen people would normally be cleaning up.

"I was at the restaurant prepping food at five thirty or six in the morning and then running food until eleven at night," TJ said. "I probably worked four sixteen-hour days."

TJ also underestimated the layoff's impact on workers who had been on hiatus. People were rusty and everyone's rhythm was off. Adding to the stress level that first weekend, the center of gravity of the restaurant had shifted. The cooks worked upstairs in the kitchen off the main dining room, but that room was still closed. The patio and tent were downstairs. Rather than a few steps to the dining room, a server or cook needed to run every dish down a narrow set of stairs, then walk another twenty-plus steps through the Cellar to get to the patio. An order delivered to the tent meant more walking.

There were glitches. People waiting to pick up takeout orders congregated near where people were eating—"exactly the kind of thing we were trying to avoid," TJ said. He already had posted several signs to help direct people, but he phoned a printer to order more. "I'm like a billboard factory here," he joked. By the next week he had signs showing people where to enter if they were there to eat at the restaurant and where to go if they were there for pickup. There was another sign telling people where to park if they were sick, immunocompromised, or just preferred that someone run the food out to them while they remained in the car. They posted the restaurant's phone number so people could call to let them know they were outside.

TJ felt like a scold asking people to wear a mask but also wondered why wearing one was so big a deal. A customer only needed to wear one while walking to and from their table or if going to the bathroom. He and everyone else working there wore them while running around all night. Some restaurants had their people wearing gloves but not Cusumano's. He also drew a firm line at disposable plates and plastic utensils, which other restaurants were using. "At that point, you're taking all the heart out of a restaurant," TJ said. He would serve food on a ceramic plate or not bother serving his food at all. His one aesthetic concession was to ditch their laminated menus. Instead, they printed their menu on paper place mats, which the bussers threw away when clearing tables.

Lackawanna County went green on Friday, June 26. Again, its residents had been lumped in with the final group of counties going green, including Philadelphia and its suburbs. Going green freed Cusumano's to open its doors to 50 percent indoor dining, but TJ and Nina decided to move slowly. They would let a limited number of people eat inside at the Cellar but otherwise would rely on outdoor dining. The restaurant was making enough to cover payroll and their other bills, TJ figured, so why push it? "We were working as hard as we could but had smiles on our faces every night because people were really enjoying themselves. Everybody was just happy," TJ said. Happy to be out and grateful there were people there to cook and serve them food, customers generally showed their appreciation by tipping ridiculously well.

"People felt sorry for us," Brenda Roscioli said. "It was fabulous."

* * *

In Tunkhannock, Mark Monsey was as busy as he had ever been. In the history of Greenwood's Furniture, no time compared to the flooding of the Susquehanna River basin in 2011. The flood caused nearly $1 billion in damage. That translated into a lot of ruined couches and dining room sets and checks from an insurance company to replace them. "We killed it for a while," Mark said.

Once he was able to reopen the store at the end of May, Greenwood's was putting up numbers just as good.

Mark had bought a half-page ad in the *Press Examiner* that ran two days before Greenwood's reopening. "Sitting in that recliner for 8 weeks?" it asked. "Kids been jumping on your sofa? Mattress shot from 4 naps a day?" The ad asked people to wear a mask. A separate flyer they posted around town said they would stagger entry to the store and preferred that people made an appointment to shop.

Mark had complained as loud as anyone in town about the government's response to COVID. Yet the same rescue plan that had given his business nearly $20,000 had also put stimulus dollars in the pockets of his customers. "June was like gang busters," Mark said. "We were just slammed the entire month."

Down the street, Glenda would have been pleased if her store did only slightly better than her usual June. It was nice to have company again when Wyoming County went yellow, yet a large portion of her clientele stayed away. The numbers picked up when the county went green on June 12, and people spent more than in the past. "I was seeing some people over and over and over," Glenda said. "Maybe it was because they had more money because of stimulus or maybe they were trying to be a part of the solution and support small business." Yet there were also regulars who still had not visited the store weeks into her reopening. When she reconciled her books for June, she saw that her 2020 revenue had been almost precisely the same as it had been in the same month in 2019.

"That's a victory," she said that summer, but added, "Last year was a horrendous year."

* * *

Luzerne County went green on June 19. By that point, Vilma Hernandez and her husband, Leonardo Reyes, had been visiting the salon for weeks to get it ready to reopen. Vilma had heard of a local effort to help businesses reopen, put together by the local chamber, the Downtown Hazleton Alliance for Progress, and other groups. What they called the Recovery & Resiliency Task Force raised $55,000 from local businesses and others interested in helping local enterprises that needed it. Vilma's Hair Salon was one of eighty-five businesses to receive a grant—in its case, $500 that Vilma used to buy the extra supplies she needed. Leonardo hung a Plexiglas barrier from the ceiling, just above a gold padded front desk that sat opposite the front door. The rest she spent on hard-to-find basics like gloves, masks, and disinfectants, which seemed to have doubled in price.

There were other expenses. To improve ventilation, they fixed several old ceiling fans that had not been working. There were also the costs of reconfiguring the salon to comply with the state's social distancing regulations. She and Leonardo did much of the work themselves, but they still needed help. The shop had six chairs, each with a corresponding station. They rearranged the main room so there was at least six feet between each stylist. There were four silver, cone-shaped hair dryers in one back room, which also needed to be moved, and sinks in the other. Everywhere around the shop, they applied yellow social distancing stickers to the floor. Whatever the $500 from the Recovery & Resiliency Task Force did not cover, Vilma put on a credit card. She would pay that back when the PPP dollars hit the salon's bank account.

In early June, the state announced that it was accepting applications for a $225 million program to help small businesses hit hard by the coronavirus, funded with a share of the $4 billion Pennsylvania received through the federal CARES Act. Small businesses with twenty-five or fewer employees and under $1 million in annual revenues were eligible for grants between $5,000 and $50,000. Hundreds of thousands of small business around the state qualified for a program that had enough money to help only a tiny fraction of them. At least half of all grants, the governor's office announced, would go to historically disadvantaged businesses that traditionally have been denied equal access to financing from lenders. It might still be a long shot, but Vilma applied.

Two of Vilma's employees confessed to her they were fearful about returning to the shop. She reassured them that they could stay home until they felt comfortable coming back—and felt relieved. Operating at half capacity meant she couldn't offer everyone their old hours. The two women spared Vilma from making hard choices.

Vilma felt joy when she reopened to customers, precisely three months after the government had ordered her to shut down. She and Leonardo had made the salon spotless for the grand reopening. As always, a photo of the Virgin Mary was displayed behind the reception desk, along with figurines of Jesus and Mary. The floor, a handsome, light tan terra-cotta tile, had been scrubbed. A half-dozen plants added a homey touch in the brightly lit shop. Once again, music played from a Spanish-language station piped in over speakers. *"Gracias a Dios,"* she said. Thank God.

Yet the good feelings of her grand reopening were mixed with worries. She knew even before opening her doors that at best they would be half-full. The green phase limited hair salons (along with fitness centers, yoga studios, and others falling in the "personal care services" category) to 50 percent occupancy. Under state rules, hair salons were appointment-only, and an establishment needed to leave time between customers to disinfect and wipe down frequently touched surfaces. A lot of her shampoos and conditioners and treatments were from Italy. Product had always served as a nice little revenue source for the salon, but, with the coronavirus, most everything she needed was on back order.

"Every day we were making changes," Vilma said. "You adapt."

* * *

With the easing of restrictions came the inevitable rise in case numbers, especially in and around Philadelphia and Pittsburgh. At the start of July, John Longstreet of the state's restaurant association heard from someone inside Tom Wolf's office that the governor and secretary of health were worried about the possible spread of the virus inside restaurants. Longstreet shared ideas the association had for tamping down their concerns, including reservation-only dining, earlier closures, and a new rule expressly directing people to remain masked inside a restaurant except when they are eating or drinking.

Longstreet thought nothing of it when someone on the governor's team reached out to him in mid-July. Making time for someone in Harrisburg had been Longstreet's life for weeks. He optimistically thought they wanted to finalize some of the ideas they had been batting around. Instead, a deputy secretary he had never spoken with told him, "We'd like to go to 25 percent capacity, eliminate all bar seating, and require that a meal be purchased with alcohol."

Taken aback, Longstreet asked her, "You're not really asking our opinion on this, are you?"

She was not. "This is going to be announced this afternoon," he quoted her as telling him. Restaurants around the state were struggling to survive at 50 percent capacity. The next day, however, they would be required to operate at no more than 25 percent.

"From then on," Longstreet said, "our strategy was to take on the governor and win in the court of public opinion."

In Old Forge, TJ absorbed the news with indifference. "We've been almost entirely outside anyway so it really had no effect on us," he said. The only possible impact on Cusumano's he could imagine was that the news might scare off some of his outdoor dining customers. "I could see people thinking to themselves, 'Hey, maybe this is really bad,' which I guess was the point of the announcement," he said.

Chapter 11

The Corner Druggist

COVID-19 torpedoed sales at small businesses around the US but not at Lech's Pharmacy, a tiny shop serving its sparsely populated patch of northeastern Pennsylvania. The challenge for other small business owners had been surviving a government-imposed shutdown and a clientele skittish about visiting their establishments—for a meal, for a haircut, to shop. But Joseph P. Lech—to everyone just Joe—was a pharmacist and therefore an essential worker.

Joe was sixty-one years old. He wished that he could shutter his shop to better shield himself from the virus. Over a career that stretched back to the early 1980s, he had served as president of the Pennsylvania Pharmacists Association and served on the board of the National Community Pharmacists Association. Joe had even testified before Congress on behalf of the country's independent pharmacists. He took seriously commandment number seven of the profession's code of conduct: if you choose to don the pharmacist's white lab coat, you agree to serve "community and societal needs."

So every morning, Joe left his home in Tunkhannock and made the thirty-minute drive through wooded hills to Laceyville, a town of four hundred at the northwestern edge of Wyoming County. He unlocked the front door on Main Street in the center of town and then locked it behind him. Since the start of the pandemic, the big CVS in Tunkhannock had let customers inside, which Joe recognized for what it was: a way of getting those needing to fill a prescription to browse its aisles and make other purchases. It was not until Wyoming County went green, on June 12, nearly three months into the pandemic, that he again allowed people inside his store.

Reopening brought its own headaches. He arranged for his stepson, a carpenter, to install a Lucite sneeze guard by the register and pharmacy counter. He bought boxes of disposable gloves that he and his people wore and purchased a Purell dispenser that he put just inside the front door. He put out hand sanitizer by the register and elsewhere in the store. Other places in town, he knew, were not following the best practices recommended by public health officials. But Joe was intent on saying they had made it through the pandemic without a customer catching COVID because they'd walked into his store.

"We did it all, the cleaning, the wiping down, the distancing, the masks, anything we needed to comply and do the right thing," he said. Of course, in the summer of 2020, in Laceyville and across much of the country, doing the right thing was the wrong thing to others, who might see an indoor mask mandate as infringement on their rights as an American.

"You'd think if it was my store, I could set the rules," Joe said. "But I guess that's not the way things work anymore."

* * *

Joe had been born and raised in Old Forge. He was more than twenty-five years older than TJ, but he spoke of the same tough town with a fighting spirt. Joe's father worked for a wholesaler that sold meat to the restaurants of Old Forge. Joe worked there, too, as a teen, delivering orders. As a kid, he played baseball with Angelo Genell, who runs Arcaro & Genell, across the street from Cusumano's, though to Joe, who moved away a long time ago, the restaurant is still Brutico's.

A career assessment test planted the idea of becoming a pharmacist in Joe's head. "It showed I had a brain for math and science, and pharmacist was one of the recommended careers," Joe said. He attended pharmacy school in Philadelphia and then moved to southern New Jersey to work for a chain called Thrift Drug. He worked at Thrift "long enough to know that it's not where I wanted to spend the rest of my career," Joe said. The job had been okay when he worked as a "floater," filling in for pharmacists on days off and sick days, but the job changed once he was assigned to a store.

"They call you assistant manager and have all these expectations so you're just working your ass off," Joe said. The same could be said of anyone building his or her own small business, but as your own boss, Joe said, "you work your ass off for what you want, not for what somebody else wants," he said. And of course there was a very different incentive structure. He could work really hard for someone else and others would profit off his labor. Working for himself, he enjoyed any monetary benefits of his extra effort.

A friend from pharmacy school was working as a drug rep in the Endless Mountains area. That's how he learned that a community not far from Tunkhannock needed a pharmacy. In 1983, at the age of twenty-three and only eighteen months after he had graduated from pharmacy school, Joe quit Thrift to open his own store. It helped that he married a woman he had met in pharmacy school whose father owned a drugstore in a small town in the center of the state. "He became a mentor," Joe said. Initially, he opened Lech's in Meshoppen, one town closer to Tunkhannock, but he later moved his store to Laceyville, in no small part to put more distance between him and the big drugstore chains.

The drugstore chains had begun their slow but steady rise by the time Joe entered the pharmacy business in the 1980s. Walgreens was founded in Chicago in 1901. CVS (originally known as Consumer Value Stores) was started in Lowell, Massachusetts, in 1963. The corner drugstore that served as a town meeting place was largely a vestige of a bygone era. The soda fountains of old had been ripped out long ago in most drugstores, a change hastened when President Woodrow Wilson signed a law banning cocaine and other opiates in over-the-counter products. Until then, drugstores had served not just ice cream sodas but also cocaine-infused drinks that gave customers "pep." Yet the chains did not dominate as they would by 2020. The pharmacy business was still a good one in the 1980s.

"It was a much simpler time," said Brian Caswell, a friend of Joe's who in 2020 served as president of the National Community Pharmacists Association (NCPA). "You could make a nice living operating an independent pharmacy." Even the chains were different then, Caswell said, or at least the small one he worked for in Kansas for his first eight years in the business. "I was able to operate like an independent and take care of our patients," he said.

Joe was still young and ambitious in the 1980s. Not satisfied with the one pharmacy, he opened a second Lech's in 1987, four years after opening the first. This Lech's was in Nicholson, a town of 850 people twenty minutes north and east of Tunkhannock. Another pharmacist agreed to run the store in return for an ownership stake in the business.

There would be more stores with other pharmacists. Joe befriended Mark Stamer, who worked for a partnership that operated several pharmacies in the area. Stamer quit to go work for Joe, who around that time introduced Stamer to his sister and became his brother-in-law. Several years later, they become business partners when Joe, Stamer, and a third pharmacist bought a place in Dushore, another tiny town in the next county over. In 2008, the same trio bought a second small-town pharmacy, in Canton, sixty miles from Tunkhannock. At that point, Joe owned pieces of four pharmacies across three counties, in addition to his original store, which he owned without partners. There may even have been a few years where he felt as prosperous as he imagined he might be when he was just starting out and dreaming of multiple stores.

* * *

The drugstore chains grew gradually until they were behemoths, crushing smaller competitors. CVS, which by 2020 ranked as the country's eighth-largest company by revenue, bought stores from the big regional chains such as Thrift, where Joe began his career, if not swallowed them whole. CVS had operated a few hundred stores in the northeast in the 1970s. By 2020, there were nearly 10,000 CVSes scattered around the country. There were another 9,000 Walgreens and 2,700 Rite Aids. In the year that Joe opened his first store, CVS reported just under $1 billion in annual sales. In 2020, its annual revenues mushroomed to $269 billion.

For decades, nonpharmaceuticals—aspirin, soap, deodorant— had been good moneymakers for pharmacies. At the end of the 1960s, for instance, sundries represented 56 percent of a pharmacy's sales. Yet the megachains, big-box stores, and later the internet intervened. Today, sundries represent barely 5 percent of a pharmacy's sales. Some owners, like Harshil Patel, who owns eight pharmacies in and around Hazleton, do not even bother to carry toothpaste, greeting cards, or chips. "It's just not worth the trouble," Patel said.

The big supermarket chains began cannibalizing the industry in the 1980s. Kroger was an early proponent of putting a druggist at a counter at the front of its stores, as were Albertsons and Publix. Eventually, Walmart and the other big-box retailers recognized that devoting a small bit of real estate to a pharmacy inside a store created a new revenue stream and, not incidentally, provided people with another excuse to walk inside. By 2020, 4,900 Walmarts had pharmacy counters. There were another 2,000 inside Krogers, 1,700 at Albertsons, and 1,100 at Publix.

There were roughly fifty-seven thousand pharmacies in the United States at the start of the pandemic. Less than twenty thousand were, like Lech's, independently owned—a trend that did not seem good for people's health. Being a pharmacist demands perfection. Dispensing the wrong drug, or an improper dosage, could prove fatal. Yet just prior to the pandemic, the *New York Times* published a report by investigator reporter Ellen Gabler, who had spent months looking at life inside these corporate pharmacy mills, filling prescriptions, administering flu shots, answering phones, counseling patients, and calling doctors and insurance companies—"all the while racing to meet corporate performance metrics that they characterized as unreasonable and unsafe in an industry squeezed to do more." Wrote one pharmacist, anonymously, to the Texas State Board of Pharmacy, "I am a danger to the public working for CVS." (Patient safety is of paramount concern, CVS said in a written statement to the *Times*. "When a pharmacist has a legitimate concern about working conditions, we make every effort to address that concern in good faith," the company said.)

Another threat has been the rise of mail-order pharmacies, which deliver a product but not a service, and the discounts insurance companies offer customers who agree to receive their medicines that way. "I remember my father-in-law in the early 1990s," said the NCPA's Brian Caswell, "telling me, 'I can compete with Walmart. I can compete with Walgreens. But what I can't compete with is when people are coerced into using their mailbox.'" Just eight megapharmacies, including the mail-order arms of several insurance companies, account for 74 percent of all prescription sales.

Yet it was not CVS or Walmart or the mail-order drug dispensaries that compelled pharmacists to descend on Washington, DC, each year for the NCPA's annual lobbying day on Capitol Hill. The real enemy making it increasingly harder for the independents to keep their doors open were the Pharmacy Benefit Managers, or PBMs—the intermediaries that set drug prices for the marketplace. Long gone were the days of flat fees for processing a prescription claim. That had been replaced by fee schedules and complicated formulas concocted by the PBMs. In 2012, Joe traveled to Washington to testify before Congress in opposition to the proposed merger of two of the country's largest PBMs, Express Scripts and Medco. Maybe it was true, Joe told members of Congress, that the PBMs were lowering healthcare costs, as their lobbyists claimed. "But then explain this to me," Joe continued. "Every year insurance premiums go up. Every year the portion the patient pays goes up. Every year we as providers are getting paid less for the prescriptions we fill. So where's all this money being saved?" PBMs never actually touched a pill but somehow hoarded an estimated 30 percent of the money spent on prescription drugs. Yet no one in authority stood up to block that merger nor similarly large acquisitions. The PBMs continued to dominate.

The PBMs determine how much a pharmacist will be reimbursed on each sale. Incredibly, that dollar amount does not always cover the price the pharmacist paid for that drug when purchasing it from the manufacturer. Hazle Drugs is a family-owned pharmacy that has been a fixture at the corner of Broad and Wyoming Streets in Hazleton since 1858 (though not always on the same corner). There, Bill Spear Jr. figured he lost money on around 5 percent of the pharmaceuticals he sold. Because the money losers tend to be pricier, brand-name drugs, Spear said, they equaled somewhere between 15 and 20 percent of his prescription revenues. When he paid $1.80 for a generic statin yet was only reimbursed $1.62, that was an easy decision. Spear ate the eighteen cents. "But when it's a brand name drug and I'm looking at a loss of twenty or forty dollars, then you have to start looking at the patient," he said. How long have they been a customer and what other prescriptions do they fill? The pharmacist is supposed to be a front-line healthcare provider, yet a third-party, Spear said, "is getting in the way of our relationship with our customers."

Pharmacists had other gripes about PBMs. The contracts were opaque, seemingly deliberately so. They included special discounts, volume discounts, and back-end rebates but also clawbacks if a pharmacy did not meet a minimum sales threshold. There were also the obvious conflicts of interest when so much of the negotiating takes place among people collecting paychecks from the same employer. Three PBMs dominate the market. Cigna, a giant of the health insurance industry, bought the largest of the three, Express Scripts, in 2018. UnitedHealth Group, the country's largest health insurance carrier, owns Optum Rx, another of the big three. CVS, which acquired Aetna, also bought Caremark, the third member of the big three. That means Caremark, on behalf of Aetna, is negotiating rates with CVS, along with every other competitor, large and small.

"It's akin to having McDonald's tell Wendy's how much they're going to be paid for a hamburger and then using that information to squeeze the competition and manipulate prices to their benefit," Brian Caswell said. There's also what Caswell and others call "steerage," when discount chains and insurance companies own PBMs and dangle deals that drive customers to its subsidiaries. "These companies steer customers into their own programs and away from the independents," Caswell said. The average independent pharmacy, according to the NCPA, reported an average of $74,800 in pretax profits in 2019. The explanation for relatively meager profits, Caswell said, is PBMs.

* * *

At Hazle Drugs, in Hazleton, Bill Spear Jr., fifty-eight years old, watched as other independents in town shuttered their doors: Hyman's Drugs, Sun Ray, the Greco Apothecary, the Wyoming Pharmacy down the street. Hazle Drugs' advantage over the independents was its compounding facility, where it formulated medication for those needing a special dosage or people who were otherwise unable to use a commercially available product. The store, which dates to 1868, promoted itself as the country's oldest continuously running compounding pharmacy. That helped counter the inevitable loss of customers when CVS and Rite Aid came to town, and then later the pharmacy counters inside Walmart and the local chain grocery store. "Customers thought they were cheaper," Spear said. "Some liked that they could get everything in one stop."

The Spears, father and son, thought about selling. They contemplated a move to the mall. Instead, they decided to remain downtown and expand. Bill Jr.'s grandfather had started as a junior pharmacist at Hazle Drugs sixty-seven years earlier. His father trained to be a pharmacist, as had he. They all worked in a wooden building that predated the Civil War. "Some buildings are old and historic," Spear said. "Unfortunately, our building was just old." At the start of the 2000s, they purchased the abandoned hotel across the street, knocked it down, and in its place built a giant, two-story, fifteen-thousand-square-foot brick building trimmed with teal and white.

"It sounds corny," Spear said, "but there really is this sense of community and loyalty and helping people as best you can."

A large pharmacy counter dominated the back of the first floor of the new Hazle Drugs, but otherwise the new place barely resembled a drugstore. Much of the ground floor felt more bookstore than pharmacy. There were carpeting and wooden shelves, several of which were devoted to women's health issues, including guides to natural menopause and books recommending natural hormone replacement therapy. The new Hazle Drugs promoted itself as "natural health specialists" and carried its own Hazle Health brand of vitamins, nutraceuticals (foods and additives with reputed health benefits), cleanses, and homeopathic and aromatherapy products. There was a "crave control" supplement for those looking to lose weight and another to strengthen bone density. A couple of years before COVID, Spear teamed up with a friend of his in Colorado who was involved in the marijuana business there. Together, they created their own line of CBD products. "Really, it's about survival," Spear said.

Upstairs were rooms for workshops and classes on nutrition, menopause, and other health-related topics. In another room, they offered nutritional assessments. The rest of the upstairs was devoted to a state-of-the-art compounding facility, where they created the vitamins, nutraceuticals, and protein powders they sold on the main floor, and the specialized prescriptions called in by doctors and, increasingly, veterinarians. Just as humans sometimes need custom-sized doses and unusual drug compounds, so do animals—who have no PBMs dictating terms. "We're doing medicines for dogs and cats all day long, every day," Spear said. Birds are also popular customers at Hazle Drugs, along with the occasional guinea pig, rabbit, and kangaroo.

The new store included a drive-through window, which proved handy in a pandemic. To serve a changing city, they hired bilingual staff. Hazle Drugs was giving flu shots and other vaccines long before most community pharmacists, and they offered what are sometimes called "memory packs" for those taking multiple pills, bundled by time and date rather than delivered in amber-colored vials. "That's not something the chain stores are going to do for you," Spear said. At the time of COVID, the store had a workforce of about twenty-five people.

"You go to Hazle Drugs because you know that if your mother is ailing, or a child is sick, Billy Spear [Bill Jr.] will show up at the store at eleven o'clock at night to unlock the door to get you the medicine you need," said Mary Malone, the president of the local chamber of commerce and a Hazle customer dating back decades. Of those using a community pharmacy, 94 percent give their pharmacists high marks. In contrast, people using a chain drugstore often don't even know the name of their pharmacist.

* * *

Joe Lech offered the same level of personal service. Almost everyone who walked into his store called him by his first name. But

Joe could not add dogs and cats to his clientele. He wasn't a com-
pound pharmacist. Even if he had been inclined to endure the
training that would be necessary to become one, his was a tiny
building that measured 1,200 square feet. He barely had room for
a small wedge-shaped desk to set up a computer, let alone the
air-lock room and ventilating hood that are required to set up a
compounding lab. There were people in the area no doubt eager to
learn about hormone replacement therapy, or get smarter about
nutrition, but Lech's was in a town of four hundred. By contrast,
tens of thousands of people lived within a fifteen-minute drive of
Hazle Drugs. Lech's sold CBD products and wooden toys from
Melissa & Doug, and the shop earned a little extra cash sending
faxes and making photocopies. But nearly all his sales were from
prescription drugs.

Joe had tried to boost revenue over the years. He added consulting rooms to his pharmacies, but "no one ever used them," his
brother-in-law and partner, Mark Stamer, said. Another year it was
a bone-density machine. "I don't think we used it a single time,"
according to Stamer. They were small-town pharmacists, open from
eight thirty a.m. to six p.m. Monday through Friday and a half day
on Saturday. People came to them to fill prescriptions and occasionally bought a bottle of aspirin.

Joe's biggest gamble came in 1995, when he was in his midthirties. He opened a Lech's in Tunkhannock, next to the Dietrich Theater. CVS had already set down stakes in town. Rite Aid was also
there. But this Lech's would be a specialty pharmacy that sold and
rented walkers, hospital beds, oxygen, and other medical equipment.

The business, however, never became the profitable enterprise
that Joe and his partner, another businessman in town, hoped it
would be. Walmart added a pharmacy in its upgrade to a Supercenter. So, too, did a regional chain when it opened a supermarket by the Walmart. Joe moved to a spot by the small hospital on
Route 6. There, Lech and Stamer, who at a certain point joined as a

partner, operated a pharmacy and also ran a side business arranging for home healthcare visits.

In 2013, the owner of a pharmacy in Lake Winola, eight miles east of Tunkhannock, was retiring. The employees there appealed to Joe for help in saving their struggling store. The same partnership behind their stores in Dushore and Canton bought the Winola store, and then almost immediately regretted it. They gave the store an upgrade, yet it continued to lose money, despite their best efforts. "It got to the point where it was affecting our other businesses," Joe said.

The year 2016 was a bad one for Joe and his partners. In a single day, they announced the closure of both the Lake Winola and Tunkhannock stores. Joe had been in negotiations with CVS to do a "file buyout"—the sale not of the pharmacy itself but its lists of customers, along with any ongoing prescriptions and insurance information. The nature of a file buyout is that if the news spills out prematurely that a pharmacy is closing, customers might leave and therefore the files are worth less to the purchaser. Joe could not announce the deal until negotiations had been finalized, but that left ill feeling among both employees and customers.

A half-dozen people lost their jobs because of the closing. A regional television station reported on the "abrupt" closure of the two stores and quoted elderly customers in Lake Winola who felt abandoned by the decision. "You've got these people who you are providing jobs to, with benefits, and you keep thinking this will turn around," Joe said. "So you persevere long after you probably should."

* * *

"Joe is very old school," Mark Stamer said. And people seemed to love him for it. Joe was not particularly tech savvy. He might wonder why someone had not responded to one of his emails and then realize that was because he had emailed himself rather than his intended recipient. The website for his Laceyville store misspells his name. Joe's system for keeping track of money involved Post-it notes on the counter. One time Mark Stamer added up the dollar amounts: Joe was owed more than $2,000.

"Joe is a great man, very well regarded in our community," said Gina Suydam, president of the Wyoming County Chamber of Commerce. Joe had sat on the board of the local hospital and served as president of the local chamber of commerce. He was a member of the Kiwanis, a service club, and an easy mark for anyone with a good cause seeking a contribution. Lech's sponsored a Little League team every year. "He's this really smart man the town is lucky to have," said Glenda Shoemaker. Joe's wife is Glenda's ex-sister-in-law and was one of her mom's first employees at J.R.'s Hallmark. "He's taught me a lot," Glenda said.

When COVID hit and Joe shut his door, customers could call or ring a doorbell he rigged up at the front door. Or they could rap on the glass. Then he or one of his people would run a prescription out to them. Normally, a customer needed to sign for a prescription, but the insurance companies dropped that rule. Joe scribbled "COVID-19" in a log and initialed the entry that served as the official record of that transaction.

At Hazle Drugs, they also locked their doors through the first two months of the pandemic. Bill Spear Jr., like Joe, was determined to make sure none of his people nor any customers caught COVID through the store. Hazle had the advantage of the drive-through window and two delivery cars, plus Spear, his spouse, and two sons, who were both enrolled in pharmacy school but pitching in during the pandemic. After the store closed for the night, each grabbed some bags and delivered them to people around the area. Spear was pushing sixty, and weight issues put him in a higher-risk category, but he took the deliveries to those he knew were sick with the virus. "If something happened to us and we went down, I don't want to think of what that would have meant," Spear said. He instructed his people to watch for anyone late in picking up a regular maintenance drug. Call them, he instructed his staff. The bilingual employees phoned those who spoke only Spanish. If customers did not feel comfortable coming into town, his people offered to have their medicine dropped off at their front door.

No one who worked at either Lech's or Hazle Drugs tested positive for COVID. At least five of Spear's people, though, had close encounters outside the store. Spear had each self-quarantine for two weeks, putting extra stress on a shrinking staff. A clerk who had been with the store for twenty years took early retirement. Two other employees quit: one to care for her sick mother, the other because she was pregnant and did not want to risk exposure.

COVID had a much larger financial toll on Hazle Drugs than Lech's. The store indefinitely canceled all its workshops and classes, and sales of Hazle Health plummeted when there were no people browsing the aisles. Sales dropped by at least 20 percent during the sixty-three days they did not allow customers into his store, Spear said. The financial loss was more than offset, however, by the $107,300 in PPP dollars that was deposited on the store's books at the end of April. Lech's, in contrast, saw a slight increase in sales. Joe chalked that up to the crowds at the Walmart (like Glenda, he refused to set foot in their store). For once, the modest size of his store was an asset, along with his willingness to run a prescription out to a customer's car. For Joe, the $40,000 in PPP dollars he received in April for the Laceyville store proved a financial windfall.

* * *

Laceyville's Main Street sits one block off Route 6 heading west from Tunkhannock. To reach Lech's Pharmacy in the summer of 2020, a visitor made a left off the highway at the house with a half-dozen Trump-Pence placards and a giant handmade sign that read, FUCK YOUR FEELINGS.

Laceyville Hardware and Floor Covering, a town fixture for decades, was still in business. So was the Community Bank across the street from Lech's. Yet the town's only grocery store had closed its doors a few years earlier, after more than four decades on Main Street. A barbershop sat vacant and dilapidated. Farther down Main Steet was the Meat Hook BBQ. The husband-wife team behind the restaurant had survived the state's red and yellow phases but then realized that they needed to restrict occupancy to 50 percent in green. With meat prices rising, they decided to call it quits that May, after six years in business.

A large American flag hung by the entrance to Lech's. A sign on the front door sign instructed people to mask up before walking inside. A second sign announced that he had masks for sale, including disposable blue surgical masks for $1. "I'll give it to someone at no charge," Joe said, if it meant avoiding an argument and convincing them to wear it inside his cramped store.

Joe dressed in a pink shirt with blue stripes and blue slacks. He is a mild-mannered-looking man with sandy gray hair worn on the longish side. He's of average size with blue eyes and a fleshy face. He wore stylish glasses and a mask his wife had sewn (he had sold more than three hundred of her home-crafted masks at the store in the previous month). Friendly and open, Joe still revealed an awkwardness that his friend and colleague Brian Caswell said was typical of pharmacists. "Pharmacy owners are often community leaders but tend to be on the shy side," Caswell said. On a ten-point scale measuring shy to outgoing, he declared Joe a five—like many pharmacists he knew.

On the topic of face coverings, though, Joe wasn't shy. "What's so hard about wearing one?" he asked, especially when a customer needed to put it on for only a few minutes. He was feeling more than a little fed up. He set the rules for his store, but, in this case, he was enforcing a state mandate. Yet that didn't matter to some.

"There's still people who refuse to put a mask on," Joe said that August. They claimed they didn't know about the rule, despite the sign on the door and the loud debate reverberating through the state. "They'll come in with no mask, no nothing. And I'm like,

'Really?' It doesn't make any sense to me," he said. Rather than get into an argument, Joe asked people to wait outside. He or one of his people—he had a staff of five, including several part-timers—would run a prescription out to them.

Joe braced for another round of arguments. A couple of days earlier, Dr. Deborah Birx, coordinator of the White House Coronavirus Task Force, had appeared on CNN. She warned that the country was entering a "new phase" of the pandemic that would not spare rural areas. She pleaded with Americans, wherever they might live, to wear a mask. In response, Trump tweeted that Birx was "pathetic" and suggested she had allowed herself to become a pawn of House Speaker Nancy Pelosi and the media. "The Fake News is working overtime to make the USA (& me) look as bad as possible!" Trump tweeted. Joe wondered if now he had to worry that a segment of his customer base might think, by asking them to wear a mask—a "face diaper," as some were starting to call them—he was siding with Nancy Pelosi, CNN, and who knows who else. At least there had been no physical fights, and for that he was thankful.

Chapter 12

Extinction-Level Threats

In Tunkhannock, the oversized parking lot of the Towne Plaza sat near empty at eleven a.m. on a sunny Wednesday morning that August. A couple of cars were parked in front of the FedEx, and another was at the Verizon store. There were a few other cars in the lot but none, apparently, to shop at J.R.'s Hallmark. The store was empty except for Glenda and an employee.

A sign on the door read, LET'S CARE FOR EACH OTHER BY STAYING 6 FEET APART. Decals marking out that distance were affixed to large rubber mats by the checkout counter, and Glenda had installed Plexiglas guards by the register. Glenda, with her aging British rocker hair, dressed in blousy, flowing clothes and stylish black leather sandals. She wore leopard-print glasses. Several thick strands of beaded necklaces hung around her neck, and she wore multiple rings on each hand, multiple silver bracelets on both arms, and a pair of drop-down stone earrings.

Across the country, retail that summer saw a bounce back in sales. Demand was pent up after all those weeks stores were shut down. Hundreds of billions of stimulus dollars were sloshing through the economy, and with travel and entertainment restricted, there were fewer ways for people to spend any extra cash they might have. Yet the rebound in sales was modest. Surveys showed that large segments of the buying public still did not feel comfortable walking inside a store. Shopping had shifted more online, sparking think pieces that postulated that the pandemic would forever change the way we shop. The number of physical stores in the US had been shrinking prior to COVID. Clothing stores and gift and card shops like J.R.'s had been on people's extinction lists for a long time. The fear was that the pandemic would accelerate the inevitable.

Glenda, after reopening her store, had gotten not quite a full month of shopping before the summer hit—always a slow time inside J.R.'s Hallmark. July had been like June, almost a normal month for her business, which was to say she experienced the usual summer blues rather than an extinction-level threat. She made her bills and had a little money left over. At least she was no longer dipping into her own savings to survive. "If a banker looked at how much money we've shoved into this place out of our own pockets just to keep this place open," Glenda said, "he'd be like, 'What are you doing? Get the hell out of there. Get out now!'" Prior to the pandemic, J.R.'s had been open until seven or eight p.m., depending on the night. She kept her regular hours when she reopened but concluded there was no point. The shop opened at nine every morning but often closed at five. "We're trying to get to a nine-to-six schedule," she said that August.

The possibility that the state might raise the minimum wage was another source of distress that summer. Someone had asked the governor about the frustration some businesses felt competing with the $600 weekly unemployment stipend. "If you want your staff to come back," Wolf answered, "just pay them more."

"That really set me off," Glenda said. Every small business owner she knew was struggling. "And yet this is the moment our governor chooses to tell us all that we're the problem, that we need to be paying our people more. In the middle of the pandemic. When a lot of us are scared we're going to close our doors."

The minimum-wage issue should have been a complicated one for Glenda. If J.R.'s closed, Glenda confessed, she herself would be a low-wage worker. Yet she adamantly opposed a hike of the minimum wage even to $10 or $12 an hour, let alone the $15 an hour that the governor and others were floating. She was barely covering a payroll of ten part-timers, some of whom she paid less than $10 an hour. Even a bump to $12 an hour would cost her thousands of dollars a year that she did not have. "My place is not for people who need to support a family," she rationalized. Her employees always had the option of earning more working at the Walmart. What she offered was flexibility and a pleasant place to work. "It's nothing to have somebody bring their kid to work or call in because their kid is sick," Glenda said. "We work around schedules. There's no retribution like at Walmart."

Yet Glenda saw the push for a living wage as a straightforward one. If forced to raise her pay, she would need to bump up her prices. Yet she was already losing business because people could find the store's products online for less money. She was against any effort to raise the minimum wage above $7.25.

Glenda also feared another shutdown. Elected officials and business owners alike had asked the courts to take away Tom Wolf's right to close businesses temporarily due to the coronavirus. But in July, the Pennsylvania Supreme Court ruled that the extraordinary steps Wolf had taken, including orders shutting down businesses, were constitutional. "The powers delegated to the Governor are admittedly far-reaching, but nonetheless are specific," the majority wrote. Not satisfied with the ruling of the state's highest court, the plaintiffs turned to the federal courts for relief. But who knew how long that might take?

"As far as I'm concerned," she said of Wolf, "he's trying to cripple small-town America with his policies." The day before had been her birthday and she confided that she was scared. "I'm fifty-eight years old and it's not like I can afford to retire any time soon," she said.

* * *

Mark Monsey at Greenwood's Furniture was sixty-five years old in the summer of 2020. He dressed in a denim shirt, knee-length tan shorts, and running shoes on a warm August day. Mark stood a slouchy six feet, two inches tall, with blue eyes and unruly gray fringe around his bald dome. A thick gray mustache turned down past his mouth, Hulk Hogan–style, sometimes making his smile look more like a snarl.

The store, with its bright green façade, occupies the first floor of a handsome, three-story redbrick building that, in 1961, at the age of twenty-nine, Tom Monsey bought from the family of the store's founder, Ray Greenwood, who had died after more than four decades in the business. The store does not seem as if it has changed much since then, starting with the old-fashioned sign stretching across the first floor of the building's façade. The filing cabinets and desks arranged in the middle of the store looked as if they had been bought by old man Greenwood. Other than the product line, not much inside the store appeared to have been updated in decades: the acoustic tile ceilings, the fluorescent light fixtures, the pegboard walls.

Mark was in the first or second grade when the family moved into an apartment above Greenwood's. "Dad hung pictures of the family in the store because this was our home," he said. Mark earned a degree at nearby Mansfield University of Pennsylvania, thinking he would teach high school, but back then at least, teaching jobs were hard to come by. He spent a few years away in Florida but returned to Tunkhannock in his midtwenties and bought a restaurant in town. He gave up on the restaurant after what he described as a "rough nine years" ("had a wife, lost her due to the food service industry") and, in his early thirties, joined the family business. When Tom Monsey died in 2005, at the age of seventy-three, Mark took charge. He was fifty-one years old.

Greenwood's competed against the chains like most every small business. Yet Mark smiled every time he saw a Raymour & Flanigan or Ashley Furniture ad on television. "The hillbillies up here, they'll say, 'Well, I don't know if I want to go to the city today, let's call Mark and see if he's got a double reclining sofa,'" Mark said. "And I'm able to tell them, 'Yes, I do.'" He matches the price he knows they're advertising on TV, and meanwhile he's saved them a trip to Scranton or Wilkes-Barre. The mortgage on Greenwood's had been paid off decades ago. "That lets me keep my prices low and compete with the big-box stores," he said. The store's motto is "Big city selection, small town service."

Mark wasn't hostile to Walmart, unlike other merchants in town. He mocked those who cast the retail giant as the end of civilization. "It would suck if a big corporate furniture store moved in down the street," he said, "but I'm not going to get a petition going because of it." The Walmart a mile away had a small furniture department, but if anything, the quality of the merchandise they sold helped his business. "They're so low-quality it's the best advertisement for me," he said. "You'll buy stuff from them, it'll break, and then you'll come buy something from us." If Walmart was bottom-tier, Mark said, La-Z-Boy and Ethan Allen occupied the higher-end market. "I stick with my medium price point," he said. "Prices my customers can afford but then they don't expect too much for the money." He sold recliners for around $500 and leather couches for maybe $800. "They beat it up and five years later, come back and buy another one," he said.

His real competition had always been Ken-Mar Home Furnishings, a family-owned furniture store in Meshoppen, the next town over and home to the giant P&G plant. Ken-Mar pitched its wares to the same midmarket customer. Yet the two brothers who had inherited the store from their parents were getting up in age, and their children, who lived elsewhere, had no interest in returning to run an aging furniture store. That store closed in 2017, after fifty-seven years in business.

If Mark had a fear prior to COVID, it was the internet. He recalled a moment four or five years earlier that sent a shiver down his back. A younger woman walked into Greenwood's looking for a love seat. "We go back and forth, I knock some money off, she's got me down to $365," he said. She responded by showing him her phone. That's the first time Monsey heard the name Wayfair, the online home furnishings company. They put a $350 price tag on the same love seat.

"She tells me, 'Match the $350 or you see this red button here? I'm going to push it,'" Mark said. He told her to go ahead, but, behind his bravado, he was petrified. Wayfair was selling furniture at the wholesale prices he was paying, and also offering free shipping. "How am I supposed to compete with *that*?" Mark asked. Even his niece, whose father worked with him at the store, ordered a sofa through Wayfair. Her experience, though, gave him hope. The sofa was uncomfortable, and she didn't like the way it looked in her home. If she had bought it at Greenwood's ("I would've given her one for nothing," Mark said, "but apparently we're not *contemporary* enough for her tastes"), he would have sent out a driver to pick up the couch, no questions asked. Sending it back to Wayfair, however, cost her around $180. In time, he also noticed that their prices creeped higher, as did those of similar sites, making him suspect that the lower price tags had been a way for online sellers to build market share. But COVID had returned that initial feeling of foreboding. Running a virtual store seemed a huge advantage during a pandemic.

Still, July had been nearly as terrific as June had been. His two delivery people could barely keep up with demand. If he had a worry in the first half of August 2020, it was that he had sold so much of his stock in the previous two months that his showroom floor was less crowded than it normally would be. Where in the past he displayed twenty-five or thirty recliners on the floor, he now showed around a dozen because he had no more stock than that. The same held true for bedroom sets and dining room tables.

"I go to reorder furniture but where it used to be a two- or three-week wait, now all of a sudden it's two months," Mark said. "I'm turning away [customers] every day."

* * *

Two other Tunkhannock small businesses had locked their doors for a final time during the first few months of the pandemic. Both were closures expedited by the coronavirus rather than caused by it. The couple behind Purkey's Pink Apple, a diner on Route 6, had already announced at the start of the year that they were retiring at the end of 2020. Two months into the lockdown, they decided to call it quits. "We hoped to sell it and keep the Pink Apple tradition continu[ing] on," Sally Purkey told the *Wyoming County Press Examiner* that May, "but I don't think people are interested right now." The woman who owned the small deli a few doors down from Greenwood's had also been looking to sell. She, too, did not bother reopening. "She just said, 'I want to be done, I'm retiring,'" said Gina Suydam, president of the Wyoming County Chamber of Commerce.

Tunkhannock's COVID case numbers remained low. More than four months into COVID, the entire county had recorded just fifty-eight confirmed cases and eight deaths from the virus. But people were still wary about mingling in public. Like Glenda, shop owners around town shortened their hours, leaving customers confused about when stores were open. Business owners were similarly flummoxed. "They're telling me how people's buying habits have gotten all weird," Suydam said. Restaurants still had no idea how to think about all those people working from home and how often they might drive into town for lunch. Restaurants that opened for lunch did so little business that they concluded it wasn't worth the effort and expense. Yet then people complained there were so few places to eat in the middle of the day.

The Dietrich movie theater was suffering. A state order still in effect limited occupancy based on the size of the space. Yet it's not like ticket takers were turning away customers. Before the virus, the Dietrich drew hundreds of people to town on a good night. That summer, they averaged fewer than fifty ticket sales a day. That hurt the Tioga Bistro, directly across the street from the Dietrich, though it's not like the Bistro could handle a crowd if it came. The restaurant had maybe fifteen tables. Under the state's 25 percent occupancy rule, that meant they could seat people at three. "We operated the restaurant like a food truck," said Maureen Dymond, who had opened the Bistro with her brother fourteen years earlier. They set a few tables out front but otherwise relied on takeout orders. The $31,600 the Bistro received through PPP proved critical.

Twigs, one block west of the Dietrich, was what Suydam described as a "date night" place for dinner before or after a movie—exactly the sort of higher-end restaurant that would struggle when people were frightened to dine indoors. Chef-owner Jerry Bogedin, the former P&G paper technician, was an angry mess that summer. "When I left P&G, I was making over a hundred grand a year," Bogedin said. Looking back, he said, "I was insane for getting into the restaurant business." He was abiding by the state's 25 percent occupancy cap but confessed that since it had been imposed, there "might have been all of ninety minutes where I had to have people wait because I was at capacity." He placed the blame for his lack of patrons squarely on Wolf, who Bogedin believed had unnecessarily frightened people when there was no evidence that restaurants were a source of widespread transmission. "Him talking 25 percent made people nervous like, 'Oh my God, it's the restaurants, it's the bars, I better stay away,'" he said.

Twigs received $113,000 through PPP. An innate mistrust of government, however, convinced Bogedin that he would need to repay that amount, no matter what assurances he was given, and he acted accordingly. (Ultimately, the loan was forgiven.) Since the start of the pandemic, he and his wife had sold their lake house and one of their two cars. They also arranged with the bank to defer their mortgage payment. "We're just scraping by," Bogedin said in August.

Bogedin was also angry at the governor over his mask order. Servers were instructed to politely ask those who entered without one to put one on. But what was he supposed to do about those who refused?

"We're not the mask police," Bogedin said. "But somehow we're the ones left to enforce it."

Bogedin was hardly alone in his frustrations around enforcing the mask policy. Every day seemed to bring another news article about an employee assaulted because of a mask mandate. The McClatchy news service published an article about owners across the country who decided to re-close indoor dining rather than confront their patrons. Closer to home, the chamber of commerce's Gina Suydam learned of one disturbing encounter at a big supermarket chain. Every Friday she joined other chamber presidents from around the state, which is how she learned about a confrontation involving the young employee the store put at its entrance to watch for people entering without face coverings. "This kid says to a guy, 'Sorry, you need to put on a mask,'" Suydam said. "The man just lifted his shirt and showed he was carrying a gun." The gun remained holstered, but her sympathies were with some sixteen- or eighteen-year-old making near minimum wage who had to wonder if he was going to get shot doing his job. Polling that summer by Womply, a marketing software maker, showed that 85 percent of local business owners required their customers to wear masks inside their establishments.

The mask mandate, Suydam said, put the business owners she was talking with in a terrible spot. No one wanted to turn away a customer in a tough economy. But if a store allowed a customer to shop without a mask, that was also a problem. Word spread through town, for instance, about a small food market that was lax about face coverings. Suydam heard from countless people who declared that they would only shop for groceries at the big supermarket outside of town or the Walmart, where mask wearing was strictly enforced.

On the opposite side of the spectrum, Suydam said, "are the people who are convinced COVID is a conspiracy and that masks are just another way to control people. They're out there trolling our restaurants and stores." In select cases, business owners themselves were among the defiant. Kimberly Waigand, for instance, the owner of the Crack'd Egg in Pittsburgh, announced on social media that she would not be requiring her employees to wear masks at work, despite a government order that she do so, nor would she ask her customers to wear them. Waigand created a hashtag for her cause (#FreeTheEgg"), a tagline ("Fighting tyranny since August 2020"), and also a manifesto: "We refuse to violate anyone's rights in order to make a living." She practically forced the courts to shut down her restaurant, which they did, at least temporarily.

Suydam herself was frustrated by the state's one-size-fits-all approach to the pandemic. "We have no nightclubs in Wyoming County," Suydam said. "We don't have crowded bars." Yet Tunkhannock and the surrounding towns needed to abide by the same rules written for Philadelphia or Scranton.

Suydam pointed me to the Facebook page of a bartender who worked at the Shadowbrook, a golf course and resort at the edge of town. The Shadowbrook has a good-sized patio. Someone could enjoy a beer after eighteen holes of golf and sit far from anyone else. Yet under the governor's rule, they were not permitted to buy a drink without also ordering food. It was not the bartender's rule, of course, or even Shadowbrook's. Yet the bartender was the one stuck explaining a mandate that made little sense.

"I get yelled at," he wrote, "all day every day."

Chapter 13

People Hate Us on Yelp

TJ was dressed in a white T-shirt, gray shorts, and running shoes. He wore a black baseball hat turned backward. He needed a shave, but in time I would learn he is one of those men who perpetually seem to be sporting several days' growth. He flashed a wolfish smile and unlocked the door to welcome me inside at nine a.m. At around ten thirty or eleven, Nina arrived. She was five months pregnant and starting to show. A couple of inches shorter than TJ, she had medium-length raven-colored hair pulled back for work. Mainly she looked tired. TJ's mother stopped by to say hello just before lunch. His father came by that afternoon. The two would return together a couple of hours later, when the restaurant opened for dinner.

"They're here like every twenty minutes," TJ said.

TJ gave me a tour of the upstairs, including the main dining room, where they had not served a meal in nearly five months. He flipped on the lights. The room looked as if only waiting for a liquidator to haul everything off to an auction house. Any tables that they had not moved downstairs were propped on foam blocks, so as not to leave rust marks on the carpeting. Stacks of laminated,

ladder-back wooden chairs sat around the room. A chalkboard promoted the featured drinks (a blackberry martini, a peach berry
sangria) that Cusumano's was hawking back in March.

The shades were drawn on the windows facing Main Street,
adding a depressing gloom to the scene. Takeout containers were
stacked high on the three-sided marble bar that in normal times
added light and energy to the room. "It really was a beautiful
restaurant," TJ said, as if starting a eulogy for his creation. "This
used to be the center of everything." The kitchen was now the only
part of the main floor they were using.

* * *

Sha-Asia Johnson was the first cook in that morning. She is a slight
black woman with a shy smile and easy laugh. She would be on till
at least nine p.m. that night, working the salad station and running
dishes downstairs, but had come in early to work on a big order
that needed to be out the door before noon. A big drug maker was
spending hundreds of dollars to buy lunch for a medical group in
Scranton. TJ asked her to come in early to help put together trays
of salad, pasta, and chicken parmigiana.

"She's getting to the point where she's good enough that I can
trust her on her own," TJ said. "She's my newest rock star." He had
been training her on the pasta station, which had her excited, but
she was also unsure of her near-term plans. Technically, she was still
in school, but TJ had not been shy about letting her know her best
education was working next to him in the kitchen. "Being successful in this business means being nimble and learning to go with
the flow," he told her. "Shit breaks, things happen. So once you've
dealt with the extraordinary circumstances of coronavirus life, a
busy Saturday night is easy."

Ang Garzon walked into the kitchen at a little after noon, wearing a green camo hat and Malcolm X–style glasses. If theirs was
a family, Ang was the shy and withdrawn sibling who often left

people wondering if maybe she was angry at them. She spoke in short, clipped sentences that often had a sting to them. Ang had felt off-rhythm her first few days back in the kitchen, but since that time, she had been enjoying the most satisfying stretch of her career. With half the restaurant off-limits, she tended to eight or ten sauté pans at once during busy stretches (with one or two pieces of meat on a stovetop grill) rather than fourteen or sixteen (with four or five meats on the grill). She savored the additional time she had to focus on each dish and felt more like a chef. Ang had also gotten something of a promotion. She still worked the sauté station, but a few weeks earlier, TJ had declared her his head cook. She would oversee the upstairs kitchen. "I'm like the kitchen manager," Ang said, with pride.

Others showed up to start their shift. Joey Graziano, the restaurant's thirty-one-year-old, rail-thin pizza maker, arrived dressed in baggy black basketball shorts and a gray T-shirt. He carried a sack from Dunkin' Donuts and a couple of bottles of Gatorade. "Nutrition," he explained with a smile, and went about setting up his station. He wiped everything down and then refilled a garnish rail with salt, pepper, garlic salt, oregano, and crushed red pepper. Next, he trimmed a half-dozen large onions, opened several six-pound cans of tomatoes, and threw it all into a giant blender (raw, rather than sauteed, onions is one secret to the sauce on most Old Forge pizza). He seasoned the mixture with copious herbs and poured it into a heavy-steel pot. He let that simmer for the next couple of hours while he grated a small mountain of cheese and prepared his toppings: broccoli, caramelized onions, fresh basil. Brian Mariotti, Cusumano's nineteen-year-old pasta cook, had little prep work that day. He was the last of the evening's line cooks to arrive.

Some chefs insist on discipline in their kitchen. That's not TJ. When younger, he worked briefly in this very prep kitchen when the restaurant was still Brutico's. "Dominica didn't like talking in her kitchen," TJ said. "I lasted like three days." Under his reign, banter and good-natured razzing were constants. ("Getting your chops busted is almost the ultimate sign of endearment in Old Forge," explained TJ's childhood friend Anthony Parisi.) TJ was often the instigator, but he was also the butt of many jokes. "I'm so severely angry when something goes wrong," TJ said. "Severely angry. Like I'm a monster." His blowups were a frequent source of teasing. TJ knew that sometimes members of the kitchen staff smoked pot by the recycling bins, but he also did not care so long as they showed up on time and could still handle the job.

When they had first reopened, TJ required everyone to wear a mask while cooking. But that rule proved difficult to enforce in a stifling kitchen during summer, especially when the upstairs fan broke. People ripped the masks off when things got too hot, and TJ did not reprimand them when they did. No one felt they were putting themselves or anyone at risk. "People weren't going out and everyone was trying to be careful," Brian Mariotti said. By the time I showed up in August, no one was wearing a mask, at least inside the kitchen.

Six months earlier, they would have had four or five servers on a Thursday night, along with at least two bartenders. On this night, Nina and Brenda Roscioli were the two waitresses, and Brie Felkowski the night's sole bartender. Felkowski, a taller woman with frosted hair and blue Armani glasses, worked as a legal assistant for a pair of local lawyers. Her day job had kept her busy through the pandemic, but she was among those Cusumano's staffers eager to get back to work after eleven weeks stuck at home. "I drank Corona the whole time. And Miller Lite," Felkowski said. "I drank a lot of things." Like the two waitresses, she wore a black T-shirt stamped with THE CELLAR on front. The back had a quote from a one-star Yelp review: "'Great food, unprofessional service.'—Samantha L."

The doors opened at five p.m., and it was as if someone had shot off a starter's pistol. The phone started ringing, and Joey Graziano slid pizzas into the oven. He used no timer or clock but instead relied on instinct. "You gotta let the pizza talk to you," Joey said. "It'll let you know when it's done." Within minutes, the first guests were seated. Nina slipped on a leopard-skin mask and Roscioli a plain black one. Felkowski kept a red polka-dot mask handy for when she needed to run out drinks or plates to help her coworkers. When just before six p.m. the phone rang, someone called out, "It's Walter." Anyone within shouting distance knew the order without being told. As always, Walter wanted stuffed peppers, and his wife asked for the grilled salmon with orange basil sauce. "We love Walter," TJ said.

More people arrived and the kitchen heated up. The patio filled up and eventually so did the tent. At around seven p.m., every table was occupied, even the one that they referred to as the "parking lot" because much of it sat outside the tent. Sha-Asia ran orders down from the kitchen, as did others. Roscioli seemed to have drawn the short straw that night. She had a table of six, where a woman she described as "very odd" was "cursing so loud the whole patio was looking at her." She also got stuck with a table of overly flirty men. The early days of the pandemic, when grateful customers left overly generous tips, had dissipated. "People are getting back to how they always were," Roscioli said. "Difficult. Very difficult."

* * *

Bob Mulkerin, the former mayor, had just started as a part-time bartender at Cusumano's in 2017. He knew TJ as a "pretty mellow guy." But then he caught a glimpse of TJ reacting to a customer who had insulted his cooking. A customer, a waitress told him, had just described his ravioli as the worst she had ever tasted in her life—so bad that she wanted the order struck from her bill.

Mulkerin watched from behind the bar as TJ made a beeline for the table. TJ makes his ravioli from scratch. Mulkerin is among those who think it's the best he's ever eaten. "He asks her," Mulkerin said, "'Like, of *all* of the raviolis you've ever had over your *entire* life, the worst *ever* in all that time is right here on your plate?'" The woman stared wide-eyed and mute as TJ kept talking. "Because I spent a part of my afternoon downstairs making them and I must be doing something really, really wrong." What struck Mulkerin was TJ seemed almost to be enjoying himself.

The customer might always be right inside many businesses but not Cusumano's, where TJ thinks most of them are wrong. He takes an item off the bill if he thinks the kitchen botched a dish, but he feels he works too hard to take a path of least resistance when someone complains.

"Maybe they ate too many appetizers and regretted ordering it," TJ said. Whatever their motivation, he rarely comps a dish, though invariably he knows he'll be reading about the experience in a one-star review on Yelp. A little before COVID, a table complained that the chicken Francese they had been served was "disgusting." He refused to comp the dish and, as expected, they posted a nasty review on Yelp. TJ responded by explaining that he had pounded the chicken himself that morning and, though he had not cooked it (Ang had), he took a bite back in the kitchen and it tasted as it should have. Not for the first time, he thought of Yelp as a plague released into the ecosystem by nerds who did not know any better.

"What a great idea, a service that lets people anonymously criticize small businesses," TJ said. Businesses out there were "dogging it," he knew, and they deserved to be called out for it. "But there are a lot of us pushing all day, giving it our all, making a product at a good and fair price but some person orders a medium-rare steak and they think it came out medium and they give you a one-star review," he said. On the door to the Cellar was a sticker that read, PEOPLE HATE US ON YELP.

"When I first opened, I used to bend over and bow down to people," TJ said. But no longer. "I work too hard, and my staff works too hard, to take that bullshit."

The pandemic only heightened tensions with customers. Limited capacity meant that when customers were seated, they were told there was a ninety-minute limit on the table. The tables on the patio were particularly at a premium. For the Cusumanos, the difference between a decent night and a bad one hinged on the ability to turn over an outdoor table at least once.

Yet night after night, TJ got into arguments with lingerers. "I'll tell them, 'Folks, thank you very much, it was nice to have you but we need this table for our next guests,'" TJ said. Around half the time people were apologetic, but the rest gave him an argument. "It's like people don't get it, that we're a family-owned business busting our butts each night to survive," he said. On the night I was there, only one table put up an argument about leaving. "We're still finishing our drinks," they complained. TJ asked them if they could finish their drinks faster because he needed the table for his next guests. When they still dawdled, he instructed the busser to clear the table, spurring them to finally leave.

"Maybe I should just start saying straight out, 'I'm struggling to make a living here and so I'd like you to please vacate the table,'" he said.

TJ remained in constant motion all night. When he wasn't seating new arrivals, he was running drinks and plates to the tables and takeout orders to the cars. At one point, he slipped next door to Cafe Rinaldi to borrow a bottle of Jim Beam. He managed to stay away from the upstairs stove, but that was not to say that the perfectionist within did not occasionally roar out. His instructions for roasting that night's vegetable, grilled asparagus, had been to roll them in olive oil, salt, and pepper, and then put them on the grill long enough to heat them up and give them a bit of char. Instead, some came down looking burnt because the kitchen was leaving them on for too long. His angriest moment came when he saw that someone had been served one of the night's specials, a New York strip in lemon herb butter, without a charred half lemon. That was Ang's error, but, rather than own her mistake, she reminded him that he was the one selling the steak with charred lemon, not her. "So that makes you the liar, not me," she said. More than once over the next couple hours, I heard TJ mutter the liar line to himself.

* * *

Cusumano's generally followed the rules as imposed by the state, but there were exceptions. The governor had instructed every bar and restaurant in Pennsylvania to remove the stools from any functioning bar. Yet it was on a stool at the Cellar's walnut bar where I planted myself when I wasn't wandering around to see what was going on in different parts of the restaurant. A couple of regulars sat on the other end of the L-shaped bar, drinking beers but never ordering any food, though Wolf had explicitly said that people could drink alcohol at a bar or restaurant only if they consumed a meal. TJ's mother joined us at the bar for a while, as did Nina's parents and a couple of others over the course of the evening. They, too, enjoyed a drink but ate no food. I wore my mask for a while, but when Felkowski served me a glass of wine, I took it off and never put it back on.

The night had been a decent one for the restaurant. Yet that said a lot about a restaurant owner's expectations in 2020. Cusumano's, TJ said, booked less than half of what it would have on a good-weather Thursday night one year earlier. The pleasant surprise was that he was making around the same profit as before. He was bringing in fewer dollars but his spending on employees was way down, which left him feeling queasy. He had not gotten into the restaurant business simply to make money.

"I don't feel so proud when I know half my staff isn't here and there are people out there suffering," TJ said.

It was past nine p.m. when Nina took a stool and smiled for the first time since the restaurant opened. "I'm not doing a good job of feeding this baby," she said, and ordered the steak sandwich with gruyere and caramelized onions. TJ enjoyed a postshift IPA. Several staffers drifted down to the Cellar for an after-work drink, and Cousin Anthony made a guest appearance. Between beers ("this one's broken," he said to Felkowki when ordering another; "this one's not working no more"), he offered an impromptu comedy set. A short muscular man with long brown hair, he kept everyone laughing with jokes about everything from the motley crew running Old Forge to meeting his wife and raising his kids. Fooling his wife into marrying him was easy, he said, as if a modern-day Rodney Dangerfield. "I kept her drunk until she was seven months pregnant and then it was too late," he said.

TJ had been at it for well over twelve hours. Yet he had a restless mind and never seemed fully satisfied standing pat. We moved to a table closer to the back of the Cellar, where he told me about a couple of deals he had in the works. The first was a boarded-up restaurant he was thinking of renting. It was in Lake Winola, a small resort town twenty miles from Old Forge, far enough that people could not order Old Forge pizza but close enough to know what it was. The property was too big for what he had in mind, but the restaurant had a small pizza kitchen in back, ovens and a dough mixer included. Through the first nine months of 2020, the *New York Times* reported, the combined revenue of Domino's and Papa John's had increased by roughly the equivalent of an additional thirty million large cheese pizzas. He would call the place Cusumano's at the Lake. "I think we could make a killing there," TJ said. He had long harbored dreams of opening several restaurants. This might be his chance.

The second deal seemed rooted more in sentimentality than business sense. He had put in his bid for GI's, the bar that had first opened as Café Cusumano in 1916. His father, Tom, had co-owned GI's while he was still in his twenties, when the idea of working all day and then much of the night seemed possible. For a while, Cousin Anthony also owned a share. "We did really well for a corner bar," Anthony said. GI's troubles began long before COVID, though. By the start of the pandemic, the bank held the paper on the property.

It was hard to imagine people crowding into a bar anytime soon. There was also his own future to consider. He was about to become a father. He and Nina were surviving the summer and presumably would have a decent fall. But what would happen when the weather turned and most people no longer wanted to sit on a patio with no real walls? Yet where others might see another monthly payment with no revenues for the foreseeable future, TJ saw a buying opportunity.

* * *

The Trump campaign wanted to troll Joe Biden by having the president give a speech in Scranton on the day his foe accepted the nomination for president. Unable to find a business in Biden's hometown willing and able to host Trump, the president's advance team settled on a family-owned kitchen supply business in Old Forge. Mike and Bobby Mariotti, grandsons of the founders, knew the Trump sons "and I guess they picked us ahead of everyone else," Bobby said. Two weeks after my first visit to Cusumano's, on the day that Joe Biden promised that under his presidency, the country would "overcome this season of darkness," Trump appeared at Mariotti Building Products, one mile from Cusumano's.

TJ had known Mike and Bobby since they were all kids. The brothers were Cusumano's regulars, and Bobby's son, Brian, was the restaurant's pasta cook and a stalwart through COVID. There was no doubting where TJ stood. He was not quite so outspoken in his dislike for Trump as his parents, who generally looked on Trump as a cancer on the body politic, but he was also a business owner in a once solidly Democratic town that seemed roughly split between those who loved the president and those who loathed him. With me, he had described Trump as a "fucking fraud" and a "dangerous monster." But TJ knew and liked people who saw positives in the president and he looked on Trump's visit from the perspective of a lifelong Old Forger. The president of the United States was coming to their town of eight thousand, and that, TJ said, "was undeniably a big fucking deal." The gears began to grind inside his head. He texted the Mariottis to float the idea of Trump enjoying a meal at

Cusumano's before or after his speech. He was disappointed but not shocked when he didn't hear from anyone on the Trump's advance team about a potential presidential visit.

His wisest move, TJ knew, was to remain publicly quiet about Trump's visit. But TJ Cusumano, if nothing else, is fiercely loyal to Old Forge, and also felt a genuine excitement for his little town. He posted on the restaurant's Facebook page that they were opening early in honor of the president's visit and added, "What a great moment for our town! We are happy to welcome President Trump to the Pizza Capital of the World!" Most of those posting in the comments section expressed appreciation for his ecumenical message but several questioned his tacit support for so divisive and dangerous a figure. A couple of posters even called for a boycott of Cusumano's, including the chef-owner of a pair of vegan restaurants in the area who happened to live in Old Forge. TJ did not know this fellow chef, but he was so offended that he would attempt to sabotage a fellow business owner during a pandemic that he phoned him. In response, TJ received a text from the man saying he was too busy to talk but added that he wished "people in our area had more sense than to support such a terrible person." TJ wrote back, "I just wanted to see if you had the guts to say that to me over the phone or if you were the coward everyone says that you are. Thanks for answering that for me."

Mariotti's is off Moosic Road on the way out of Old Forge toward the interstate. The business, which had received $1.15 million in PPP funding that April based on a payroll of ninety workers, was recording record sales, Bobby Mariotti said. To greet the president, several gleaming metallic blue truck cabs stamped with the Mariotti logo were parked behind a podium. Attendance was limited to this event on private property (TJ did not request an invitation), but thousands, according to media reports, lined the roads into the facility, waving American flags and Trump 2020 banners. Trump took the stage at around three p.m.

The speech was typical Trump fare. Biden was under the control of the "radical left" and favored a "socialist takeover of the US economy." Biden had angered many on the left when rather than call for an end to fracking in Pennsylvania, he only proposed a pause on new exploration. But Trump said that Biden's proposal to shut down fracking in Pennsylvania would cost 670,000 jobs. (According to the Pennsylvania Department of Labor & Industry, there are fewer than 50,000 fracking jobs in the state, including support positions.) Trump seemed to hit on every hot-button issue including the "Chy-na virus," immigration, Black Lives Matter, and phony witch hunts. "If you want mobs and criminals, you got to vote Democrat," he said. Biden's great-great-grandfather had been an engineer who helped design the layout of Scranton's streets. Biden was born in Scranton but moved away when he was ten, after his father found a job cleaning boilers for a heating and cooling company in Delaware. His family still spent every summer and holidays in Scranton. But speaking at Mariotti Building Products, Trump castigated Biden as a hypocrite who had "abandoned" the region.

"He keeps talking about, 'I was born in Scranton. I lived in Scranton,'" Trump said. "Yeah, for a few years, and then he left for another state."

The patio at Cusumano's was packed with patrons dressed in full Trump gear when at four thirty p.m. Brenda Roscioli took a quick breather outside. That's when she noticed state police on motorcycles gathering on top of the hill. More police were gathered at the borough hall one block away. She found TJ, and together they saw Secret Service agents and bomb-sniffing dogs walking toward them. By the time the presidential motorcade came rolling down Main Street twenty minutes later, every last customer and most of Cusumano's staff were outside. The president's limousine stopped on Main Street, right in front of the restaurant.

"Whatever you think of the guy," Roscioli said, "it was a wild experience seeing Trump get out and wave."

Trump headed into Arcaro & Genell, one of the older pizza restaurants in town. TJ was not surprised. The owners were staunch

Republicans and openly supported Trump. The president picked up several trays of Old Forge pizza for the Air Force One ride back to Washington, including a pepperoni, a sausage, and a white (no tomato sauce, heavy on the cheese).

Thirteen days after Trump's appearance, the COVID rate in Old Forge jumped sixfold, according to a study published by the health news outlet *Stat*. A team of researchers at Stanford looking at Old Forge, among other Trump rally sites, documented a similar spike in COVID-19 cases and also deaths.

The day left TJ with mixed feelings. Trump in town, spreading his bile, only served to roil bad feelings in Old Forge. Yet for one day, at least, it was like the coronavirus magically did not exist. A couple of post-COVID Saturday nights might have been busier, but the day of Trump's visit was far and away his best Thursday in he couldn't remember how long.

Chapter 14

It Takes a Village

The wider world seemed aligned against small businesses in the US, but the list of groups that assist them is long and includes what are called Small Business Development Centers. Think of SBDCs as small consulting houses that help even up the sides on a lopsided playing field. Larger businesses have teams of marketing people, finance departments, and other advantages over small ones. The SBDCs, some of which date back to the 1970s, operate with money from the SBA and also state and local governments, universities, and economic development nonprofits. At no cost, a small business can have access to consultants who generally bring decades of experience to the task, whether that's helping a wannabe entrepreneur create a business plan or serving as a lifeline to a seasoned operator navigating the choppy waters of a crisis.

"We've all had barely a minute to breath since this all started," Lisa Hall Zielinski, the director of the University of Scranton's Small Business Development Center (most but not all SBDCs are housed at universities), said in the summer of 2020. Zielinski had a staff of five consultants who helped businesses scattered across eight counties, including Lackawanna and Wyoming. Theirs was one of sixteen SBDCs in Pennsylvania and nearly one thousand nationally. An SBDC based at Wilkes University, in Wilkes-Barre, served Hazleton and the rest of Luzerne County. Family-owned businesses in the region could also rely on support from the Family Business Alliance, based at Wilkes University and Penn State Scranton.

Any number of advocacy groups were promoting the interests of small businesses in Washington, DC, and state capitals around the country. Founded in 1943, the National Federation of Independent Businesses is the oldest and largest with several hundred thousand members. The NFIB generally takes conventional pro-business stances against taxes and regulation. Its more liberal counterpart is the Main Street Alliance. Founded in 2008, the Main Street Alliance, which has around thirty thousand members, pushes for more livable wages, better child care, and more affordable health care for all, based on the belief that a healthier and more prosperous community leads to a more robust small business environment. The California-centered Small Business Majority also champions a more progressive small business agenda. Every advocacy and trade group seemed to offer regular webinars during the pandemic and created guides to help small businesses navigate the thicket of agencies and government programs that could provide financial help and other resources.

Trade groups played a similar role. TJ had paid little attention to the Pennsylvania Restaurant & Lodging Association before the pandemic. But the group, recognizing that businesses were cash strapped, suspended collection of dues and unlocked its website so that any restaurant, bar, or hotel seeking help could log on, regardless of membership status. Soon TJ became a regular visitor. The association sourced PPE when it was hard to find and did a good job, TJ said, synthesizing the jumble of information coming from different government agencies. "The guidance they gave was always really helpful," he said. Similarly, the Pennsylvania Chamber of Business and Industry created a "Bringing PA Back" site open to anyone. It, too, provided webinars on everything from PPP to unemployment compensation to the latest best practices for operating responsibly in a pandemic.

The local chambers also did what they could to help mom-and-pop businesses. In addition to webinars, the Wyoming County Chamber of Commerce sponsored a #takeout2020 campaign that had them handing out thousands of dollars of vouchers for area restaurants. The chamber in Hazleton also offered online seminars aimed at helping local businesses regain their footing and gave away several thousand dollars in gift certificates to help local businesses. The Greater Hazleton Chamber of Commerce was also one of the prime movers behind the newly formed Recovery & Resiliency Task Force that had provided Vilma Hernandez with a small emergency grant. The group raised another $64,000 from community members to enlist the services of two bilingual business development consultants with a goal of helping up to fifty local business owners develop and implement a recovery plan.

"The silver lining in COVID has been this sense that together we will get through this," said Mary Malone, president of the Hazleton chamber. The virus had hit Hazleton particularly hard, and almost the entire community came together, she said. The one exception among businesses was Amazon. As the head of a local chamber, Malone's job essentially is to say complimentary things about businesses operating in the area. If nothing else, she typically avoided uttering anything negative. Amazon's AVP1 plant was a major employer in the area but she was so frustrated over the company's behavior early in the pandemic that she did not care.

"Amazon blocked us at every turn," Malone said. "I have nothing good to say about Amazon."

* * *

Malone was hardly the only prominent Hazletonian with a negative view of Amazon. Kevin O'Donnell spent his entire career at CAN DO, recruiting large corporations to the area and then hyping them locally. O'Donnell had adopted a kind of see-no-evil approach to business in his forty-seven years with CAN DO, twenty-six of which were spent as the organization's president and CEO (he retired at the end of 2020). But he, too, singled out Amazon. Every other business seemed willing to spare a plant manager for a couple of hours, or at least someone in authority, to attend the occasional association meetings CAN DO held in its various industrial parks. But Amazon, O'Donnell said, rarely if ever showed up. "It was a little disheartening," he said. "It was even sometimes difficult to get them to talk to another business in the park if an issue or something came up."

Cargill's giant meatpacking facility outside of Hazleton, like the Amazon distribution center, had been an early vector for the spread of COVID. "But these two large companies couldn't have dealt with it more differently," Malone said. Local leaders spoke regularly with the Cargill plant manager. "Some would say maybe Cargill should've acted faster but they agreed to shut down their plant for two weeks and pay their employees," Malone said. "They worked with us, they worked with our local healthcare systems to retool regarding their setup. They did their best to keep us informed on what was going on inside."

Amazon, by contrast, acted as if being a global colossus meant not needing to deal with the yokels. Upward of two thousand locals worked at the Amazon fulfillment center, yet Malone said no one part of the Recovery & Resiliency Task Force received even a return phone call from Amazon. "I don't think anyone in the company cared anything about what was going on in Hazleton and what role they might be playing in spreading COVID," Malone said. Amazon declined to temporarily shut down to sanitize the building, as Cargill and plants around the country had done following a widespread outbreak.

Amazon workers were more frustrated than local officials. The company refused to share even basic information with them, including the number of people who had been infected at the site or where in the warehouse transmissions were clustered. Asked why, a company spokesperson told NBC, "We don't think that number is super valuable." Employees who raised questions about workplace safety inside fulfillment centers elsewhere in the country were fired.

Jim Dino, a reporter with the Hazleton *Standard-Speaker*, spoke to a half-dozen employees who were working inside the Amazon plant during the first weeks of the pandemic. Several criticized their employer on the record. They complained about a lack of masks and cleaning supplies. Several said the company was not bothering with social distancing or other basic preventative measures. Dino, who retired after thirty-eight years with the paper in 2021, contacted Amazon before publishing any story. He described the various Amazon spokespeople he spoke to as automatons who read from the same script.

> *Our top concern at Amazon is ensuring the health and safety of our employees.*
> *Since the earliest days of the pandemic, we have worked closely with local authorities to help fight this terrible disease.*

"They were about the biggest violators around when it came to COVID-19 practices but they just denied, denied, denied what people were telling me was going on," Dino said.

Eventually, the area's state senator intervened, and local inspectors were sent into the Amazon plant, ostensibly to check for municipal code violations. The people he was speaking with, Dino said, told him that was the step that finally brought about change. "Only then did management give everybody a mask and start taking people's temperature and putting tape on the floor and all that good stuff," Dino said.

The Hazleton fulfillment center featured prominently that May during a *60 Minutes* segment looking at Amazon's treatment of its workers through the first couple of months of COVID. Employees working at the Hazleton site had counted at least seventy confirmed positive cases, but the company stuck with its "not a particularly useful number" talking point. Under pressure, though, the company announced that it was setting aside $4 billion for "COVID-related initiatives to get products to customers and keep employees safe."

Amazon could afford the extra expenditures. With people afraid to shop in stores, Amazon saw its revenues soar by 41 percent in the second quarter of 2020, and its profits during those three months doubled to more than $5.8 billion.

"They were making money and didn't care what happened to their employees," Jim Dino said. "Their attitude was, if something happens to them, we'll just get new ones."

* * *

Meanwhile, Vilma's Hair Salon continued to limp along as summer turned into the fall. There were no drop-ins at a shop where that had been the norm. Everything was still appointment-only. Vilma continued to bring in barely half of what she was making before COVID. She still hadn't received replenishment of the product she sold. Occasionally, she checked on the status of shipments she was expecting from Italy. They were perpetually "en transit," figuratively if not literally lost at sea.

Other small businesses in Hazleton were also struggling. The VIP Healthy & More, a juice and sandwich shop near the center of town, had always been less a dream than a pragmatic decision by two Latina women in their thirties, working dead-end jobs in the industrial parks for $12 or $14 an hour. The store stayed closed for the first two months of COVID and continued to struggle even once it reopened. Theirs was a snug lunch and snack spot on Wyoming, one block from Broad. The offices of the *Standard-Speaker*, two doors down, was indefinitely closed, as were most offices in the eleven-story Hayden Tower at the corner of Broad and Wyoming and the seven-story building across the street from the Hayden.

Relief came through the $5,895 VIP received through PPP. Jimmy's Quick Lunch, a fixture of Broad Street since 1937, was still standing. But with no downtown lunch crowd, sales were not even half of what they had been before the pandemic. Owner Jimmy Grohol, sixty-seven, might have been far more worried about the future if not for the $50,000 from PPP.

The Shop 2 was a couple doors down from Jimmy's. Two nurses had opened this antique store in 2010, and eventually gave up the medical profession to devote themselves full-time to its success. One, Carmine Parlatore, was the sister of baseball's Joe Maddon. Neither Parlatore nor her partner, her cousin Francine Umbriac, was getting rich from the store, but, Parlatore said, "we covered our expenses and made a little money and I enjoyed it immensely." They could have reopened at the end of May, when Luzerne County went yellow, but waited until June and the green phase. They then wondered why they'd bothered. "If we had five people in the store in a day, that would be a lot," she said. The Shop 2 never had employees, so they did not apply for PPP. The bills kept coming, but they were not generating the revenues to pay them.

Between the Shop 2 and Hazle Drugs at the corner of Broad and Wyoming sat the Poppy Press Coffee Company. Owner Tamara Hersberger, fifty-three, had done a little bit of everything before getting into the coffee and sandwich business: operations manager for a family-owned business, human relations, lean manufacturing consultant, furniture restoration. Tamara had her first child when she was eighteen years old, and she and her husband had seven more kids over the next eight years. Tamara had long been a regular at a café called the Dragon Fly. When she learned it was for sale, she bought it for what she remembers was around $65,000. She renamed the shop Poppy Press, in honor of her father, whose recent death had spurred her to think about buying a business. She opened her doors in October 2019.

"We were really making it," Tamara said. Then COVID hit. It

felt to her as if someone had bent over and pulled the plug on her business, causing everything to stop with a jolt.

Tamara is a stout woman in her early fifties with blue eyes, a round face, and blonde hair she wore pulled back. She did not bother with takeout in a largely abandoned downtown. Instead, she put her effort into getting the Poppy Press ready for the green phase. She spent $3,000 on outdoor seating that would let her seat twelve outside. She rearranged the tables and stools inside so no one was sitting within ten feet of one another. She received $17,732 through PPP but brought back only a single employee. "All my foot traffic is from the *Standard-Speaker*, from the Hayden Tower, from the other buildings, yet nobody is down here," Tamara said. She closed for July 4 and decided not to reopen. She donated hundreds of dollars' worth of perishables to food banks rather than throw them away.

The man Tamara had bought the property from was understanding. Pay what you can, he told her, and we'll work it out. But she had other bills she couldn't put off: gas, electricity, the cable company for Wi-Fi, the exterminator who came once a month, her work insurance. With her doors closed, she looked for any catering she could scrounge up: a bridal shower, a birthday party, a memorial. "I'm living on whatever I can make this week," Tamara said.

* * *

Since the Maloneys had started Sol Cacao, the summers had always been about survival. With no opportunity to offer in-store samples, 2020 seemed destined to go down as their toughest. But the horrific video of George Floyd's murder, and the protests that followed, proved an inflection point in the fight for racial justice and a recognition by some of structural inequities. For three chocolate makers in the Bronx, it brought sudden attention that translated into orders.

"After George Floyd, there was this move to support local black businesses," Daniel Maloney said. "For the first time, we got visibility and had people—I mean, people we would never even imagine—reaching out to us and supporting us."

Bloggers and others who wrote about chocolate were among those contacting the Maloneys. People of color generally were the workers who planted and harvested the planet's cacao beans, which grow in tropical climates. But the owners were overwhelmingly white. The Maloneys were featured in an article *Eater* ran about "chocolate makers decolonizing the industry." *New York Makers*, an online magazine, spotlighted the bespoke approach to producing chocolate taken by these three brothers who had set up shop in Port Morris. A local news site profiled the bean-to-bar makers behind the Bronx's first chocolate factory.

"We had been telling our story for five years," Dominic said.

"And finally people were listening," Nicholas said, finishing his brother's thought.

The surprise for the Maloneys was that the horror of George Floyd's death was so deeply shared (a poll in June 2020 showed that 71 percent of white Americans agreed that racial discrimination was a "big problem"). The resulting racial reckoning meant the country, or at least many (Trump spent much of the summer decrying the "mobs" that had taken over the country's biggest cities), were looking more deeply at institutional racism and the wide range of privileges whites blindly enjoyed at the expense of people of color. Many tried to do their small part by buying the Maloneys' chocolate bars. Stores the Maloneys had contacted in the past got in touch with the brothers. Others cold-called Sol Cacao—something that had never happened in its first half-dozen years. Normally, discussions with a store stretched on for months, but a couple put in an order shortly after first contact.

The summer saw a change in how Sol Cacao sold their bars. Individuals had always had the option of buying directly through the Sol Cacao website, but online purchases had never amounted to more than 10 percent of their sales. The rest they sold wholesale to stores. That summer, though, online orders equaled half their revenues, if not more. Mothers found them on the spreadsheets listing African American–owned businesses that New York City moms started sharing soon after George Floyd's murder. People read about them online and bought bars for themselves and others. The globe was suffering, and chocolate, as it has long been, seemed a way for people to show they cared.

"You could definitely see the human spirit play out in terms of gifting," Daniel said. "We're getting a lot of notes saying, 'Hey, I want to send bars to my colleagues who have been there for me,' 'I want to send these to someone to say thank you for support through hard times.'"

Another market opened up that summer: corporate customers. Several businesses had approached them for fifty or one hundred bars they could send directly to customers or include in a gift basket. One large corporation hired the brothers to do a virtual tasting for its sustainability department. That led to more jobs like it. "People were looking to get outside their confined space and find different things for team-building," Daniel said.

Revenues between May and September were more than three times what they had been one year earlier. "The summer saved the company," Daniel said. They earned back all the money they had lost in the first couple of months of the pandemic. "That gave us hope that we could get back on track in the fall," Dominic said.

Chapter 15

10 Percent Capacity

John Longstreet at Pennsylvania's restaurant association was
not lobbying the state to drop its 25 percent capacity limit,
which had been in effect since mid-July. He was *begging* them
to reconsider. Under the state's rules, servers, bartenders, and cooks
were included when doing a head count. Longstreet asked people to
imagine a restaurant (not unlike Cusumano's) that sat one hundred
people. "When you factor in staff," Longstreet said, "at 25 percent,
they're left with four or five tables. At that point, the economics of
opening don't work."

There was a similar push to resume bar seating, a restriction
Longstreet and his people saw as equally arbitrary. What difference
did it make if someone was eating at a bar or a table? Bar patrons
could be seated at least six feet apart. A bartender would be wearing a mask. Any establishment seeking extra precautions could add
Plexiglas barriers, as restaurant and bar owners were doing in other
parts of the country. Members of Longstreet's association were fum-
ing that customers still needed to order food if wanting a drink,
but, Longstreet confessed, "we weren't as forceful in fighting that."

The ban on bar seating, along with the rule requiring a food

purchase to drink, remained. But in September 2020, the state announced a relaxation of its capacity limit. Starting on Monday,
September 21, restaurants could increase indoor occupancy to
50 percent. To increase its occupancy, however, a restaurant needed
to self-certify that they were following all the protocols laid out by
the state.

Longstreet was incensed. Retail didn't have to self-certify. Neither did manufacturing concerns, or construction companies, or even
massage parlors or hair salons. "That was one more way the restaurant industry felt singled out and forced to go through these extra
hoops," he said. Adding to everyone's frustration was the state's
self-certification portal, which was not ready until two weeks after
the September 21 start date. A restaurant could open on the twenty-
first but would not know until October 5 precisely what they were
self-certifying.

The governor's people reached out to Longstreet when fewer
restaurants than they expected self-certified. Longstreet was not
surprised. There were legal ramifications to vouching on an official
state form that an establishment was strictly adhering to the rules.
More than a few of his members were reluctant to sign a document
that could be used against them in a lawsuit. "As I was saying a lot
back then, 'The state earned the distrust of our industry,'" Longstreet said.

* * *

TJ Cusumano had no problem clicking a few boxes on a website
if it meant he could operate at 50 percent capacity. The decision
to reopen for indoor dining, however, was not an automatic one.
He first needed to hear what his staff was thinking. "I didn't want
to put myself or my people in an environment of being exposed
because now we would be serving the public inside," he said. The
kitchen staff had made it clear they were all in favor of indoor
dining and, not incidentally, the extra hours it would mean. It was

time to find out what Cusumano's front-of-the-house people were thinking.

In mid-September, around fifteen people—the restaurant's servers and bartenders, along with a couple of bussers—gathered in the Cellar to talk about the reopening. TJ had Joey Graziano cook up trays of pizzas, and he invited people to serve themselves from the bar. "Someone asks, 'What are we all doing here?' and I said, 'I don't know, just drinking and eating,'" TJ remembered. "Because we really didn't know what we were doing." TJ sat at the bar with a notepad in front of him, but first he put it out to the group: What did they think about indoor dining?

There would be no great debate. Most of the restaurant's waitstaff and its bartenders were eager to get back to work. Cusumano's had made it that far without a known case of COVID, and they trusted that everyone would be sensible enough, and take the necessary precautions, to keep it that way. TJ shared what he had in mind. They would use every other booth along the walls and set up fewer tables in the center of the room. At 50 percent, they could seat maybe thirty people in the main dining room and another twenty in the Cellar. There was also a back room upstairs they used for private parties and overflow on busy nights. They set up another few tables there. TJ and Nina figured they would need roughly twice the staff to handle both indoor and outdoor dining. Everyone working the front-of-the-house would be required to wear masks when they interacted with the public.

Down in the Cellar, TJ wrote down people's names and their availability in his pad. Jessica Barletta certainly wanted the hours. Her dance studio was still only at two-thirds of her prepandemic registration numbers. "I have parents who aren't comfortable yet," Barletta said, and she could hardly blame them. The schools in Scranton were closed to in-person learning, so why would it be okay to send them to a dance class? She worried about another shutdown and feared that even if the governor didn't order them closed, her numbers would fall anyway come winter, when the cold weather meant she could no longer keep the windows open for better ventilation. She was happy for any extra work.

The guidance counselor, Shawn Nee, put himself down for shifts. He had two kids in college and a third only a couple of years away. Cousin Anthony took his usual Thursday-night shift and picked up Sundays as well. Among those saying they preferred not to work was Bob Mulkerin, the former mayor. With a full-time office job in Scranton, he didn't really need the money. "I kind of announced my semiretirement that night," Mulkerin said.

The expansion of the Devil's Pit behind the restaurant represented another big change that fall. A side venture cooking barbecue had morphed into a new business for Cusumano's: an outdoor patio and bar. With help from his uncle Larry, Cousin Anthony, and other tradesmen in town that he plied with free food and beer, TJ created a stone barbecue pit that let him lower and raise the meats and included a large smoker. They also built a long stone and wood bar, edged with steel beams. They put out some tables and planters. By the start of October, Cusumano's started pushing the Devil's Pit on its Facebook page, where the restaurant had more than ten thousand followers. It opened at one p.m. and closed, TJ wrote, "when we run out of food, booze, and energy!" He expanded the menu to include smoked turkey, salmon, and kielbasa.

Live entertainment was the next step. Next door, Pat Revello was offering outdoor music on weekends and some Wednesday nights, drawing good-sized crowds. The addition didn't make him much money ("you have to pay for the band, pay rent on a tent, and heat it," Revello said), but it brought in paying customers, which helped keep Revello's alive that summer and into the fall. TJ turned to Fuzzy Park, a local husband-wife duo he liked. After a couple of Sundays, he began referring to them as his house band.

Cousin Anthony worked as the Devil's Pit bartender on Sundays. He had not known what to think of TJ's latest brainstorm, but the music, the food, and the opportunity to eat and drink outdoors proved a winning combination. People were desperate for any bit of joy after so many months of isolation. "He's really killing it," Anthony said. TJ's hope was that the Devil's Pit would become permanent, a seasonal fixture that drew additional people to the restaurant whenever the weather was good. Already people were reserving the space for daytime celebrations: birthdays, an anniversary, a family reunion. "Not everything that's coming out of COVID is bad," TJ said.

* * *

Those early weeks of the fall were in ways an idyllic time for TJ and a moment for celebration. Nina was seven months pregnant when, in early October, their friends and family threw a party for each of them. Nina's baby shower would be a feast inside the restaurant for nearly one hundred guests. Another seventy-five showed up outside at the Devil's Pit for TJ's "diaper party" (literally, a party where guests piled up mountains of Huggies, Pampers, and Luvs). TJ dressed in jeans, a torn sweatshirt, and a baseball hat worn backward. As always, he needed a shave. "I can't help myself," he said when someone teased him about holding a pair of tongs at his own party, tending to sausages sizzling on the grill. Partway through the party, TJ grabbed a guitar he kept hidden away in a small office under the stairs and, along with two of his oldest friends, Lou Moriano and Anthony Parisi, sang a couple of songs, including a credible version of the Band's "The Weight," just as the trio used to do at parties as high schoolers. The entire kitchen crew was there, even a friend of Sha-Asia's who had started at the restaurant only a couple of weeks earlier. So, too, were most of the restaurant's bartenders and servers, along with Pat Revello and Russell Rinaldi.

His kitchen crew was also something TJ was feeling good about that fall. Sha-Asia continued to impress him, and Ang was doing a good job handling her dual roles as sauté chef and kitchen manager. He had only good things to say about Brian Mariotti at the pasta station and Joey Graziano downstairs making pizzas. Levi Kania, who had been with him almost from day one, could be a source of tension. The two squabbled like an old married couple that had long ago stopped censoring their true feelings. But he also knew Levi could handle almost any task in the kitchen. "I've got like an all-star team right now," TJ said.

He had also picked up another cook whose kitchen skills he respected: Sam Egan, who was doing his second tour at Cusumano's. Sam had studied to become a teacher at Central Connecticut State and was fifteen credits from graduating when it was his time to student teach. "That's when I realized I hated other people's children," Sam said. He had been cooking for more than two decades the first time he came to work for TJ but left to be the cook at a bar a friend of his opened in Scranton, where Sam had grown up. After a year, though, he had called it quits. "How many times can you have the same fight?" he asked. Sam had returned to Cusumano's in August. "He's a real chef and just the best guy in the world," TJ said.

TJ had Sam come in at nine a.m. to anchor his daytime prep crew. Everyone else working the kitchen (including TJ) dressed in shorts and T-shirts and running shoes, but every day Sam wore checkered chef pants, a white smock trimmed with black-and-white checks, and black clogs. The uniform, he explained, granted him a kind of authority. "With the clothes, they treat you differently," Sam said in a gritty West Scranton accent that made him sound a bit like an old-time gangster. He was the only member of the crew that TJ trusted to bake focaccia or the pizza shells. He also made the sauces and could prepare and cook anything else the upstairs kitchen might need to survive the night. "He's my everything man," TJ said.

Yet these were hardly carefree times inside the restaurant. Indoor dining was proving a bust. They had maybe two good nights in three or four weeks. They could blame the governor, but the reality was that only once had they had to ask a party to wait because they were at 50 percent capacity. The patio was carrying the restaurant, along with the Devil's Pit. The tent was still up, but a table out there had become a kind of booby prize. What would happen when the temperature got cold?

Adding to the sense of gloom was the town's first restaurant casualty. Billy G's, two blocks away on Main Street, closed. Chef-owner Billy Genovese had reopened for takeout after staying shut for two months, but the economics of his establishment no longer worked when he couldn't sell his bread and coffee services, or his expensive brandies and the cigars he stored in a humidor that had set his investors back $3,000. Billy G's shut down for good even before Pennsylvania upped capacity to 50 percent. "The restaurant was so successful and then, all of a sudden, nothing," Genovese said. The shuttered restaurant was where Moosic, the main road into town, dead-ended on Main Street. That meant TJ was reminded of the closure every time he drove to or from the highway.

* * *

The kitchen at Cusumano's was a place where little seemed to be off-limits as a topic of conversation: girlfriends, vulnerabilities, embarrassing moments. But politics was the one subject that was necessary to avoid that fall. TJ had at least a couple of Trump supporters on his payroll, and his staff included a twenty-two-year-old black woman ("everything you think I think about Donald Trump is probably right," Sha-Asia said) and an openly gay woman who posted memes on Facebook casting the president as unhinged and dangerous.

Still, the topic of Trump versus Biden couldn't be avoided completely. The two campaigns, including money from their companion super PACs, spent more than $200 million on television ads in Pennsylvania. That meant every hour multiple ads ran for both Trump and Biden in this battleground that Nate Silver's site, FiveThirtyEight, declared "by far the likeliest state to provide either President Trump or Joe Biden with the decisive vote in the Electoral College." The campaigning was even more intense in the northeastern corner of the state. Trump had been the first Republican to win Pennsylvania in twenty-eight years, and Lackawanna and Luzerne Counties had made the difference. Barack Obama had beat Mitt Romney by nearly thirty percentage points in then solidly blue Lackawanna in 2012. Four years later, Hillary Clinton barely won the county with 50.2 percent of the vote. That flip to the Republican column represented twenty-three-thousand-plus votes—more than half of Trump's 2016 margin of victory. Trump won Luzerne County by nearly twenty points in 2016 compared to Obama's five-percentage-point victory in 2012. That represented a swing of more than thirty thousand votes—roughly two-thirds of Trump's margin of victory.

"You talk about it but don't talk about it," Brian Mariotti said. Instead of articulating their political preferences, they shared facts as neutrally as possible: Trump was in the hospital for COVID, Eric Trump was speaking at a mall in Wilkes-Barre, Jon Bon Jovi was singing at a Biden rally twenty minutes from Old Forge. They'd be more likely to talk about Bon Jovi's music than his endorsement of the Democrat. "It's like everybody's being on their best behavior," Sha-Asia said. They spoke less about COVID as well after TJ imposed a moratorium on the topic. One staffer had been a COVID denier, and his crackpot theories were driving everybody crazy.

"This job can be such a pain in the ass sometimes," TJ said—and a lot more than teaching cooks to prepare a medium-rare steak consistently.

That night proved a lousy one for the restaurant. At around five thirty p.m., TJ and Nina welcomed a wealthy couple eating at the restaurant for the first time since the start of COVID. Nina took their table—and then made a face like she wanted to retch after walking inside with their order. The man had rubbed Nina's belly without asking, as if it were his right, because, he said, "I miss feeling my wife's belly when she was pregnant." A couple took a table in a corner of the Cellar; a few Cellar stalwarts sat at another. TJ's parents were there, and also Nina's. At least there was life downstairs even if half of those gathered inside the Cellar were not paying customers.

Upstairs, the scene was grim. At six p.m., there were only four people eating in a dining room that in normal times could accommodate eighty. The subdued lighting and gray tones that normally lent an elegance to the room gave it a depressing gloom. Two men dressed in suits took a table a half hour later, but there were few guests either upstairs or downstairs after that. "We were having better nights when it was just the tent and patio and we didn't have upstairs," TJ said. One of the two servers working the upstairs sat on a ladder-back chair placed to offer him a perfect view of the dining room, in case his one table needed something. The other server spent much of her time standing at the kitchen window, talking with the cooks, who also did not have much to do.

"There's a bunch of regulars we still haven't seen since this all started," TJ said. "And it's not like this is a time people are looking to try new restaurants." The difference between cooking for a restaurant at 100 percent occupancy and one at 50 percent, TJ said, was only one or two cooks. A half-occupied restaurant might make money. On this night, however, peak occupancy never cracked 10 percent.

"I have no idea what's happening," TJ confessed at the end of the night. Including takeout, they had not done fifty plates on the night. "I don't know if this is a trend we're just at the beginning of, or maybe it's just a bump in the road." He had barely made payroll during the past two weeks. "It's only a matter of time before Nina and I will have to stop taking a check," he said.

The winter months loomed. The tent would be coming down the following week and the Devil's Pit would go into hibernation until the spring. The patio had a stone fireplace, and TJ had bought several heat lamps he would scatter around the space. Yet who knew if people would agree to eat out there in a month or two, when it meant wearing a heavy coat through dinner. COVID rates were rising both in Pennsylvania and around the country. He did not want to think about what might happen if there was another big surge in cases. "That's just a nightmare scenario," he said.

Despite their reluctance, other restaurants had turned to food delivery apps such as Grubhub and DoorDash. DoorDash, for instance, collected $879 million in fees in the third quarter of 2020—only a few million dollars short of the total dollar amount it generated in all of 2019. But where restaurant profit margins hovered in the 3 to 5 percent range, the delivery apps typically took a 25 to 30 percent cut of an order. Posh, a restaurant in Scranton, deemed the cost worth it. They had done almost no takeout or delivery prior to the pandemic. There was no profit on an order through Door-Dash or Grubhub, the two services Posh used, yet it helped cover employee salaries and avoid food spoilage. "I'm already paying my staff whether I get ten orders or fifty," said co-owner Joshua Mast. "I'm not happy to lose 30 percent on an order but I am happy our staff is busy."

TJ, however, couldn't fathom signing up for a service that took so large a percentage of a restaurant's take. Rather than use one or more of the delivery apps, he asked a dishwasher to be his restaurant's new delivery guy. TJ offered him a daily stipend plus any tips he picked up. "He was like, 'Great, I hate washing dishes,'" TJ said. The restaurant had its first delivery driver in its history.

TJ made another change to batten down the hatches ahead of winter. This one would prove less popular with customers, assuming they even noticed: a surcharge whenever someone used a credit card rather than cash to pay for a meal. The credit card companies charge a business owner a fee on every credit card transaction. In normal times, TJ was willing to absorb that as a cost of doing business. "But with business really sucking," TJ said, he added a 3.5 percent charge on all credit card purchases. The one customer who complained was incredulous. He told TJ he viewed the surcharge as price-gouging in a crisis.

"I tell him, 'Well, we're struggling and right now I can't really afford to pay for your points or your miles or whatever you're getting through your credit card rewards program,'" TJ said. It was the merchant, he explained, and not the credit card company that paid for all those cash-back and rewards programs people enjoyed. "I told him if he didn't like it, he could pay cash or use a debit card," TJ said (there is no merchant fee on a debit card transaction). "I also gave him the option of not eating here anymore."

There was more disappointing news in October. His plan for selling Old Forge pizza in Lake Winola at Cusumano's at the Lake had fallen through. An inspection by the health department uncovered arsenic in the water, among other problems. TJ pulled out of the deal, killing his idea of bringing in extra cash. He was less disappointed when a roadblock stood in the way of his purchase of GI's, the bar several generations of Cusumanos, including his father, had owned. A bank snafu while the bar was in foreclosure had messed up ownership of the liquor license, and he felt relieved he had an excuse to walk away. "There was almost a higher power saying, 'Don't do it, stupid,'" TJ said.

The monthly mortgage payment on the small blue ranch house TJ and Nina owned around the corner from the restaurant was under $350. That would help them survive the winter. Yet they had both bought new cars just prior to COVID. TJ had a fully loaded black Chevy Silverado Z71 extended-cab pickup truck with gleaming mag wheels and Nina a black Jeep Cherokee. That meant two sizable car payments that were manageable when the restaurant was generating a profit but loomed as a burden through COVID.

TJ was feeling exhausted nearly seven months into the pandemic. There had not been a day in the prior month, he confided, that saw him do less than eight hours of work. On some days, he worked nearly twice that long. "And that's counting Mondays and Tuesdays, which technically are my days off," he said. There had been the usual hassles and nonsense of running a restaurant. But add to that the reopening of indoor dining, the construction of the outdoor bar, and other headaches. The liquor control board expected him to pay full freight on his 2020 liquor license, as if it were like any normal year, prompting him to reach out to his state rep. "Of course, I never even heard back from her," he said. After the good luck he had had taking in Sha-Asia, he had taken a chance on another Lackawanna College student. This one, a tall, awkward white kid, proved a dud in the kitchen. As a favor, he let the student complete his hours washing dishes rather than fire him. "And then after the internship is over, the guy turns around and files unemployment on me," he said.

TJ could not work any harder, yet it was not enough. "It's like every day I wake up and am like, 'Oh, yeah, it's not a normal day,'" he said. "It's coronavirus again. It's like fucking *Groundhog Day*, and every day starts with a punch in the gut."

Chapter 16

The Fall Surge

P eople are tired of hearing Fauci and all these idiots," Donald Trump said two weeks before Election Day during a call with campaign staff. Several weeks earlier, in testimony before the US Senate, Robert Redfield, the head of the Centers for Disease Control, had declared masks vital in the fight against COVID, at least until vaccines were widely available. Trump's response was to contradict his own choice to head the agency.

"He made a mistake," the president said of Redfield's testimony. "It's just incorrect information."

Daily case numbers were setting new records by the third week of October. Hospitalizations due to COVID were also on the rise. Yet Fauci and his fellow "idiots" had been sidelined in favor of the new coronavirus guru inside the White House, Dr. Scott Atlas. Atlas is a radiologist, not an expert in public health or infectious diseases, but he was a Fox News regular who argued that the coronavirus was overblown. Among his other claims was that the country was testing too much, lockdowns hurt more than they helped, and deaths attributed to COVID had been grossly exaggerated— precisely what Trump wanted to hear. Atlas had been named a special advisor to the president that summer, and almost immediately spurred a debate about adopting a strategy of herd immunity. Epidemiologists were horrified, but that became the de facto Trump policy. Let the virus spread unchecked until it dies off naturally because enough people have had the disease.

"We're not going to control the pandemic," White House chief of staff Mark Meadows said on CNN when asked about the surge of cases in late October. COVID is a "contagious virus," Meadows said, and therefore until there was a vaccine, government's role was to help fund therapeutics to treat those who catch the disease. Four members of the vice president's staff tested positive for COVID, but Vice President Pence stuck to his campaign schedule and chose not to self-quarantine. While the Biden campaign practiced social distancing and therefore drew far more modest crowds, Trump held outdoor rallies that drew twenty thousand or sometimes more, which some epidemiologists declared super-spreader events.

* * *

Mark Monsey's father had always warned against putting anything on the walls of Greenwood's Furniture that might be the least bit controversial. Even hanging a picture of a favorite NASCAR driver could be a mistake. "Because if someone doesn't like Dale Earnhardt Jr. you've probably lost that person as a customer for life," Mark said. He had hewed to that advice for years but made an exception for Trump. He kept a Trump hat perched on a filing cabinet next to his desk and doubted it hurt business. As a test, he suggested going to the Second Wind, the bar next door to his shop. "I bet every person you talk to would tell you they like Trump," Mark said. "He's one of us, a local, blue-collar, redneck, hillbilly, beer-drinking, gun-toting, card-carrying American. Or at least he makes us feel he is."

Mark complained about his business in the weeks leading up to the election. He was still turning away customers because his suppliers were behind on orders. But he could hardly blame Trump for a broken supply chain in the furniture business. "I'm happy with the job he's doing," Mark said. Sure, the president had made mistakes handling COVID, but it had been decades since the schools even mentioned the 1918 pandemic. *Anyone* would have been dubious of experts recommending a shutdown of the economy to fight a virus. "If somebody came to you in January of 2020 and said, 'There's going to be this plague,' you think you'd be, sure, okay, a plague, let's shut down businesses for months. Whatever you say," he said sarcastically.

Mark was glad a businessperson was occupying the Oval Office when COVID hit. As Mark saw it, Trump listened to the health experts in the early days of the pandemic, but soon economics and other issues came in to play. He imagined Trump listening intently to Fauci and other members of the White House's coronavirus task force but respectfully disagreeing. Trump, Mark said, "had his eye on the big picture," and therefore was the perfect chief executive to help restart the economy. "I don't know that anybody would have done better," he said.

Glenda, at J.R.'s Hallmark, also gave the president the benefit of the doubt in his handling of COVID. "I think Donald Trump did the best he could," she said. It got to the point that she felt sorry for him. She started her day with *Good Morning America*. How was it, she asked, that for every ten stories about Trump, nine were negative? Sometimes she tuned in to CNN, where ten of every ten Trump stories were critical. "The media is so biased against him, it's not funny," Glenda said. It had gotten so bad she stopped watching the news altogether. "I couldn't stand it anymore," she said. She already had a struggling store to rile her up without adding politics.

A vote for Trump did not come naturally to Glenda, who hailed from a family of Democrats. Her mother's father had been a big shot in the local Democratic Party. Her mother always voted straight Democrat and was upset when Glenda told her she had voted for Trump over Hillary in 2016. "She almost had a heart attack," Glenda said.

Yet Glenda refused to feel defensive about her decision. It was her mother, she said, who needed to open her eyes. Janet Shoemaker acted as if she had no use for Trump, but she didn't complain about a spike in the stock market and the impact it had on her retirement savings. "She's bragging to me about how much she's making even as I have no money because the store is going to crap," Glenda said. Glenda had warned her mother, "Everything is going to hell if Biden wins." A moderate Biden might have been someone Glenda could support, but he had been replaced by someone who championed a $15 minimum wage. "I saw that and said, 'Holy crap, that's going to be a lot of people out of business,'" she said. She thought about all those years she worked at the McDonald's in town.

"You're talking about some kid in school whose gonna sit behind the counter and go to the bathroom ten times a day because he wants to be on his phone," Glenda said. "I think they've lost their minds if they think a $15 minimum wage is the answer.

"I tell my mom, 'The Democratic Party is not the Democratic Party of your day.' I don't feel like I trust them or any politician anymore."

Glenda continued to wear a mask while at the store. All her employees did. A few times, a customer walked in bare-faced, but she believed that was because of absentmindedness, not defiance. "One of us will say something and they'll go, 'Oh, crap,' and they're rushing back to their car to get their mask," she said. Mark took a different approach to masks at Greenwood's. He had looked it up: the governor's guidance provided a medical exemption to mask wearing and expressly stated that businesses "are not required to provide documentation of such medical condition." If someone walked into his store without a mask, he assumed they had a medical reason to go around without one and did not say anything. "I don't think it helps but I'll put the freakin' thing on just in case Big Brother is watching," Mark said. He slipped up the black gaiter he wore around his neck when anyone masked walked into his store. He slipped it down when talking with someone who wasn't wearing one.

That was better than some business owners in town. Glenda refused to walk inside the establishments of several she knew were far more lax than Mark. One of her employees told her about a woman in town who tested positive for COVID. She saw her outside without a mask. "She tells me this and I'm like people are—" Glenda said, cutting herself off before using an unflattering adjective. She dropped the point and resumed: "It's a strange little town."

Glenda had had a decent October. Sales about matched what they had been the year before. But she worried that even the modest amount of business she was doing was deceiving. The county courthouse had shut again. The local paper reported on a coronavirus outbreak at the local nursing home. "I don't know if people are shopping when they can, just in case everything is closed down again in December," she said.

Glenda steeled herself for the weeks ahead. She made 40 percent of her money each year between Thanksgiving and Christmas, but who knew about this year. One oddity of her business is how far in advance she must buy product. She started in January or February and finalized the bulk of her holiday ordering by July, when no one had a clue what might be happening in December. Buy too little product and she would chide herself for lost sales. There was also the risk that people would be disappointed for how little they found on her shelves "and then they've got another reason to forget me and go online." Yet spending too much on goods could prove disastrous. If she sold only a fraction of her merchandise, she would not have cash to pay her bills, "and then everything starts falling apart."

One concession Glenda had made ahead of the holidays was to join Hallmark's Ship from Store program. For at least a couple of years, the mothership had invited its Gold Crown stores to participate in a program that let local store owners fulfill the orders for those in the area who had bought items at the Hallmark website. Hallmark sent boxes and packing materials to participating stores, along with a special tape machine and even a large table for handling the shipments. The company picked up the cost of shipping but also took a 25 percent cut of each sale.

"I always refused to do it because I hated what it stood for," Glenda said. "But then there comes a point where the ship is sinking and no matter how much you want to stand on your soapbox, it doesn't make sense anymore." She signed up for the Ship from Store program and vowed that 2021 would be the year they figured out a way of selling their product through a J.R.'s website. That way she could sell items online without Hallmark siphoning off a full quarter of her sales.

"We're smart girls here," she said. They would first handle sales from Hallmark.com and then figure out Shopify or some other e-commerce platform. "That might be our ticket to taking me to retirement," said the fifty-eight-year-old Glenda.

First, however, she needed to survive the next couple of months—if the media allowed that to happen. "I might even make it," she said, "if the news doesn't scare the crap out of everyone to the point they're staying home and shopping on their computers." She vowed that if the governor ordered another lockdown, she would remain open if Walmart did. "I've been telling people, 'I'm not going to lay down like last time,'" Glenda said. If nothing else, she would do curbside delivery and maybe even let people inside for appointment shopping. "When for a human being is enough enough that you just can't do it anymore?" she asked. She diagnosed herself that fall as suffering from PTSD.

* * *

In Hazleton, Vilma had nothing good to say about the national government's handling of the coronavirus. She cautiously avoided naming Trump and instead criticized those in charge in DC for failing to act until it was too late. "They should not have waited until it affected so many people before they did something," she said of the US government.

Vilma was relieved to live in Pennsylvania. She saw Governor Wolf as a man who moved cautiously and heeded the science, searching for a balance between people's health and their livelihoods. Unlike many other small business owners, she had nothing negative to say about the governor. "I feel that small businesses have been supported," she said. "I don't want to die." She saw a spike in numbers and braced for the worst.

"I hope it doesn't happen," Vilma said. "I trust it won't. But I would not get upset if the governor closed us again for our own safety. As a precaution."

Masks were never an issue inside the salon. A red sign on the shop's front door told people they were welcome inside only if they wore one. Most arrived wearing their own face covering, but a customer was free to grab one from the shop's supply. Every day began the same for the salon's workers, whether a stylist or the one responsible for sweeping up hair. Each employee washed her hands, grabbed a blue surgical mask, and then sprayed, wiped, and cleaned up her station. That was their routine all day. They sprayed and wiped after they finished with a client and before welcoming the next one.

Eventually, the two employees reluctant to come back to work returned. The government had cut off their supplemental unemployment payments at the end of July and, economically, they had no choice. For Vilma that meant shaving hours. On a good week, she was still bringing in only half of what she made before COVID, and already she saw the drop-off in business as COVID case numbers crept up. Everyone would suffer, but she recognized that the pain was hardly distributed equally.

"In a salon, not everyone has the same income," Vilma said. "Some make more, some make less." The hairdressers were generally fine, but she worried about the employees who washed hair and cleaned up the shop.

"We receive new rules and there are new norms, and we adapt to keep going," Vilma said, largely because she saw no other option than to continue working.

* * *

The battle for Pennsylvania's twenty electoral votes seemed as close as the experts predicted it would be. The contest rested on a "knife's edge," the Trump campaign declared. The two candidates spent more time there in the final weeks of the campaign than any other state, with a disproportionate number of appearances in northeastern Pennsylvania. Trump's sons, Donald Jr. and Eric, made appearances in the area in the final two weeks of the election, as did Melania. Jill Biden appeared at a "drive-in rally" in Moosic, the town next to Old Forge. By Election Day, both Trump and Biden had visited the state more than a dozen times. Each closed his campaign in northeastern Pennsylvania. Trump chose the Wilkes-Barre/Scranton International Airport, four miles from Old Forge, for his final "Make America Great Again" rally. "Pennsylvania, it's up to you," he told the crowd. On the morning of Election Day, Biden visited his childhood home in Scranton, where he wrote on the living room wall, "From this house to the White House, with the grace of God."

Chapter 17

Makersville

There's a distinctly industrial feel to the Bronx's Port Morris neighborhood, despite the best effort of real estate developers and others spying its moneymaking potential. Former factories and giant warehouses had been converted to lofts. Several more had been carved up to provide space to smaller enterprises like Sol Cacao. But they were still outnumbered by the lumber yards, plumbing supply companies, and scrap metal places whose inventories were locked each night behind corrugated steel fencing topped with razor wire. The New York City Department of Sanitation operates a giant facility a couple of blocks from Sol Cacao. All City Recycling has a yard one block the other way, toward the East River, which serves as the neighborhood's eastern border. The rumbling Bruckner Expressway demarks the community's western border. Its southern border is Bronx Kill, the narrow body of water that separates the Bronx from Manhattan.

Long before they sold their first chocolate bar, the Maloneys had fallen in love with the idea of setting up shop in a converted industrial area thick with artists and fellow makers. But DUMBO and Williamsburg, both in Brooklyn, were well outside their price range. So, too, was Harlem, where they also looked because saying Sol Cacao was a "Harlem-based" enterprise seemed a phrase imbued with almost magical powers for three young black men starting a business in New York City. But even a small, five-hundred-square-foot space they found there was renting for $6,000 a month.

The Bronx, by contrast, offered far more start-up-friendly rates. The Bronx Brewery had opened there, as did the maker of a moonshine-style rum from Puerto Rico called *pitorro*. Another entrepreneur, Ralph Rolle, who had played drums for Sting, Queen Latifah, Biggie Smalls, and Aretha Franklin, was behind a company called Soul Snack Cookies. The Maloneys visited Port Morris in 2018. After one visit, they decided that's where they needed to be. "Everyone was doing their own thing, and everyone seemed to be thriving," Daniel said.

Sol Cacao occupies a large room on the second floor of a block-sized, two-story black building at the bottom of Port Morris, near where the East River hits Bronx Kill. The trestles for Amtrak stand one block to the east along the river. Due east, in the middle of the river, sits the infamous Rikers Island. "This feels like New York more than a lot of other parts of New York," Nicholas said. It reminded Dominic of Williamsburg when they were growing up—specifically the largely vacant industrial stretch that creatives had found in search of cheaper workspace. Their workspace was around the dimensions of a good-sized studio apartment, except this one has a row of the "speed racks" restaurants and banquet halls use to hold trays and an industrial-sized refrigerator where they store racks of bars. Sacks of fermented cacao beans sat on pallets in the back of the room. A large wooden table dominated the center of the room. That's where they "fold" the bars—their shorthand for wrapping a bar in gold foil and slipping it into the heavy-stock white paper they use for packaging.

"It's one of the few things we all do together," Daniel said. It's there that they'll laugh together or have serious talks about the business. "Some of our best conversations are when we're folding bars," Daniel said. The equipment to make the chocolate was in the front part of the room: a roaster, to cook the beans; a "cracker" that separates the husks and then turns solid beans into a kind of chocolate paste; and the tempering machine they used to heat and cool the chocolate after they have added sugarcane.

Near the entrance, the brothers had set up a couple of chairs and a gray couch under a framed poster that read, NEVER STOP DREAMING. The round-faced Dominic, the firstborn, was dressed in a maroon-colored knit shirt and black-and-gray checkered pants on a chilly afternoon in early November. Nicholas, the middle brother, wore jeans and a white-and-blue acid-washed shirt. Daniel, the baby of the family, was in jeans and a dark blue sweater. He tended to serve as narrator of their story with his two brothers playing the role of color commentators.

The surprise when visiting their production space was how small everything seems. The cracker had been a big splurge a few years back after they had received a big order from California. Until then, they took turns turning a crank by hand, the mention of which caused all three of them to cry out in unison, in mock-strained voices, "Your turn!" Yet the new machine was barely larger than a toaster oven. The roaster was a more substantial piece of equipment weighing around fifty pounds, but so modest was it in size that it sat on a table.

"There's no real middle in chocolate," Daniel explained. There's only industrial- and hobby-sized. The customers for chocolate-making equipment either shop at a hobbyist website or they're Ghirardelli or Hershey, buying industrial-sized machines that help them mass-produce more bars in a day than the Maloneys sell in a year. The brothers drew a contrast with coffee making, which was a more mature industry, offering a wide range of grinders and roasters, manufactured by an array of companies. In the chocolate business, there's one main manufacturer, and much of its equipment needed to be customer-made. "We're still in a lot of ways in the early stages of chocolate," Dominic said.

Dominic, as Sol Cacao's one full-time employee, was the company's chief chocolate maker. It was Dominic who figured out the ideal temperature and roasting time for each type of bean, and Dominic who invariably ladled the chocolate into the molds. "He's always experimenting," Nicholas said of his brother: raising the temperature but cooking the chocolate for less time or fiddling with the sugar-to-bean ratio. His two brothers boasted about Dominic's expertise. He spent so much time around the chocolate he needed only to sniff the air to know what kind of beans they were cooking or how far they were in the process. His brothers helped with roasting, cracking, and folding and took on other tasks. Nicholas worked on packaging and did the bulk of the deliveries. Daniel handled customer relations, marketing, "and whatever else Dominic needs me to do."

The Maloneys braced for an end to the special status accorded many black businesses in the aftermath of George Floyd's murder. The attention and heightened sense of justice was decades overdue, but they also recognized that there might be a kind of half-life to people's attention span. By the fall, polls showed that the portion of white voters who supported Black Lives Matter was back to what it had been before Floyd's death. It seemed inevitable that the country would allow itself to get distracted by something else.

Sales, however, remained strong through the fall. Individuals were continuing to order bars through the website at unprecedented rates. One of Sol Cacao's earliest partners, Chelsea Market Baskets, a specialty gift store inside New York's Chelsea Market, began to feature their bars more prominently. Their corporate business also continued to grow. "We'd have companies wanting us to send [bars] to all 250 of their employees or customers," Daniel said. Prior to the pandemic, a three-thousand-bar month was a strong one. That fall they needed to produce closer to five thousand bars in a month to keep up with demand. The Maloneys were virtually out of beans again at the start of November. This time the reason was demand. That Tuesday, they'd received more than 1,300 pounds of beans—by far the most they had ever bought. They had a backlog of bars that needed shipping (it takes roughly five days for them to turn cacao beans into a chocolate bar ready to be shipped), but mainly they wanted to be prepared for a small deluge of new orders. *Martha Stewart Living* magazine had listed Sol Cacao in a "20 Chocolate Bars Perfect for Gifting" feature running in its November issue. The brothers started talking about hiring a couple of people, at least part-time. They even investigated the possibility of buying a larger, industrial-sized machine, like any growing player.

Chapter 18

The Hammer and the Dance

Maybe the planet's most famous small business in early November was Four Seasons Total Landscaping in Philadelphia. At 11:22 a.m. on November 7, four days after Election Day, and with Biden up by thirty thousand votes in Pennsylvania, the Associated Press called the election for Biden. The television networks, Fox included, quickly followed suit. (The final tally had Biden winning Pennsylvania by eighty-one thousand—nearly twice Trump's margin of victory in 2016.) By happenstance, Rudy Giuliani, Trump's personal lawyer, had scheduled a news conference scheduled to start at eleven thirty that same morning. Presumably, the Trump campaign meant to book the luxurious Four Seasons Hotel, five blocks from the Pennsylvania Convention Center, where Philadelphia's votes were being counted. Instead, at this other Four Seasons, across the street from the Delaware Valley Cremation Center and a few doors down from the Fantasy Island adult bookstore, Giuliani indignantly proclaimed on behalf of the president, "Trump won't concede." By Monday, the Trump campaign was in a US District Court in Harrisburg seeking a federal order that would block the state from certifying the 2020 election.

In Tunkhannock, Glenda Shoemaker didn't doubt the validity of the vote count even as she was convinced Biden's victory would put her out of business. If he did not double the national minimum wage, she was convinced he would cook up some other set of policies with Nancy Pelosi, whom Glenda did not particularly like. "More bad news on top of bad news," she said of Biden's victory.

Mark Monsey was not sure what to think. His drinking buddies at the Second Wind, or at least the most vocal among them, were convinced that the Democrats had fabricated just enough mail-in votes to ensure Biden won Pennsylvania. He did his own investigating online. "Was there cheating, lying, stealing, or anything else going on? I don't know," Mark said. But he was also convinced that nothing that went on would be widespread enough to claim the election had been stolen. "I've resigned myself to the fact that Biden probably did win," he said. Like Glenda, he thought Biden's election was bad for business, but, taking a not-so-veiled swipe at the Black Lives Matter marches, he said, "I'm not going to go around looting, or stealing, or burning any business down."

Trump handily won Wyoming County, but his winning margins there and in other rural parts of the state weren't as lopsided as his campaign had hoped. Biden picked up several percentage points more than Clinton had in Wyoming, and also Sullivan and Bradford Counties, where Joe Lech co-owned pharmacies. Biden also did three to four percentage points better than Clinton had in both Luzerne and Lackawanna Counties. The Trump campaign had been hoping that the rushed confirmation of Amy Coney Barrett would be Trump's ace in the hole should the election end up in the US Supreme Court. Yet the court declined to hear appeals of lower court rulings against the Trump campaign in Pennsylvania, including one that would have nullified all 2.6 million of the state's absentee ballots. Efforts by state lawmakers and members of Pennsylvania's congressional caucus to hand Pennsylvania to Trump also failed.

* * *

There was still a pandemic, even if the president, by all accounts, did little besides watch TV, tweet, and rage at whoever dared to get near him. The day after Election Day marked the first time the US logged more than 100,000 new daily infections. That Friday, the country crossed 150,000 cases. Trump was posting dozens of tweets a day, but none mentioned the steep rise in positive cases nor that members of his administration (his chief of staff, his HUD secretary, the lawyer tapped to lead his efforts to overturn the election results) had tested positive for the virus. He did respond to the news, shortly after the election, that Pfizer-BioNTech announced development of a vaccine with an efficacy rate of nearly 95 percent. He accused Pfizer, along with the US Food and Drug Administration and the Democrats, of conspiring to suppress the announcement until after people had voted.

By mid-November, it felt like the spring all over again. The country was averaging as many deaths as in May. On November 16, pandemic-related hospitalizations reached an all-time high. At 11:55 that night, Trump tweeted, "I WON THE ELECTION!" Meanwhile, Wolf and other governors were on their own.

Some governors adopted the same laissez-faire approach to the virus as Trump. They did very little to try to mitigate the spread of COVID. Others, like Wolf, practiced what one blogger referred to as "the hammer and the dance." People were free to congregate so long as they took proper precautions. But when case counts climbed too high, the authorities needed to lower the hammer to tamp down the spread.

Pennsylvania's state legislature continued to try to rein in Wolf to prevent further COVID-related restrictions, if not undo those in place. In the fall of 2020, both chambers passed legislation that would allow people to sit at a bar and enjoy a drink without having to also consume a meal. The bill would also allow eateries to impose occupancy limits based on social distancing guidelines, as the state's restaurant association had been advocating, rather than seating capacity. Wolf vetoed the bill, calling it "another meaningless attempt to change a necessary tool for fighting the pandemic." Dozens of Democrats had voted in favor of the bill—enough to override the governor's veto—but most changed sides on the vote to override, which failed.

The federal courts delivered a mixed verdict on lawsuits filed by those who opposed the governor's shutdown orders. A federal judge in Philadelphia ruled against a group of business owners who contended that Wolf overstepped his authority in demanding they close their doors. "We are skeptical of claims seeking to challenge emergency government actions taken to combat a once-in-a-lifetime global health crisis," the judge, who had been appointed to the bench by Bill Clinton, wrote. A few weeks later, a federal judge in Pittsburgh, a Trump appointee, declared the same business closures unconstitutional. He also ruled that Pennsylvania's stay-at-home order was a violation of the Fourteenth Amendment ("nor shall any state deprive any person of life, liberty, or property, without due process of law") and that Wolf's limit on large gatherings violated the First Amendment's freedom of assembly clause.

The US Supreme Court, however, declined to hear any challenges to Wolf's right to shut non-life-sustaining businesses. Court watchers were not surprised. The justices had refused to hear the case in May, and a subsequent ruling made it clear the court was reluctant to intervene in local decision-making. Elected officials should be granted leeway when enacting policies "fraught with medical and scientific uncertainties," Chief Justice John Roberts wrote in a California case challenging restrictions on religious gatherings. The legislature was free to change the law (subject to a gubernatorial veto) or pursue a ballot initiative that would let the people decide. Until then, the governor of Pennsylvania had far-reaching legal powers to deal with an emergency.

* * *

Pennsylvania, like every other part of the country, was feeling the pain of the coronavirus as November turned into December. The state recorded nearly 150,000 new cases of COVID in November— more than the combined total of the prior five months. "The commonwealth is in a precarious place right now," Wolf said at a news briefing a few days before Thanksgiving. "We need to make sure that we're doing everything we can to save lives." Around the state, small businesses braced for another round of lockdowns.

"You know, Wolf will find a way to mess everything up again for small businesses," Glenda said.

Public support for Wolf's handling of the pandemic had waned since May, when more than seven in ten people in the state approved of the job he was doing. The erosion of support was inevitable when Wolf became the face of the pandemic. The governor and his people had made its share of serious mistakes. Because hospital beds were at a premium early in the pandemic, nursing homes in the state were told they "must" readmit residents when discharged from a hospital, even if they still tested positive for COVID. They were just following CDC guidelines, the Wolf administration claimed, but all those empty hotel rooms around the state would have been a better alternative for housing the infectious. Wolf appeared at a Black Lives Matter vigil in June, earning him plaudits but also scorn by those casting him as a hypocrite for ignoring his own ban on mass gatherings. One week before the election, Trump mentioned Wolf's name at a rally in Allentown, one hour south of Hazleton, which sparked an impromptu chant of "Lock him up." Wolf had been granted Hillary status. By November, Wolf's approval rating for his handling of the virus dipped below 50 percent.

The first flash of the hammer came just before Thanksgiving. That Monday, Wolf and Levine returned to the emergency management center for a news conference. In the prior week, the number of deaths in Pennsylvania attributed to COVID had quadrupled. The average daily case count was seven times higher than it had been two months earlier, and there were reports around the state of over-whelmed hospitals. Already, Philadelphia announced that it was shutting indoor dining, along with gyms, casinos, and museums, through the end of the year.

In Harrisburg, Wolf announced a one-night suspension of al-cohol sales at bars and restaurants. "The biggest day for drinking is the Wednesday before Thanksgiving," Wolf said. "I don't like addressing that any more than anyone else does, but it's a fact." To tamp down the spike in infections, the state was banning the on-site consumption of alcohol starting at five p.m. Restaurant and tavern owners around the state were angry, but it was also a single lost night, albeit traditionally a big one.

A week later, word spread about a major news conference in Harrisburg, causing more worries among small business operators around the state. TJ saw it mentioned online, so he made sure to tune in. In Tunkhannock, Glenda broke her self-imposed morato-rium on the news and watched on her phone. "Like a lot of small businesses, I don't think I can survive another month or two of being shut down," she said. She had to sell tens of thousands of dollars of product between Thanksgiving and Christmas if she had any chance of paying her bills. She braced herself for a replay of the spring.

Inside the governor's office, though, they still had not made up their mind what course to take. So instead of any big announce-ment, TJ, Glenda, and others around the state who tuned in heard Rachel Levine do little more than remind everyone to wash their hands and be extra vigilant with caseloads so high. "I was hopeful that over the weekend, they had come to their senses," the Pennsyl-vania restaurant association's John Longstreet said.

Longstreet sent an email to Wolf's chief of staff, who reassured him, "No decisions are being made." A wary Longstreet wrote him back. "I said, 'Well, if you're considering anything, let me just ask for two things,'" he said. The first was that the governor's office not do anything before Christmas. "December is also when a lot of restaurant owners build up their reserves," Longstreet said. They didn't need the state canceling Christmas after the year most of them had had.

The second thing Longstreet asked for was advance warning of any new policy. He reminded the governor's chief of staff of the pain the state caused that summer when it gave restaurants and bars barely eight hours' notice of a reinstatement of the 25-percent-capacity limit. Food had been discarded and people's lives disrupted. When the Philadelphia's mayor banned all indoor dining through the end of the year, he at least gave restaurants the week to prepare for a six-week shutdown.

Yet daily cases were back over ten thousand a day in Pennsylvania. "COVID-19 Hospitalizations Jump 57% in Pa. as New Cases Keep Climbing," read an *Inquirer* headline in early December. When during the summer and early fall, ten or twenty people were dying from COVID each day across the state, Pennsylvania was now logging more than two hundred. The state registered its deadliest day since the start of the pandemic, and the next day broke that new record.

Three days after Levine's solo performance, the governor joined her at the emergency center. Wolf and his staff had learned from the first lockdown. Stores that sold furniture or Hallmark cards or jewelry were far safer places for people to shop than big-box stores packed because the state had shut everyone else down. This time the state spared retailers and also hair salons. Vilma in Hazleton could still operate at 50 percent capacity.

Wolf, however, had bad news for restaurants and taverns. The state was again shutting down indoor dining. Again, the state gave little advance warning. Wolf announced his shutdown order on a Thursday. By Friday at midnight, all of Pennsylvania's restaurants needed to close their dining rooms until January 4. Restaurants had little more than a day to redraw their holiday plans. The governor also announced the reclosure of gyms, theaters, concert venues, casinos, museums, and bowling alleys.

John Longstreet was disappointed and also angry. He thought about restaurant owners around the state and also all the bussers, servers, cooks, and others who would lose out on hourly wages and holiday tips. He understood the need for state-imposed mitigations but was dubious that shutting indoor dining would have much if any impact on transmission rates. Ten months into the pandemic, there was little known about the rates of transmission through restaurants, but the anecdotal evidence suggested they were low. Based on several months of data through contact tracers, New York State released information that showed that restaurants were believed to be a factor in only 1.4 percent of the cases they saw, compared to 74 percent attributed to household gathering. Closer to home, two suburban counties outside of Philadelphia also sifted through data from their contact tracers. Again, there were few suspected transmissions through restaurants (or gyms, for that matter).

There had been pockets of noncompliance among Pennsylvania businesses since the start of the pandemic. A poll by the state's restaurant association suggested that defiance ten months into the pandemic would be more widespread. Roughly 1,500 establishments across the state responded to the survey. One in seven stated they were ignoring the governor's latest shutdown order. Most would do so clandestinely and hope that people at the liquor control board or county health department were too overwhelmed or too tired to bother with a small operation like theirs.

Some, however, were public about their intentions, including Michael Passalacqua, the owner of Angelo's, an Italian restaurant in suburban Pittsburgh. Initially, Passalacqua had closed his dining room in accordance with the governor's order. A week later, he posted a seven-minute video on YouTube explaining why he had changed his mind. He had spent $20,000 on tents, he explained, and spilled another $10,000 on single-use menus, paper products, and other items to reduce the risk of infection in his restaurant. Now he would be reopening his dining room one week into the governor's shutdown order, if for no other reason than for his staff. "My employees have been decimated," he said. Some twenty-six thousand employees, according to the restaurant association survey, were laid off because of the December order. Restaurants were forced to throw away an estimated $1.5 million in food.

His people wore masks, Passalacqua said. He insisted that his customers do as well except for when they were eating. He would take the same public health precautions he had been taking since the start of the pandemic. This act of civil disobedience was entirely out of character, said Passalacqua, who served on the restaurant association's board. But, he said, "I can no longer sit on my hands while other restaurants are protesting and risking themselves and their license[s] and everything about their business[es]."

Chapter 19

Starvation Mode

November proved a dismal month inside Cusumano's—so much so that TJ felt compelled to pick up construction work for the cash. That became a trend during the pandemic: successful small business owners working side jobs because their normal business was not producing enough money. A few miles away, Joshua Mast and Paul Blackledge, the couple behind the Colonnade and a revival of the old Scranton Club, a pair of event spaces in downtown Scranton (which also housed their restaurant, Posh), had both been working side jobs since almost the start of the pandemic. Over the years, the local press hailed the pair as trailblazers who helped revive the city with their resuscitation of two downtown properties to their former glory. Mast served as the president at Scranton Tomorrow, a downtown civic organization, and Blackledge was active in the local chamber of commerce. Yet since early in the pandemic, Blackledge donned a red vest five days a week as a salesclerk at the giant Lowe's on the outskirts of town. Mast worked for a local supermarket as a "picker" who fulfilled online orders. He worked a second job demoing products at a Walmart.

The fall of 2020 felt a lot like the previous spring inside Cusumano's and every other restaurant in Old Forge. "People stopped eating indoors," TJ said. "They're scared." The patio still brought in some money that November, but the restaurant was surviving on takeout. "It's no secret to people in town that people are dying left and right," TJ said. Every time the phone rang, it seemed they heard more news about someone else in the hospital with the bug, if not the death of someone's parent or uncle. TJ did not think it really mattered what Wolf did or said. "Every restaurant in town is seating about 10 percent," he said. With barely enough to cover everyone else's salary and his other bills, TJ again stopped giving himself a paycheck.

"It's been grim on our end," he said at the start of December. "We're all in starvation mode here."

The construction job started as a favor to a friend who set up conveyor and racking systems in warehouses, primarily for supermarket chains. The friend asked TJ to help for a day. But TJ enjoyed the work ("like building a giant Erector Set," he said, referring to the old craft toy by that name) and also needed the cash. The friend mentioned he had more jobs, and on the spot TJ told his friend he would work full days on Mondays and Tuesdays and half days on Wednesdays and Thursdays, so he could spend the afternoons and evenings in the kitchen. The construction work paid him around $500 a week.

TJ didn't bother opening the restaurant on the Wednesday before Thanksgiving. The governor was right. That was a big drinking night. But it was not much for food sales. Even before opening his doors, he knew a ban on alcohol sales meant he would lose money by bothering to staff the place for the night. Part of him was relieved to have the night off. The restaurant had been selling takehome turkey dinners since 2018. That first Thanksgiving, they had sold nine turkeys. The next year they received orders for fourteen or fifteen. In 2020, Cusumano's had commitments for 177 turkeys, along with vast mounds of stuffing, gravy, and other trimmings.

He and his people had plenty to keep them busy. "That saved us—for a week," TJ said.

TJ laid off Sha-Asia just after Thanksgiving. She was back in school, and, with the end of the semester approaching, she could use the time to focus on her schoolwork. Still, the moment filled TJ with dread. She checked off every box as an employee: skillful with a knife, someone who pitched in wherever she could make herself useful, someone he could depend on. She had quickly become a favorite. TJ hoped he could bring her back in January, but that assumed the state's mitigation efforts worked. He slashed the hours of everyone else in the kitchen. People who had been working forty or forty-four hours a week were down to thirty-two hours. The waitstaff and others worked fewer hours as well.

TJ never thought about joining any rising restaurant rebellion. He was up for a good fight but not when it meant risking everything he and Nina had spent the prior seven years building. He also thought it was futile. With case numbers so high, people did not feel comfortable eating indoors, at least in Old Forge, Pennsylvania. If there was a sword to fall on in the final weeks of 2020, indoor dining was not it.

TJ was not angry at Wolf like so many other restaurateurs. By then, he had figured out that running a restaurant during a pandemic meant being plugged into what was happening in Harrisburg. He had been braced for a second shutdown since right after Thanksgiving, and he'd ordered food accordingly. "I can't tell you," TJ said, "how many texts I got from different people. 'My sister is a lobbyist in Harrisburg.' They'd be like, 'I heard from so-and-so, today is the day.'" On December 9, the governor's office announced that Wolf himself had tested positive for COVID-19. That was the moment that made TJ certain the governor would lower the hammer. Twenty-four hours later, Wolf (who was asymptomatic) announced the statewide closures. "In my opinion, he should have shut us down four weeks earlier, when cases started spiking hard again," TJ said. He threw away no food because, to his mind, he'd had days of warning, even if the governor had not yet made it official.

"It's a real shame the governor has turned into the villain for so many people when from day one it really should have been the president and the CDC handling this," TJ said. In a vacuum, he said, Wolf "really stepped up and is doing something. He's doing his best in impossible circumstances."

A year earlier, Cusumano's pulled in between $18,000 and $23,000 revenues a week. A few months earlier, $11,000 in receipts represented a good week. "Now we're working on $6,000 a week," TJ said. Even with staff cuts, his weekly payroll came in at just short of $5,000. At the start of December, he added up the bills he needed to pay that week and saw that he was $5,000 short. To cover it, he wiped out a big chunk of his savings. "That's money I've been saving pretty much my entire adult life," TJ said. "Money I needed to use because the business could no longer sustain itself." He'd vowed never to raid his own savings to pay for the business, but even as he said it to himself, he knew that those were just words. He would pay his people for their work, just as he would pay his vendors so he could keep on cooking. Yet his reserves were not deep. "Another week or two like this, and I don't know what we do," TJ said. He applied for a $5,000 grant from the county and a loan through the SBA's EIDL program.

The original plan was for Nina to work until she went into labor. "She's tough," TJ had told me back in October, when she was almost seven months pregnant and still working her share of tables. "She's in great shape." But with cases spiking, she heeded the governor's shutdown order and spent the remainder of her pregnancy at home. That represented hundreds of dollars in lost income each week.

As a precaution, TJ changed his hours. He worked at the restaurant from six to ten each morning, when he knew he would be the only person in the kitchen. He left instructions for his people, who took care of any takeout orders that came in, along with those few people willing to brave the patio in the frigid weather. He then returned after everyone left, to count the night's receipts. "I really didn't want to bring the virus home," TJ said.

He considered hibernation for the winter. Other restaurant owners around the country had chosen to shut down until outdoor dining was again a possibility. Financially, it was possible. His bank would let him freeze his mortgage for another few months. That left mainly the utilities, which would not be much with the lights and gas off. Yet he knew he was in the wrong town for that approach. "In our area, people respect grit and determination," TJ said. "It would look weak if we folded up and only came out when the weather was sunny again."

Instead, he began working on a new way of bringing in extra dollars. Long before the pandemic, he had entertained the prospect of jarring his Sunday gravy and salad dressings and packaging his gnocchi. He would use the pandemic as his excuse to start selling his own Cusumano's brand of products to grocery stores. He hired someone to secure the licensing he needed from the state to get into the business and spoke to a friend about creating a label.

TJ tried to remain optimistic about December. There would be no tables of revelers in the restaurant or downstairs in the Cellar. There would be no holiday parties to cater. Yet people still wanted to celebrate, and many had more free time. He took his second shot at the meal kit business with something he dubbed "Easy Eats from Cusumano's." His first offering was gnocchi and meatballs. For $45, a customer received a quart of sauce, five meatballs, and the ingredients to make homemade gnocchi for four. A three-minute instructional video they posted on the restaurant's Facebook page walked people through the process. The restaurant also advertised seasonal specials on its Facebook page: a stuffed pork chop with apples and sage, a chicken breast stuffed with spicy sausage and leeks. TJ also worked on special menus for Christmas Eve, Christmas Day, and New Year's Eve. Maybe something he came up with could entice customers to celebrate with them.

* * *

TJ's complaint was not the lockdown but the lack of a corresponding program to help restaurants and other small businesses suffering through a second round of lockdowns and revenue drop-offs
through no fault of their own.

Since the passage of the $2 trillion CARES Act in March, there
had been talk in Washington of another huge relief package. Economists were saying that trillions were needed to avoid an economic
catastrophe. A writer for the *Atlantic*, after talking to a range of
experts, put that figure at $10 trillion. (Think of $10 trillion not
as a big number, the magazine counseled, but "the appropriate dosage for a once-in-a-century economic affliction.") In May, House
Democrats had passed the $3 trillion Heroes Act, a bill that Mitch
McConnell, then the Senate's majority leader, declared "dead on arrival." McConnell imposed a cap of $1 trillion and insisted any new
bill include liability protection for businesses operating during
COVID, to shield them from lawsuits related to the pandemic. A
separate bill to help restaurants was bouncing around Congress as
well.

The restaurant bill had its roots in a new group started early in
the pandemic by a Manhattan chef who felt frustrated that bailouts
targeted airlines and other industries but not restaurants, which
employed far more people. A Trump conference call with restaurant industry representatives that only included the large national
chains helped give momentum to what was called the Independent
Restaurant Coalition. Star chefs joining the group included Tom
Colicchio, Marcus Samuelsson, Nina Compton, and José Andrés.
Their ask was a $120 billion restaurant relief fund created solely for
small and independent restaurants. New York's Chuck Schumer,
then the Senate minority leader, was among those behind the bill.

Negotiations between the parties dragged on through the summer and into the fall. A key sticking point was the $600 weekly
unemployment supplement, which had expired at the end of July.

Democrats favored an extension while most Republicans adamantly opposed a plan that gave lower-wage employees a financial incentive to stay home rather than return to work. The two sides, along with Mnuchin, claimed to be talking, but there was never news of progress.

Presumably, a second rescue package should have been a priority. Restaurants were suffering, along with bars, hotels, wedding venues, movie theaters, and a long list of businesses operating in other sectors. Yet the broader economy had proven more resilient than expected and had rebounded faster than the economists had predicted it would. Glenda Shoemaker saw it by tracking her mother's retirement account: the stock market had covered most of its prior losses. Factories reopened, if they had ever closed, and construction continued, though with extra mitigations. Those hardest hit weren't white- or blue-collar workers but those part of the service economy, on whose behalf the political system rarely bothered. In early October, Trump broke off talks with a tweet: "I have instructed my representatives to stop negotiating until after the election when, immediately after I win, we will pass a major Stimulus Bill that focuses on hardworking Americans and Small Business."

The second wave of COVID sparked more warnings about the dire consequences for small businesses without another big economic relief package. Job growth had stalled, and, with cases rising through the fall, there were worries about another round of massive layoffs. The economy's biggest retailers and restaurant chains were in a better position to capitalize on the coronavirus and, as predicted, picked up market share. The country's fifty largest publicly traded companies saw a 2 percent growth in revenue in the first nine months of 2020. By comparison, small business revenues shrank during that same period—by 12 percent, according to data from thousands of smaller firms collected by Womply. Without a second big stimulus package, some predicted, hundreds of thousands of more small businesses could close.

Democrats ceded to Republican demands that a package not exceed $900 billion, which rekindled negotiations. The debate over a larger $2 or $3 trillion package could wait until the new Biden presidency and maybe a Democratic majority in the Senate (this was before runoff elections in the Georgia Senate races). The final deal was good news for small businesses, in whose bank accounts roughly one-third of this money would end up. Congress earmarked $285 million for a second round of PPP loans (this time, a business qualified only if it had fewer than three hundred employees, and if that was still too expansive a definition, at least the chains were not permitted to participate as in the spring). Another $15 billion was set aside for Economic Injury Disaster Loans to small businesses in low-income communities needing up to $10,000. The bill also directed that a $600 stimulus check be sent to all but the most well-off Americans (children included), a good portion of which presumably would end up in the tills of small business owners. A compromise was reached on the supplemental unemployment payment: $300 a week rather than $600. There was no release of liability, despite McConnell's demand that it be included.

The bill passed the House and Senate a few days before Christmas. By then, Trump had retreated to Mar-a-Lago. The bill was flown to Florida for his signature, but then an embittered Trump blindsided even White House officials when he posted a video on YouTube calling the bill a "disgrace," though his Treasury secretary had been among its primary architects. A brooding president sat on the bill for five days before finally signing it into law a couple of days after Christmas.

* * *

December had proven a better month than TJ might have hoped. The restaurant's salvation that December were the holiday menus TJ had put together for Christmas and New Year's. For the Christmas orders, Cusumano's booked around $12,000 in sales over two days. New Year's had proven even more profitable. His New Year's

Eve special was a surf-and-turf that included four lobster tails, four filet mignons, and four twice-baked potatoes for $179.99. He had sold somewhere between 110 and 120 combo dinners, which brought in another $20,000.

"It's a lucky thing that we're in a small and supportive town," TJ said. "Because if we weren't, we would've had to close." He ended the year letting the kitchen people work their full hours. He was even able to give holiday bonuses: an extra $100 for each of his line chefs and $200 for Ang as head chef.

Yet there was still January to get through. The new year began with the birth, on January 1, of Livia Rose Cusumano. At that point, the only money the Cusumanos could count on was from TJ's side work building conveyor and racking systems. He did not imagine much of an indoor crowd anytime soon, and he could count on only so many takeout orders. He would not let himself contemplate hibernation, but he did broach the idea of turning Cusumano's into a one-man pizza place.

"It would be just me coming into the restaurant by myself, making the dough, working the phones, and getting home by eight thirty," he said, adding, "We're not that far away from that."

Chapter 20

"Surviving Long Enough to Survive"

There was good news for Vilma Hernandez that winter: her beauty salon received $20,000 through the state's small business relief fund, financed by a share of Pennsylvania's CARES Act money. Vilma bumped everyone's hours and used a portion to restock masks, sanitizers, and other supplies. But mainly the grant offered Vilma peace of mind. The salon had reached a kind of equilibrium point but one that had the business living on the financial edge. Now she had a cushion to protect her from hard times. She took comfort from the images in mid-December of healthcare workers receiving their first COVID-19 vaccines. Vilma was a healthy woman in her fifties who would have to wait her turn. But seeing shots going into people's arms felt to her as if a clock had begun. It was just a matter of time before Vilma and her people would be inoculated.

The two women who owned VIP Healthy & More, the juice and sandwich shop just off Broad on Wyoming Street, also had reason to celebrate. It had been a miserable 2020, but they, too, had received a grant though the state's small business relief fund. They were awarded $5,000—a modest dollar amount, but theirs was a low-overhead operation. The money, on top of a similar allotment through the PPP program, would carry them through the winter.

A third local recipient of the same small business program was Jose Francisco. Jose was the thirty-one-year-old, high-energy proprietor of a nightclub on Broad Street called Second Base. Born and raised in Passaic, New Jersey, a working-class city just north of Newark, Jose moved to Hazleton at age twenty-one. Eight years later, he took over Second Base. "I've dreamed of being a club owner basically since I'm like five years old," Jose said. Second Base served Dominican dishes during the day and, prior to COVID, stayed open until two a.m every night.

The state's emergency order required bars and nightclubs to close by midnight. Jose needed crowded dance floors to make money, yet there were also the social distancing rules he needed to abide by. He had planned to reopen when the county went green, but his chef disappeared. "I can only guess he was scared off by the corona," Jose said, "because I'd never hear from the guy again." Because of the requirement that people eat if they wanted to drink, business was abysmal when he finally reopened in August. "It's really hard to get people eating a full meal when they know they're going to go to sleep in an hour or two," Jose said. Before COVID, he had a dozen people working for him. At the start of 2021, he had maybe four or five, and none were back on full-time schedules.

Jose had been feeling desperate that fall. He had found a bank that submitted a PPP application on his behalf, but the computer always flashed the same message: "under review." It read that way for months and then rejected his application for reasons that were never clear to him. "To be honest, if there's no help for me, then that's the end," Jose had said in October. He had four kids. He would not bankrupt himself to save his club, even if it had been a dream since childhood. "I have to protect my family," he said. "I can't be left with nothing." It was not until he learned at the start of 2021 that he was receiving $10,000 from the state that he allowed himself something like optimism.

"That lets me survive long enough," he said, "to find out if I can survive this thing."

* * *

Broad Street had its first big casualty of the pandemic when the Shop 2 consignment shop announced it was closing permanently in October. The co-owners, both in their sixties, still did not feel comfortable going into people's homes in search of antiques to sell, and they did not see that changing anytime soon. "I had another ten years in me," co-owner Carmine Parlatore said. Six months after closing, they still had not taken down the store's Facebook page. Doing so, Parlatore said, meant fully acknowledging that her business was "kaput." Because of COVID, a well-preserved throwback building with beautiful hardwood floors had been shuttered. Broad Street had another vacancy.

Jennifer Donald-Barnasevitch at Smith Floral, also on Broad, had thought her prospects were similarly dismal. The wedding business was virtually nonexistent, and perversely, the same could be said about her store's funeral business. People were dying at a higher rate, but the pandemic meant smaller gatherings and therefore fewer flowers sold. It was the garden center part of her business that carried the store through much of 2020, followed by a terrific Christmas. She credited a trend that small shop owners around the country were reporting: customers increasingly recognizing the importance of local business to the community. Some customers stated it outright, like the woman who bought Christmas ornaments from Smith Floral for her thirty-five employees because she wanted to support small business.

"That's definitely been the vibe and that's really helped us," Donald-Barnasevitch said. "People want to shop small." A "silver lining of the pandemic," she said, was the country waking up to the dark side of an economy dominated by the likes of Amazon, which booked more than $385 billion in sales in 2020. Her accountant surprised her that January when he told her she'd actually earned more money in 2020 than she had in 2019. With time to reflect, it made sense. She had fewer employees, which translated into lower costs but also meant she logged longer hours. "I worked really, really hard so I earned that extra money," Donald-Barnasevitch said. There was also the $35,000 in PPP she received.

Tamara Hersberger at the Poppy Press Coffee Company was still struggling. She remained closed through most of the fall. "I'm coming downtown, hanging out and getting the feel," Tamara said. "Nothing was happening." Hers was a beautiful shop with exposed brick walls, hardwood floors, and heavy wooden tables. Oversized Edison bulbs dangled over a blonde wood bar and stools. The works of local artists hung on the wall. Downtown people loved spending time inside her café but there was no upside in offering muffins and coffee in the morning and a full lunch menu when there were no office workers to caffeinate and feed.

Tamara contemplated calling it quits, but the thought of permanently closing made her moan as if in pain. With the office buildings downtown still empty, she turned her attention to catering. She still had the kitchen, even if the rest of her restaurant was not of much use to her. The big assisted-living center a block away hired her to make sandwiches and sides for a staff event, and she ran large containers of chili and mac and cheese and her Buffalo chicken wings to one of the hospitals. A doctor's office put in an order. A local tool company hired her to do a series of customer appreciation events. "That's when I knew I had something," Tamara said. She used some of the $18,000 in PPP she had received to buy a portable food cart. She dressed it up with paneling and flowers so it looked more like a portable café and hauled it behind the Chevy pickup truck she drove. It still wasn't enough, though. She needed more than the two or three small catering jobs she was doing on average each week.

Her kids sparked Tamara's big brainstorm idea. With eight grown-up kids, she said, "I can't go buying all these presents." So she made them what she called "boards"—cutting boards piled high with scones, muffins, quiche, cheeses, or cakes, depending on each kid's preferences. "They were like, 'Mom, you should do these,'" Tamara said. Her first offerings were New Year's Day boards for $45. There were themed boards (bagels, cream cheese, and lox, say, or a French-themed board with Brie, quiche, and French toast) or a customer could mix and match their own with items from her menu.

"I'd do fifteen to twenty a weekend and that would pull me through," Tamara said. For the moment, she was making it.

"It helps that it feels like everyone's going through the same thing. Otherwise, you'd take it personally that you're failing."

* * *

There were two Lech Pharmacies: the one in Laceyville, which Joe ran, and the one in Nicholson, where the same pharmacist had served as manager for twenty-seven years. But the man's parents were in poor health. Rather than put them both in a nursing home, he decided he would take care of them himself, so he announced his sudden retirement in early 2021. Joe respected the decision, but that did not make the task of taking care of a second store any easier.

"We're replacing a guy who has been part of the community there for almost thirty years," he said. In the interim, Joe was spending more time in Nicholson and using temps until he could find a pharmacist willing to move to the area and accept rural pay, which is less than in the big city.

Revenues were down at both Lech Pharmacies. The two shops he co-owned with partners were barely in the black. That was less because of COVID and more because of broader trends. In November, Amazon announced it was getting into the prescription drug business. Amazon Pharmacy, as they were calling it, offered free two-day delivery to all Prime members. Soon Joe was feeling the impact of another big entrant into the market. Since COVID, he said, he was hearing at least once a week from someone who told him, "We're glad you're here." But those customers were invariably older. "Younger people who grew up online and with the phone are just as happy to avoid coming into the store," he said. They want the pills they need, and do not care if it's from Lech's or Amazon.

There were the usual annoyances that were inherent to a world dominated by the pharmacy benefits managers. Joe's big complaint in the winter of 2021 was the pricing of ninety-day prescriptions. The prices had changed to the point that he was losing money on a lot of the prescriptions he filled. "It's not like we're all making all this money and fighting to keep these huge profits," Joe said. "We need a fair deal so we can keep our doors open."

Bill Spear in Hazleton had little choice but to accept the terms dictated by PBMs and insurance companies. There were plenty of nearby drugstores to serve a customer if a pharmacist chose not to pick up a contract. Yet Joe had leverage as the only pharmacist for miles around, and he encouraged other rural pharmacists to do the same. He canceled a contract he had with Blue Cross, even though it represented 20 percent of his business. "We're in a rural area, you need us," he told the carrier—and less than one month later, he had been granted better deal terms. The same happened when he dropped one of the health insurers that Procter & Gamble, the county's biggest employer, offered its people. "Within the week, the insurance company is on the phone asking me, 'What's going on?'" Joe said. That, too, led to a more favorable PBM contract.

Yet deals like that were harder to come by. Increasingly, the PBMs reminded Joe that people have mailboxes, where they can receive their medicine, and also telephones, if they need consults. From the vantage point of an office in another part of the country, the eighteen-mile drive to and from Tunkhannock was no big deal, and there was another small pharmacy in the next county that was only ten miles away. He won his fight over better pricing for ninety-day refills, but decades of jousting over rates had taken its toll.

"I'm sixty years old," Joe said, "and I don't know how much longer I want to keep fighting these fights."

* * *

Mark Monsey had his usual gripes. The summer and fall were six of the best months in the fifty-nine years Greenwood's had been in the Monsey family. "But I was selling all my furniture and nothing was coming back in," he said. The global supply chain had seized up during COVID, and home furnishings, along with flooring and appliances, were among the businesses disrupted. The manufacturers were promising delivery in four to six weeks, but that had been months earlier. He cut back the store's hours from nine to seven each day to nine to five. "I had no product to sell so what was the use?" Mark asked.

"Christmas was kind of a total dud," he said. His customers had money in their pockets. They came by the store to shop. He just didn't have the recliners or dining room sets or washer-dryers to sell them.

Down on Tioga Street, Glenda Shoemaker had surprised herself with a strong Christmas. "Sales were up," Glenda said. "Not much. But up." Her participation in Hallmark's Ship from Store program had helped. She earned less on those sales than from her in-store customers, but they were also people who found her through Hallmark's portal. In a single day, she and her staff had picked, packed, and shipped 140 items. But her walk-in business was also strong. "People would tell me straight out, 'We're shopping now because we want you to be here a year from now,'" Glenda said. Mark Monsey and his wife stopped by to buy holiday items. So, too, did Joe Lech and his spouse.

"I think COVID had something to do with more people

shopping small businesses," Joe said. He was selling more over-the-counter aspirin and toothpaste since the start of the pandemic. For the same reason, he thought Glenda saw more customers that holiday season. "People didn't want to go to Walmart and deal with the idiots who weren't wearing masks around here," Joe said. "And so they shopped local."

Or at least enough of them did so it made a difference to Glenda's bottom line. Walmart more than doubled its profits in 2020, and Target enjoyed its best year in more than a decade. Sales grew by several billion dollars at T.J.Maxx. Dollar General, one of the country's fastest growing retailers, notched an extra $2 billion in 2020. People may have been stopping by a favorite small business or two to drop some money, but otherwise they seemed to be spending the bulk of their discretionary dollars with the same small universe of giants.

Glenda allowed herself to feel something like optimism. She had survived Christmas and had money in the bank. There were times she regretted returning her first allotment of PPP, and now she had a second chance. "Would it be this huge amount that covers everything I lost? No," Glenda said. "But it could make everything easier to go through."

Chapter 21

Maxed Out

Dining rooms around Old Forge reopened on January 4, 2021, the day the governor's prohibition was lifted. Indoor dining had been shut down for barely three weeks, but the demand for a table was high everywhere in town. With the reopening, at least one of the governor's orders became irrelevant, at least in Old Forge. As if by mutual agreement, restaurateurs around town dropped the 50 percent cap on indoor dining. Some cheated the number higher, while at least one ignored it completely. "We were at 100 percent on Friday and Saturday," one Main Street restaurant owner confessed. The staff rebuked those who failed to wear a mask and tried, unsuccessfully, to stop customers from congregating near the entrance or even in the dining room.

"It was like homecoming weekend," this chef-owner said. "Everyone hugging."

TJ was slower than others to reopen. Nina was exhausted and recuperating after an arduous delivery. Nina and the baby didn't arrive home until the day dining rooms in the state could reopen. TJ recognized that his place was with Nina and the baby. If he was out of the house, he was at the side job he was working for extra cash. His kitchen crew handled a takeout-only menu that first weekend. He didn't allow patrons back inside the restaurant until January 13.

The same pent-up demand that filled the town's restaurants that first weekend filled his the following one. He, too, abandoned the 50 percent guideline. "We instructed our staff to seat people wherever there's seats available and if people are uncomfortable and they don't want to sit there because they're too close to somebody, then they can leave or they can come back at a later time," TJ said.

"From the start, I've said let us open fully or close us down," TJ said. He had had it with the back-and-forth: 50 percent, 25 percent, 50 percent, then 0, and technically back to 50 percent again. "Make it a level playing field," he said. "Everyone does takeout until a widely distributed vaccine has been injected in a high enough proportion of arms and then there's some sort of immunity. And then you open the floodgates and then we're back.

"It's this in-between and back-and-forth stuff that's driving me crazy," TJ said.

* * *

Finally, there would be good news for Cusumano's that winter. The SBA sent TJ an Economic Injury Disaster Loan for more than $50,000. He would need to pay that money back, but the monthly repayment on the thirty-year loan came to barely $400 a month. "My water bill is more than that," he said. He considered that "free money," given the peace of mind and sense of stability it gave him. He had a good-sized cushion that would help him ride out the rest of the pandemic.

The internet portal for applying for a second round of PPP opened on January 11. TJ had signed up for an alert at the SBA website to ensure he was in the first batch of applicants. New rules imposed by Congress dictated that to qualify, a business must demonstrate that its 2020 revenues had fallen by at least 25 percent.

"Unfortunately, I qualified," TJ said. This time businesses were eligible for up to 3.5 times their average monthly payroll rather than 2.5 times. Less than two weeks after applying, TJ had another $60,000 in his bank account. In this second round of PPP, recipients did not have to devote the lion's share of the money to employee salaries. They were permitted to spend the money on a greatly expanded list of business expenses, from the mortgage or rent, to paying suppliers, to buying new equipment. To win conservative support back in December, though, a provision had been added that allowed businesses to use PPP money to offset any property damage caused by looting or vandalism in 2020.

The year 2021 saw the swearing-in of the 117th Congress, giving Democrats slim control of both the House and Senate. In March, seven weeks after Biden's inauguration, Congress passed the $1.9 trillion American Rescue Plan. The package, which passed without a single Republican vote, included another $50 billion for PPP, bringing total funding for the program to just under $800 billion. "I have not met a small-business person who isn't working harder than they ever thought they'd have to work," New Jersey senator Cory Booker, a Democrat, said during debate over the bill. "That's from small restaurateurs all the way to people who started businesses online. And we just have to make sure that we are doing things to help them and not just crafting these programs that only the bigger companies can access." Another $16 billion was set aside for grants to theaters, music clubs, and the like under a shuttered venue arts program. The bill also included a generous tax credit for businesses of any size that saw more than a 50 percent decline in revenues in 2020.

Toward that end, the rules governing PPP had changed once again. When setting up the program, Congress did not require lenders to collect demographic data about the program's recipients. Some did anyway, revealing a program that disproportionately favored white men. A more in-depth analysis by the Federal Reserve Bank of New York looked at counties with high proportions of black-owned businesses (the Bronx, Queens, and Wayne County/ Detroit in Michigan). The portion of businesses receiving a PPP loan in those counties was "starkly" lower than the averages, in part because firms owned by people of color were less likely to have a commercial account with a bank. The San Francisco Fed analyzed majority-white zip codes and found higher-than-average loan numbers.

The SBA announced that it would give priority to applications received from smaller financial institutions that served low-income communities and groups that otherwise lacked access to financing. This time around, 43 percent of the approved PPP loans went to people of color. Another change was prompted by scammers, who had siphoned off billions from the program. The worst violators, like those using the money to buy vacation homes or Lamborghinis, were facing criminal charges. The SBA added automated safeguards that served as a check on fraudulent applications even as it would cause more of them to be rejected.

* * *

Biden gave his version of the small-business-is-the-backbone speech in February, barely one month after taking the oath of office. He declared small businesses the "backbone of our communities"— and with COVID, he added, "far too many are on the brink of closing their doors." He offered an additional step to help smaller businesses. "When the Paycheck Protection Program was passed, a lot of these mom-and-pop businesses got muscled out of the way by bigger companies that jumped in front of the line," the president said. A full 70 percent of the sole proprietors and independent contractors were women or people of color, yet they had largely been locked out of the PPP program. For the next two weeks, Biden announced, the SBA would accept applications only from businesses with fewer than twenty employees. The Biden administration also set aside $1 billion specifically to help employee-less enterprises in low- and moderate-income communities. A ban on applications from convicted felons was also lifted. Only those who were in prison or had been convicted of financial fraud would be automatically turned down.

Congress's $1.9 trillion rescue package included the Restaurant Revitalization Fund that the Independent Restaurant Coalition had been pushing since almost the start of the pandemic. Some restaurant owners were disappointed. They had been asking for $120 billion, but just under $30 billion was apportioned to the program, and restaurants would need to compete with food trucks, saloons, taverns, wineries, and inns if at least one-third of their revenues were from food and alcohol sales. Restaurant owners could complain, but many sectors seeking special bailouts (gyms and hotels, for instance) had come up empty. The great advantage the restaurants enjoyed were politically powerful allies, including Chuck Schumer, who was the new Senate majority leader, and Congresswoman Nydia Velázquez, the New York Democrat who chaired the House Small Business Committee (in 1992, Velázquez became the first Puerto Rican woman elected to Congress).

Much like it had done with PPP once the White House was in the hands of a Democrat, the government gave a head start to any application from a restaurant or any other qualifying food- and alcohol-related businesses that were majority owned by a woman, a veteran, or those the government described as "socially and economically disadvantaged." For twenty-one days, only those who self-certified as belonging to one of these categories could apply for a grant through the Restaurant Revitalization Fund. Pots of money were reserved for applicants that brought in less than $50,000 in revenues a year and those reporting less than $500,000.

TJ spoke to his banker soon after passage of the Restaurant Revitalization Fund. The formula was simple: deduct 2019's gross revenues from 2020's, subtract any PPP dollars received, and theoretically a restaurant was due the difference. That made him eligible for a check of roughly $100,000. "I may even survive this thing after all," TJ said near the end of January.

* * *

TJ worked construction for several more weeks in January and into February but gave notice because the restaurant was demanding more of his time. He declared Valentine's weekend as "decent"—if nothing else, good enough so that he did not have to dip into his PPP or EIDL money to cover his expenses. His older customers were getting their vaccines, and business picked up in March. By April, the weather had turned warm, and people again were asking for the patio rather than settling for it as the best worst option.

TJ had always been frugal in his approach to business. That helped him remain open while restaurants elsewhere closed. He had his parents to thank for that. They had their whole lives invested in their inventory, and he saw the stress it caused. As a result, he ran lean like some corporate behemoth with a just-in-time operation. He lived in fear of sunk costs—money invested in inventory. In the early days of the restaurant, he carried wines that he priced at $200 or more. "That was torture, watching a bottle of wine sit on a shelf, knowing how much I've paid for it, waiting for the right customer to come in and buy it," he said. Now he ran a small, compact wine list of $35 bottles and $10 glasses. He was constantly running out to pick up basics he needed for that night's dinner.

Meat prices had skyrocketed. He felt embarrassed to be charging $52 for his dry-aged prime New York Strip, but his cost for that cut of meat was roughly $28, and restaurant economics dictated that he should have charged significantly more. Veal caused a similar dilemma. He used a formula-fed veal raised on a farm in south Pennsylvania, where the animals were more humanely treated and the meat a beautiful pink. When veal prices jumped by one-third, he needed either to raise his prices further or drop it from his menu.

"At a certain point, how much could I charge?" TJ asked. He took veal off the menu for a while. He brought it back, but, with veal at $19 a pound, he charged $29 for a veal chop (roughly twelve ounces of veal) and then spent his evenings apologizing to people for the price.

TJ continued to skirmish with the occasional customer. That spring, on TJ's birthday no less, a customer complained that the $52 dry-aged prime strip he had asked for rare had been overcooked and demanded that the kitchen cook him a new piece of meat. With the steak cut open on the man's plate, TJ knew it looked the proper shade of red. He even grabbed a meat thermometer to test what his eyes were telling him: 115 degrees, which is below the recommended internal temperature for a rare steak. He told the man he would cook him a second steak, but he would be paying for the first one. A harsh online review—and TJ's lengthy response—followed.

TJ had been thrilled when a pharmaceutical giant booked his back room for a dinner for twenty—the first since the start of the pandemic. "Like finding money on the ground," Bill Genovese had said of these lucrative events, which were Billy G's bread and butter during its short life on Old Forge's Main Street. But the rep who arranged the dinner complained that the service wasn't what they'd expected and specifically mentioned the fifteen-year-old busser who had not cleared the plates fast enough between courses. She demanded that TJ reduce the bill. "They're some huge multinational pharmaceutical company bringing in billions, and they're squeezing a family-owned restaurant for a few dollars?" he said. The two engaged in what TJ described as a "yelling fight."

With PPP and the EIDL loan, the Cusumanos had money in the bank. Feeling rich, they devoted money to upgrading the restaurant. TJ was always sifting through sites that listed restaurant equipment for sale. "The sad thing is with COVID there's a *lot* for sale," TJ said that spring. He fell in love with a sixteen-burner stove that he bought on eBay for under $5,000. They also bought a new pasta machine that let the kitchen cook six pasta dishes at once. ("I can't even think of how we made it without it," he said.) Most of the rest would remain in the restaurant's bank account as a cushion against any further hard times.

* * *

TJ's perspective was that of someone who had endured a catastrophic storm. He feared he might lose everything in a shipwreck but now stared out at calm seas and a bright sun. "I can't pinpoint it," TJ said at the start of May 2021. A couple of months earlier, he was limping along, and everything was a struggle. The next day he was adding up receipts that showed him clearing $8,000 on a Saturday night. That was not quite prepandemic levels but vastly more than during the bleakest days of winter.

TJ had secured the approvals he needed to jar and sell his Sunday gravy and other products. But he decided to shelve the idea indefinitely. "Time-wise and staff-wise—everything-wise—I'm totally maxed out," he said. As is, they hadn't set a day for Livia's baptism, though Catholic doctrine dictates newborns be baptized within a few weeks of birth.

There was also news in the kitchen: Ang Garzon was gone. She had quit the previous weekend with little warning, and people still seemed in shock. The crew blamed the stresses of the previous couple of months. "It's been nonstop," Brian Mariotti said. TJ should have been angry because of the sudden departure of his sauté cook and kitchen manager—a key member of what in the fall he called his all-star team. Instead, he felt relieved. He had grown tired of their regular squabbling and her knee-jerk defensiveness. Levi Kania, who had started working at Cusumano's as a dishwasher when he was fourteen, would now anchor the upstairs kitchen. He was twenty-one years old.

For her part, Ang said, reaching thirty spurred her exit. The time had come, she decided, to get serious about retirement savings. She had no inkling of the Cusumanos' plan to include her in a 401(k) just before COVID hit. She quit, thinking she would find a job at one of the big warehouses in the area. With so many employers hard up for workers, they were paying around the same as she was earning at Cusumano's—$17 an hour, plus benefits. Instead, she took a job as the chef at the Thirst T's Bar & Grill, a Scranton-area place specializing in wings and burgers. There were no benefits, but there she was also the top chef. "I guess it was just time to move on," she said.

Sha-Asia had colored her hair blue on one side and red on the other. She also added a small gold nose ring. "I couldn't do anything like that while I was in school because the instructors said it was unprofessional in the hospitality business," she said. She still did not have her two-year culinary degree. She had thought she was attending school on a full scholarship but learned that somehow she owed the school money. She needed two more classes to graduate but was not permitted to enroll in them until her account was squared away—and for the time being, she was not paying it. "I told her," TJ said, "as long I'm still alive and you're willing to work for me, you've got a job here." Sha-Asia appreciated the vote of confidence, and she continued working in the kitchen. But she had ambitions beyond Cusumano's. She was considering a four-year degree. "I'm a very driven person," she said.

TJ had been vaccinated in March—as soon as he was eligible. He chose not to ask his staff what decision they had made. This was May, before vaccines became another way for the country to divide itself into hostile camps. He knew Sam Egan, who was in his midforties, had gotten the shot. But the rest of his kitchen staff were young and healthy. He assumed they felt invulnerable to the virus and would fail to recognize any bigger obligation to the community. Some might be persuadable but certainly not his best dishwasher. "He's telling me he's not getting a shot because the government's using it to implant chips in all of us," TJ said.

The second weekend of May was a busy one inside Cusumano's. There was overtime that weekend for anyone who wanted it. In addition to the usual Friday-night crowd, the kitchen needed to prep for a rehearsal dinner for fifty in the Devil's Pit, under a tent that had been rented for the night. That Saturday, Cusumano's opened its doors during the day for a pair of events: a First Communion luncheon in the Cellar and a large birthday celebration for a two-year-old. Between the two events, they needed to feed nearly one hundred people before the restaurant even opened its doors for dinner. Cusumano's had two more First Communion celebrations booked for Sunday. Including the bar bills for the rehearsal dinner and the three First Communions, he brought in more through just these side events than during entire weeks the previous fall and winter. As of Easter, Pennsylvanians once again could buy a drink at a bar without ordering food—unless it was in Philadelphia, which set its own guidelines. The governor also upped restaurant capacity to 75 percent. TJ had been ignoring that number since the start of the year, but the lifted rules on drinking augured well for the Cellar.

That night, the pulse of the restaurant beat much faster than it had through the first year-plus of the pandemic. Three or four cooks was no longer enough, so he had Sam staying late on Friday and Saturday nights, to make the appetizers in the downstairs kitchen. "Lately, I work and I sleep," Sam said.

TJ had also hired an "expeditor" to serve as air traffic controller on Saturday nights. He was a young black man named LaSalle who Sha-Asia had worked with at McDonald's. TJ loved him if for no other reason than he pitched in any way he could to keep the kitchen running efficiently, as a good expeditor must. "He'll run stuff down if there's a to-go order, he'll go down to pick up appetizers Sam cooks," TJ said.

There's always something inside a restaurant. On this night it was a broken dishwashing machine, which meant washing everything at the smaller dishwashing station in the main floor kitchen, adding to the stress level. Occasionally, TJ ventured upstairs to check in with LaSalle, but mainly he planted himself on a stool in the Cellar and buttonholed any upstairs people who came downstairs for something. At a little after six p.m., Brian grabbed more pasta. "How's it going?" TJ asked.

"Not too bad."

"It's early yet." Thirty minutes later, Jessica Barletta, who had been working as a waitress since before the Cusumanos bought the restaurant, was downstairs to pick up a half tray of pizza for her table. "Everything okay?" TJ asked.

"Everything's on time," she told him.

"It's early yet," he repeated.

TJ jumped up to check on the downstairs kitchen. He noticed that Sam was low on calamari, so he grabbed a knife and started cleaning and cutting more as a guard against running out. With a full house upstairs and a crowd downstairs, he could not help himself. At the first hint that the kitchen was lagging, he gave up his bar stool in the Cellar and took his place behind the stove beside Levi. Finally, there was a buzz in the restaurant that might have made him think COVID was a thing of the distant past. The bar upstairs was crowded; the bar in the Cellar was full. Every table was occupied, and people on both floors were eating, drinking, and laughing.

The next morning, TJ was up early to make a nine a.m. run for supplies at the Restaurant Depot. Over breakfast before the store was open, his voice hoarse, he said, "I'm exhausted but I'm not complaining."

Chapter 22

Wait Till Next Year

Fourteen months into the pandemic, on May 13, 2021, the Centers for Disease Control issued new guidance for face coverings: fully vaccinated individuals no longer needed to wear a mask or practice social distancing unless required to do so by local regulations and rules. The next day, Pennsylvania adopted the CDC's relaxed COVID guidelines, lifting the requirement that stores, restaurants, and workplaces require face coverings. Two weeks later, Tom Wolf announced that 70 percent of the state's population eighteen or older had received at least a first dose of a COVID vaccine—joining nine other states. The significance of that milestone was clear to Vilma Hernandez. The state lifted many of the lingering COVID-related orders, including the emergency rules it had imposed on hair salons and other personal care businesses at the start of the pandemic. Vilma was free to operate her salon under the old rules that governed her shop before the pandemic.

Those first months that Vilma's was free from the COVID rules proved joyous ones for Vilma and her staff. Everyone still wore masks, but the shop was lively as it had been prior to COVID. "For so long, customers didn't feel comfortable getting their hair cut but now they're happy in my shop," she said. "People want to leave their house and finally take care of themselves." At last, the hair products that seemed forever en route had arrived, just in time for a return to the way it used to be.

"People were eager to get out and enjoy themselves," Vilma said—and they visited the salon both to feel good again and to look their best when they stepped back into the world. Vilma did not mandate that her employees be vaccinated, but she also did not have to. Perhaps because of how they made a living, they all got their shots once they were eligible for them.

There were issues, as there always are when operating a small business. She lost three of her people. Salary-wise, she could not compete with what jobs in the industrial park were paying. None were longtime stylists but instead junior people who mainly washed hair and cleaned up around the shop. Their absence put pressure on everyone who still worked there.

Yet that also meant everyone was making good tips in a busy salon. Vilma even picked up new customers, which was unexpected. Revenues reverted to where they had been prior to COVID. "I'm just thankful we were able to get back to where we had been," Vilma said.

* * *

Two constitutional amendments on the state ballot in Pennsylvania that May asked voters to curtail the governor's emergency powers. The governor had declared a disaster emergency on March 6, 2020—and every three months had renewed that order. Russ Diamond, the conservative state legislator who had led chants to lock up Secretary of Health Rachel Levine, was among those feeling fed up with "the 'two weeks to flatten the curve' nonsense of Tom Wolf's data-free edicts, mandates, and lockdown." Wolf vetoed all bills that the Republican-controlled legislature passed to help free the state of his dictums. Their answer was to use Republican majorities in the House and Senate to put constitutional amendments on the ballot and let the voters of the state decide.

Both amendments passed with 52 percent of the popular vote. Under the first, a simple majority in the legislature can terminate a disaster declaration whenever they want. The second limits any disaster declaration to twenty-one days rather than ninety and gives the legislature sole power for extending it. A few weeks later, the legislature used its newly granted power to end Wolf's coronavirus disaster declaration.

* * *

Tamara Hersberger had reopened Poppy Press Coffee Company in Hazleton just before Thanksgiving—only to close two weeks later when the governor shut down indoor dining. She reopened on January 4 but with limited hours. She opened at seven a.m. as usual but closed at two p.m., and then only Monday through Friday. This time she would not blame Wolf but a sudden lack of people willing to work for minimum wage plus tips. She needed minimal help while she was handling food orders in the back. But even finding the one or two people she needed was proving a problem.

Tamara was hardly alone, of course. Businesses across the country in the spring of 2021 faced worker shortages. Fast-food chains dangled signing bonuses to lure employees. Wealthier companies offered free college tuition and parental leave. Applebee's gave a free appetizer to anyone who agreed to sit down for an interview. A storied amusement park in Pittsburgh had been paying its summer people $9 an hour. To compete, it increased pay to $13 an hour and dropped its requirement that employees buy their own uniforms.

Everywhere around Hazleton that spring were yellow-and-white flyers promising anyone who joined Amazon a $1,000 signing bonus and pay of $16 an hour. Amazon upped the ante with the promise of health coverage on the first day of work. Cargill advertised meat-cutting jobs that paid as much as $25 an hour (or $17 an hour for people who preferred working in the part of its Hazleton operations where they made chocolate). Other big businesses with a presence in Hazleton—the T.J.Maxx and Lowe's, a Panera Bread and Taco Bell—raised their wages.

"How am I going to compete with that?" Tamara asked. More than once someone had started working but then gave notice a few weeks later to take a job in one of the industrial parks. A couple of people she hired did not last that long: they accepted a job but never showed up for their first shift. Tamara made do with one person. In a pinch, she ran food out to the counter or one of the tables.

By the start of April, Tamara had had it. She announced on Facebook that she was limiting her menu to coffee drinks and pastries and closing every day at eleven a.m. She also decided to remain dark on Wednesdays. "I just didn't have no more to give," she said.

In her Facebook post, Tamara blamed the federal government for her troubles. The $300 weekly supplement the government had promised the unemployed, she wrote, had made it "almost impossible to find help." That was an assertion that by then had become a popular talking point among conservatives. No doubt many under-paid minimum-wage workers were happy to sit at home watching TV while collecting an extra $300 weekly on top of whatever unemployment the state was paying them (working minimum wage for forty hours a week paid $290). But twenty-five states ended the $300 unemployment benefit early and saw little change in hiring. People were viewing the world differently more than a year into the pandemic. Some had enough of a financial reserve to be more choosy or change career paths. Others chose better-paying options, even if it meant being a cog in some giant corporate machine. Child care was still a huge stumbling block in the way of parents return-ing to the workplace, and of course some still felt at risk working indoors at a café or a warehouse.

"We'd be killing it if I had the people," a frustrated Tamara said that May. She tried not to think about how much more she would be bringing in if she had the people to do a full lunch like before

COVID. She stayed open mainly because she feared the message she would send if she did not. "If I stayed closed too long people would just think of me as gone," Tamara said. The irregular hours, though, were proving frustrating to her customers.

Tamara's salvation that spring was her catering business. Word of her gift boards spread, and she got smarter about shaving costs. Rather than buying the cutting boards wholesale, she found a local able to make them for her. "I never thought it would be nearly as big as it is," Tamara said of her boards business. She also added picnic baskets to her offering. That was an idea she got from a customer who asked if that was something she did.

The portable café she pulled behind her truck continued to bring in money. But barely six months after buying it, she was ready for an upgrade. What she had dubbed the Poppy Express was nothing but a trailer dressed up as a portable café. She still needed to cook everything at her storefront. That spring, she found a small Airstream that she worked on converting into a portable kitchen, complete with a grill, a small oven, and several burners. She had already booked a summer wedding in the Poconos, one hour away. Her responsibility was the rehearsal dinner, a breakfast the morning of the wedding, and a day-after brunch.

Tamara confessed that she was thinking of abandoning central Hazleton. "It's the catering and the boards that are keeping me going," she said. She asked herself why she bothered with Poppy's. "The choice right now seems between coffee for like ten or fifteen regulars or extra time for a $700 catering job," she said. "So why don't I close that front door?"

The refusal of many to get vaccinated, and the life it gave the Delta variant (deaths by the end of the summer would be back above two thousand a day, which matched numbers from the early months of the pandemic), hurt her business. Yet Tamara was in no position to complain. She was among those reluctant to get vaccinated. She mentioned a sign she had seen at a local farmers' market near her house: BEWARE OF THE ZOMBIE. "That really spooked me," she said. She also had her mother's voice in her ear. "My mom won't get it," she said. "She's in her seventies but she's like, 'Nope.' We have big faith in our family. She's like, 'If I'm gonna die, Jesus is gonna come and get me.' She says she's more worried about aliens."

Tamara explained her hesitancy as rooted in the fear of missing work. "I've seen people get really sick from the vaccine," she said.

"I can't afford no time off. I'll just die. Let me just die if I have to put another note on my door saying that I'm closed."

* * *

Dominic, Nicholas, and Daniel Maloney were still pinching themselves in the Bronx. After years of slow growth, everything was working for Sol Cacao.

"This has all been confirmation for us that you shouldn't quit until you have nothing left," Daniel Maloney said. "That even when your back's against the wall and you don't know what you're going to do to stay alive, you stay open because you never know when the opportunity comes along that changes everything."

Christmas had been as strong as the Maloneys had hoped it would be. They'd more than doubled their normal output of bars. "December was the biggest month in our history," Daniel said. "And that momentum just kept going." They used the extra money they made during the holidays to buy the large cracker they had been coveting. The machine set them back around $10,000, but it was the kind of industrial apparatus inside the factories of larger producers. When it arrived in February, "we were able to triple our production in a day," Dominic said.

More good things happened for the Maloneys that winter and through the spring. Someone from Google reached out to them and invited Sol Cacao to take part in a new badge program that helped people support certain kinds of businesses. Sol Cacao was certified as both a black-owned and family-owned business and also earned a badge for sustainability. "They tell us the algorithms elevate us to the top of the search engine [if someone plugs in one of those criteria]," Daniel said. In April, the company won a Bake-Off of local enterprises cosponsored by MasterCard and the New York City FC (Football Club), the city's team in Major League Soccer. Their company logo was sewn onto the uniform sleeve of every member of the team, and they were invited to an on-field, opening-day ceremony that, Daniel said, "basically had us lighting the torch." But the real benefit was the services of MasterCard's digital marketing team. As they saw it, they were receiving the equivalent of a $50,000 consulting contract but at no cost.

The Maloneys still spoke to stores about carrying their bars, but that was no longer their prime focus. They would not say no if Whole Foods told them they were ready to get behind their product and give them better real estate in a store. But getting on a store shelf had gotten even harder than when they had started. They had grown fond of what Daniel called the "workaround": engaging with customers, whether individuals or corporations, who discover them online.

"This idea," Daniel said, "that someone sitting at home can come to our product and feel an excitement for our product—that changes the whole dynamic."

Individual orders stayed strong. The repeat orders were particularly gratifying. People were trying their product and reordering because they were drawn to quality. "For the first time, we were getting the feedback," Dominic said. "We always knew that we were making some of the best chocolate but now it was recognition from a much larger audience." Yet individual orders only accounted for maybe 20 percent of sales that spring. The larger orders paid the bills. A lot of those were corporate gifts, which continued to be a bright spot for Sol Cacao. "It's a continuation of this trend of people wanting to support black-owned businesses," Daniel said.

By the spring, Sol Cacao was regularly stamping out more than three thousand bars a month. They were near the capacity of what the three of them could do. They again began talking about hiring an employee or two to help them with production.

Yet the Maloneys continued to face monumental challenges. They were still competing with Big Chocolate and the lower costs enabled by scale. The FDA requires a maker to include cacao beans in some form but not much: a company could call its product "chocolate" even if it was 90 percent something else. "A lot of these commercial brands are sticking pretty close to the bare minimum 10 percent," Nicholas said. More worrisome were handcrafted dark chocolate bars in the hands of industry giants: quality bars they could sell at a lower price than Sol Cacao.

The American consumer also presented a challenge to a company selling a product aimed at connoisseurs. Research shows health benefits of chocolate, at least in moderation, "but that's a hard sell in the US," Dominic said. "We've made chocolate almost sinful: 'I'm a chocoholic.'" Market research showed that older consumers were more likely to eat higher-quality chocolates. "The elderly recognize that it's good for the brain and good for the heart," Nicholas said.

The brothers introduced a new Colombia bar that spring—their fourth. Daniel described this bar as having an earthy taste with hints of vanilla and a zestiness on the back end. "People are telling us, 'That's my favorite now,'" Daniel said. "People are really loving it." The Maloneys also reinitiated talks with growers in Trinidad. "We have a little more brain space where we can work on other things," Daniel said. The three dreamed of a bar that was 85 or 88 percent cacao beans, though for the time being, they were sticking with bars that were 70 to 72 percent cacao.

"To most people, chocolate is just a sugary treat," Dominic said. "But I think there's space right now where there are people who want to know where their food comes from and be part of a movement that's not only helping them find these great chocolates but also empower farmers and also know what they're buying was grown with integrity and in a sustainable way."

For the Maloneys, chocolate was commerce but also a cause.

* * *

COVID was no longer the biggest challenge for Joe Lech and his partners. But earning a living as an independent pharmacist, especially one operating in a rural area, remained iffy. Their store in Dushore was the only drugstore in Sullivan County, yet "our eyes are just barely above water," said Mark Stamer, Lech's brother-in-law, who spent most of his time there. To make extra money, Stamer (but not Joe or their other partner) had gone through the requisite training needed to administer the COVID vaccine. "The state considers us a medically underserved area," he said. So they would help the community and also bring in another $40 or so for each shot administered.

The Canton pharmacy, in Bradford County, was having an even harder time than Dushore. In a town of 1,800, it was one of two pharmacies. The Lech's in Nicholson was losing business. About the only one of Joe's stores that was holding its own was his eponymous store in Laceyville, where he spent the majority of his time.

Joe and his partners put the Canton and Dushore stores up for sale. A group in New Jersey indicated their interest, but they were waiting to see the end-of-year financials. If that did not work out, the three of them discussed the possibility of approaching the rival pharmacist in Canton about a file buyout, which meant closing the store. Joe's biggest worry—"my worst nightmare," he said, was that nobody would be interested in Dushore, which was the only pharmacy in the county.

"I'll bet you've got people traveling fifty, sixty miles round-trip to go there," Joe said. "If there's no pharmacy in Dushore, people are screwed."

Mark Monsey, at Greenwood's Furniture, was dressed casually as always, in jeans, a gray sweatshirt, and running shoes. It was May, but his Trump hat still held a place of honor atop a file cabinet next to the desk where customers filled out paperwork to complete sales. "I think if I took it away people would complain," Mark said.

He received his vaccination as soon as it was his turn and felt he had gotten his shot just in time. There had been a spike in COVID cases across Wyoming County in April, and he was thankful for the protection. "Half the people who come into the store aren't wearing masks," he said. Some had been vaccinated but certainly not all the maskless.

Mark described his business through the first five months of 2021 as "bleak." Greenwood's received $18,500 in a second round of PPP. Wyoming County sent him a check for $12,000—his 2019 earnings compared to 2020, minus the PPP dollars he had received. Yet his revenues were down by $20,000 or more in some months. "I'm in the black some months but not every month," he said.

The supply chain continued to be a problem. He was convinced the big makers were letting their bigger customers jump the line at his expense. "I talk to the drivers that do the deliveries, and that's what they're telling me," he said. When the phone rang, whoever answered sounded like a broken record. "We're waiting on the factory." "We can't even guess on when it might come in." "We'll let you know as soon as we can." He had been waiting for some items since the summer.

Compounding the store's problems was a spike in costs. With supply limited and demand high, Mark said, "my prices are through the roof." His cost of buying mattresses and box springs, when he could even get them, was up by about 25 percent. There was a similar inflation at work for appliances and dining room sets. Customers paid more for an item but Mark also absorbed some of the price increase. He figured that inflation was cutting his margins by 5 or 10 percent.

"It's so crazy because people have money up the wazoo," Mark said. "We're selling everything I can get my hands on. I'd be setting all kind[s] of records except I've got nothing to sell."

* * *

Glenda Shoemaker had reason to feel upbeat. That January, she received $27,500 through PPP. "I don't know if I should say this but I almost feel like I'm better off than I was before this happened," Glenda said. Not that that caused her to feel optimistic about the future. In January, she signed a one-year lease on the store. "I was scared about signing anything for longer," she said.

Glenda had survived 2020, but she was still braced for the worst. "I wouldn't be here without PPP," she said. And yet she recognized that it was unlikely that there would be a third round anytime in the future. "I'm wondering what happens next year when there's no check," she said. In May, she was already fretting about Christmas. Adding to her stresses was the new role she had taken on. A member of Tunkhannock's borough council had resigned that February, and Glenda was appointed to fill out her term. "I didn't think I could say no," she said. She complained that she worked seven days a week and said she "hates" politics but successfully ran for a second term when the first was up.

Glenda expressed resentment toward her fellow business owners. She could confide in Gina at the chamber, but the mind-set of the other shopkeepers in town was stoic silence. "I probably shouldn't say this because I'll make everybody mad but one thing this thing has taught me is you think you're part of a community but instead I feel like I'm standing all alone in my store," she said. She had reached out to other business owners but all she really heard was that things were fine. She thought this idea of keeping bad news bottled up ended with her mother's generation but maybe not.

Glenda's big news that spring was that someone had made an offer on the store. Someone she knew from high school with money had a sister moving back to town. He also had a daughter. Would she consider selling the store for the two of them to run?

Another person might have jumped at the chance. Most would at least have put a happy face on the business. Glenda instead explained to the man why buying her store was a bad idea. He would look at the books anyway, she figured, so why pretend? "I looked at him and said, 'Number one, your sister is my age. Does she really want to work seven days a week?'" Glenda's second point was that he was wrong to imagine that both his sister and daughter could make a living running J.R.'s. "I told him, 'This store can't even support one person,'" she said. "I told him the truth: 'This store can't even support me anymore.'"

She didn't want to sell. What else would she do if she didn't run J.R.'s Hallmark? "The thing about when you run a small business is you have more control over your life," she said. "It's you here every day, you talk to your customers, they see you as part of the community." There was also her sense of self. If she wasn't Glenda Shoemaker, proprietor of J.R.'s Hallmark, "who would I be?"

Chapter 23

Dream Small

I n Tunkhannock, Glenda had everything riding on the 2021 holiday season—and had the invoices to prove it. She spent more than she ever had buying Hallmark products to sell, and she set a store record as well loading up on non-Hallmark items. "We're packed with merchandise, which scares the crap out of me," she said that November. "But I made the decision that we were going to make it or we were going down trying."

Staffing proved an issue in the second half of 2021, as it did for so many businesses. Several of her people quit to take better-paying jobs, leaving Glenda to scramble in search of replacement workers. The Delta variant hit that summer, followed by Omicron at the end of the fall, causing more staffing issues. "This one's gone for ten days, this one's out for three weeks," Glenda said. "So I'm working seven days a week and running around like a crazy person." The store still did not have a website—but how was she supposed to take that on when she was chronically understaffed?

In mid-December, Glenda herself tested positive for COVID. "The most important week out of the entire year," she said, "and I couldn't be at my store." For the first couple of days that she was home sick, Glenda stayed in touch with her staff by phone. "But then I wake up and I can't breathe," Glenda said. She spent eight days in the hospital, most of them in the ICU and on a ventilator. "You see what's on the news but they don't prepare you for what getting this thing [COVID] is really like," she said. Whether she had been vaccinated was something Glenda declined to answer when asked. "I almost died and that's all some people wanted to know," she said.

Despite Glenda's ill-timed hospitalization, J.R.'s Hallmark had "a very good end of year," she said. She was especially grateful to several longtime employees who ran the shop in her absence. "They told me, 'Glenda, we're just doing what you taught us to do,'" she said.

She had survived another unpredictable year, just in time to start worrying about 2022.

The start of the new year had been especially bad, even considering that January is perennially a slow month for J.R.'s. Wyoming County recorded more than one thousand positive cases in January—the most in a single month since the start of the pandemic. Sixteen people died from COVID in January, and area hospitals did not have the staffing to handle the influx of patients (Glenda would wait two days in the local ER before an ICU bed opened up in a facility closer to Scranton). "People are scared to death to go out," Glenda said.

Glenda returned to the store after another week spent recuperating at home. She did not struggle with fatigue, like others experiencing long COVID, but more than one month after first getting sick, she was still having breathing problems.

"You come back from something like that and tell yourself, 'I'm not going back to that person I was who was always working,'" Glenda said. But a couple of her new hires had quit ("I don't think they realized how hard they had to work") and even as she was still sometimes relying on a portable oxygen tank to help her breathe, her hours crept back up.

"There's no other option if you have no other people to do what needs to get done," she said. Not for the first time, Glenda questioned her own sanity. "Why are we still fighting to run these family businesses? Why are we so stupid?" she asked.

"They call it the American Dream but they leave out the part of having no life."

* * *

Life inside Vilma's Hair Salon in Hazleton had, by the middle of 2021, returned to something resembling normal. Vilma and her people still wore masks while they were working, and the salon remained chronically understaffed. She was spending a couple of hundred dollars each month on masks, gloves, and sanitizer. But revenues approached pre-COVID levels. Because of lower payroll costs and despite her additional expenses, some weeks the shop banked more money than prior to COVID.

Delta had a "minimal" impact on the salon, Vilma said. Omicron, however, proved devastating. Luzerne County, like the rest of the country, saw its highest rates of transmission of COVID since the start of the pandemic. The timing of the Omicron surge proved especially bad. The holidays are typically a bustling time inside the shop. Her revenues, Vilma calculated, fell by 40 percent in December and January.

Yet as always, Vilma expressed optimism about the future. "Everything comes down to faith with my mother," her son Ivan said. "'God will provide.' 'God is in control.' 'With God's help, we can handle it.' With my mother, it's always the positive." Her salon was still open—something that was not a given in 2020. And for that Vilma felt eternally grateful. *"Gracias a Dios."*

* * *

The Maloney brothers enjoyed another strong summer of sales in 2021. That was followed by a busy fall and an even better holiday season than they had in 2020. Perversely, Delta and then Omicron helped drive sales. The decision by businesses to delay their plans to have their people return to the office hurt any number of small businesses located in business districts. For Sol Cacao, however, it drove corporate sales. "Corporations wanted to gift their employees something at home," Daniel Maloney said. "And we were very fortunate to get a lot of those orders." Where corporate sales had been virtually nonexistent before COVID, they accounted for roughly half of the company's revenues by the second half of 2021.

Sol Cacao was aided by a trio of grants the company received in 2021. The first was a BeyGOOD award from a Small Business Impact Fund created by the NAACP and the singer Beyoncé, to help black-owned businesses in five cities, including New York. A few months later, they received a small business grant from Amazon—a site offering chocolate bars produced by big makers such as Hershey and Ghirardelli at a fraction of the price Sol Cacao charged. Both grants were for $10,000. The extra cash allowed the Maloneys to buy two pieces of equipment: a tempering machine for finishing the chocolate and a second industrial-sized cracker (to turn solid cacao beans into a chocolate paste). That allowed them to increase their manufacturing capacity just in time for a holiday rush fueled by a marketing grant from Spectrum cable company that allowed them to advertise at no cost on a range of channels the service carried.

"We went through packaging faster than we ever had," said Daniel, who quit his engineering job that August to devote himself full-time to Sol Cacao. "We went through more beans than ever." That meant many twelve- and fifteen-hour days just to keep up with orders. "But we were finally back on track with our projections and where we needed to be."

Again, the brothers spoke about hiring someone to help with production. They had hesitated in the past because they worried that while the previous month had been a good one, the next one might prove a disappointment. "We really want someone who can grow with the company," Daniel explained. "We don't want to just hire someone and then feel like we have to let them go or reduce them down to one or two days a week." Yet Daniel declared themselves ready to finally act. "We need to bring someone on board to really grow the business," Daniel said in February 2022. "And now we feel like we have the cashflow to make that happen."

If the Maloneys had a worry heading into the new year, it was the price of the cocoa beans they bought from small specialty farms that served as their suppliers. They were purchasing more beans than they ever had, but the $4,000 to $5,000 a ton they paid prior to COVID had shot up to as much as $7,800 a ton. "We didn't change the price because with so many orders, we're doing okay," Daniel said. "But we'll need to increase it this year for sure."

Larger producers no doubt saw their prices increase as well, but they generally bought in bulk from industrial farms that charged them much lower prices. The giants enjoyed economies of scale and other advantages that accrued with size. The Maloneys were confident they made high-quality bars that could compete with those produced by any rival. Yet Sol Cacao's biggest hurdle to success, as it is for virtually every small maker, is price. And bumping the cost of their bars by even one dollar would hurt them in their battle for market share.

* * *

Nothing seems to change for the independent pharmacist except that it gets harder with each passing year to compete with the chains. Still, Joe Lech received heartening news in the second half of 2021. His "worst nightmare," as he had put it, was that they would be forced to close their Dushore location, leaving Sullivan County without a drugstore. Yet a pharmacist in her midthirties indicated she was interested in buying the store from Joe and his two partners. She had grown up in Sullivan County and lived there with her husband and child, even as she commuted an hour each day to work at a CVS.

"She hated working for a chain and so came to work for us," Joe said. "That's how we came to find out her life dream was to own her own pharmacy." It seemed as if divine intervention had come into play. "It's tough to get somebody willing to come all the way out here without any connection to the area," Joe said. "And here's someone from there who's involved in the community. It really is an ideal fit."

Joe and his partners still had found no buyer for the Canton store, in Bradford County, which they also had put up for sale. Short of another local who knocked on their door to tell them that running a pharmacy in a remote rural area had always been a life-long dream, they would need to find a group looking to do a "roll-up"—snap up multiple pharmacies that would be run not by a pharmacist-owner but staff pharmacists that they either inherit or hire. A couple of groups were looking at Canton, but, by early 2022, none had done more than express interest.

"What people are looking for when they buy a business is one that's making a profit they're happy with," Joe said. He didn't finish that thought, but he did not need to. There were two pharmacies in a town of 1,800 in a sparsely populated stretch of Pennsylvania, in a world dominated by the PBMs, chains, and an encroaching Amazon, among other threats. "I'm just happy we're still there," Joe said.

* * *

In Old Forge, TJ enjoyed what some were calling the Great Awakening. After well over a year of avoiding in-person contact, people were ecstatic to experience simple joys like meeting friends in a restaurant or watching a movie in a theater. That worked out well for a restaurant with a nice-sized dining room, an outdoor patio, and a popular rathskeller. "We had a great summer," TJ said.

That's not to say the restaurant was fully back to where it had been in 2019. "I can name off the top of my head at least a dozen regulars that still haven't come back," TJ said in the fall of 2021. "They were some of our best customers and they're not even really doing takeout." Bookings for private events from the pharmaceutical industry had not returned to pre-COVID levels, nor had the "bereavement/funeral luncheons" Cusumano's promoted on its website. Another disappointment in mid-2021 was the rejection of their application for restitution through the Restaurant Revitalization Fund. A group of white restaurant and bar owners had challenged the program in court because of the twenty-one-day head start the SBA gave those restaurants and bars owned by underserved communities. The rule was overturned, throwing the program into chaos. The 177,000 qualified applicants the SBA turned away included not only the Cusumanos, but many of the disadvantaged restaurants that the government had rigged the system to help.

The Delta variant, TJ said, had only a modest impact on his business. Omicron, however, blew a giant hole in the restaurant's bottom line. Some 120 reservations were canceled between Christmas and New Year's Eve. TJ estimated that he lost $15,000 in receipts in the final ten days of the year.

"That's money that's never going to come back," TJ said. Still, he and Nina revived their idea of a retirement benefit for their staff. Any employee with at least two years' experience (including themselves) could participate in a plan that has the restaurant matching people's contributions up to 3 percent. "It'll cost probably an extra $1,500 a year for every employee that participates, but it's a tax deduction, and a nice little tool for a small business to retain people," TJ said.

Among those who would not be participating was Levi Kania, despite seven-plus years with the restaurant. TJ was happy with the job Levi had been doing as his sauté cook since Ang's departure yet the two got into a fight when Levi asked for a Saturday night off to attend his girlfriend's college graduation party. TJ said, of course he would have said yes if Levi had not taken off two Saturday nights already that summer. Also, TJ said, Levi already had vacation time scheduled for September. TJ gave Levi an ultimatum: show up for work that night or he would be out of a job. "It was the stupidest thing," Levi said. "The last straw." Levi chose his girlfriend. "So I fired his ass," TJ said. (Levi is now cooking at a well-regarded, high-end restaurant in nearby Wilkes-Barre, where he is learning the "French brigade" hierarchal approach to cooking.)

That put TJ back behind the stove, not just on that night but indefinitely. Rather than promote someone from within or find an experienced cook in a tight labor market, TJ replaced Levi with himself. "We're doing really well with me behind the line," TJ said. "The food is better and we save so much money on payroll. It's like we're putting an extra $800 in our pockets every week." TJ enjoyed being a chef again. He could rely on Sam as a backup, and Sha-Asia had even taken a turn or two as the restaurant's sauté cook. "It feels good to be back in touch with the food I'm serving," he said in early 2022.

That was one way the pandemic had changed TJ: rekindling his passion for cooking that had first drawn him to the restaurant business. Before the pandemic, TJ dreamed of opening more restaurants. There was his scheme to sell his sauce, dressings, and gnocchi in the grocery stores. He put all those plans on hold. He was a father, and the three of them were living comfortably with TJ working a manageable fifty or fifty-five hours a week.

"Maybe in the future," TJ said of his many plans. "But right now I'm happy with what I have. I don't want to spread myself thin and possibly upset something that's good."

Onward

A person needs to be crazy to start a small business. The hours are often brutal, and the odds dictate that the venture will fail. The lucky ones last eight or ten years, rather than three or five, before a liquidator arrives to auction off a business's remains. Working for someone else is simpler and typically less stressful. Have a good week or have a bad one and an employee receives the same-sized paycheck. Corporate jobs often include perks such as healthcare and retirement benefits, and there's never a moment when an employee must dip into their personal savings because the business cannot make payroll. True, someone else may be profiting off your toil, which is what helped propel Joe Lech to open his own pharmacy. But you also don't have to endure the anxiety that comes with never being certain that you'll earn enough to cover next month's mortgage.

It's not small business that we celebrate in the US but the kind of person who starts one. It's the founders themselves we admire and venerate in the US—the dreamers or innovators or pragmatists who would rather wager on themselves, despite the risks, than feel stuck in a job that barely pays a living wage, or squeezes the life out of them, or just stands in the way of what they see as their true calling. Maybe they desire to better themselves or their family. Maybe they start a restaurant simply because they have always loved to cook or they take over a pharmacy because they feel a deep satisfaction knowing they are an integral part of the community. Whatever their motivation, they are independents who bushwhack their own path rather than take the well-paved route of working for someone else. The historian Ben Waterhouse argues that what he describes as the "popular mythology surrounding small business" harkens "all the way back to Thomas Jefferson and [hails] the virtues of independent yeoman farmers at the time of the founding." As a nation, we threw off the yoke of a repressive monarch to venture out on our own. We admire the self-reliant and the scrappy and the brave who create something out of nothing, or go down trying.

In their 2018 book, *Big Is Beautiful*, Robert D. Atkinson and Michael Lind argue that a landscape dominated by large companies is good for the US economy. Large-scale enterprises, they point out, bring efficiencies to the market. Bigger companies generally offer better prices and typically pay their people a higher wage. Someone is more likely to receive benefits working for a large corporation than a small business. The sad truth is that chains can more accurately be described as the "backbone" that connects us across the country. The giants are the engines that drive the economy. Relative to them, mom-and-pops like TJ's and Glenda's and Vilma's have a relatively minor impact on the overall economy. It's impressive that the Maloneys are on pace to sell maybe half a million dollars of chocolate in 2022, but that doesn't compare to the more than $8 billion that Hershey booked in 2020. The Maloneys had no employees at the start of 2022. Hershey's employed fifteen thousand. The only small businesses that the government should help, Lind and Atkinson argue, are start-ups that have every intention of growing into large businesses.

Yet Atkinson and Lind point out that one only needs to put

the word "big" before something to make it sound nefarious to the American ear: Big Pharma, Big Tobacco, Big Oil. The pollster Frank Luntz has tested the words "small business owner," "job creator," "innovator," and "entrepreneur." "Nothing tests better than 'small business owner,'" Luntz said, "because it represents all of those." It's small businesses that somehow connect us to the country's founding and ties into an American affection for the underdog, even if the reality is we favor the better prices and conveniences offered by the giants that are crushing them.

COVID, of course, made everything harder for these intrepid souls who had had it hard enough before a hypercontagious virus hit the planet. Guidelines changed, norms shifted, and views on everything from vaccines to the existence of COVID itself hardened into political ideology, placing small business owners in the middle of a culture war. In retrospect, hibernating with the door shut in the early weeks of the pandemic seemed the easy part for any business that requires face-to-face contact. The widespread availability of vaccines in the spring of 2021 was a blessing but also added new challenges. Shop owners, restaurateurs, and other small business owners found themselves having to police their customer's behaviors and enforce ever-changing standards and restrictions on masks, occupancy levels, and vaccine status. Small business owners had always had to deal with angry customers, but now they sometimes found themselves subject to verbal abuse if not in the middle of a fight. Carmine's is a red-sauce Italian eatery a few blocks from my family's apartment; it's a neighborhood place we've gone to for big family gatherings. What the *New York Times* described as a "melee" broke out outside of Carmine's in the fall of 2021 over New York City's requirement that every indoor diner show proof of vaccination.

Businesses of all sizes also had to decide whether to require their own employees to be vaccinated. A vaccine mandate proved a non-issue for Vilma, whose employees had voluntarily been inoculated, and a nonstarter for Glenda, who herself was a vaccine skeptic. TJ struggled over what to do. The decision would be easy if he ran a medical clinic, he said, or served as a school principal. Ultimately, though, he decided against imposing a vaccine requirement.

"I believe everyone should get vaccinated," TJ said. "I believe in all the science behind it. I just don't believe that if you're a pizza maker in the basement or washing dishes semi-alone in a corner, you should be fired if you won't get vaccinated." Yet he feared that sharing that view too loudly would alienate customers who felt differently than he did.

"COVID created this whole extra layer of reasons for people to get mad at you," TJ said.

* * *

Every successful small business requires both good timing and good fortune. COVID gave fate a chance to change its mind. Every business's plight in 2020 had been determined years or decades earlier, before any business owner gave a second thought to the possibility that an airborne illness would cause businesses around the globe to shutter their doors. Those who had chosen to get into the restaurant business were not as fortunate as those who had decided to operate a hardware store, a pet shop, or a shoe repair place, all of which generally performed well through the pandemic. Yet their luck was not as bad as those who had the misfortune to dream of opening a bar, a dance studio, or a wedding venue. Small manufacturers tended to be the luckiest. Cindi Heyen, the Cusumano's regular through whom I first heard about the restaurant, runs the Scranton-based JED Pool Tools, which since 1989 has manufactured pool and spa accessories. JED saw a 44 percent increase in its 2020 sales, making it "by far our best year ever," Heyen said.

"The vast swath of manufacturers I worked with had a good 2020, if not a record-setting year," said Gene Marks, a small business consultant and *Philadelphia Inquirer* columnist. Most of the businesses he worked with were deemed essential, and those that weren't, he said, included "many who cheated and opened up anyway." Businesses merely inconvenienced by COVID received the same help from the government as those PPP recipients whose businesses were shut down for months. "Even if they were doing fine, [the] government picked up a lot of their employee costs," Marks said. Another random factor determining success: Was a business's landlord the inflexible type who insisted that a business pay the rent in full, even if their doors were shut, or did they recognize that by working with a business, they could avoid a long-term vacancy?

Geography proved another crap shoot. The small business owner who rationally chose to open a sandwich shop or coffee place in a central business district faced the prospect of surviving with virtually no customer base. The choice of storefronts in a big city could determine a restaurant's future. Did its owners have the misfortune of having chosen a spot with a bus stop directly in front of it or something else that prevented its owners from building an outdoor dining structure? Whether a business operated in a red or a blue state was also a factor. At the start of 2022, seated diners were still down at least 40 percent from prepandemic levels in more liberal cities such as New York, San Francisco, and Philadelphia, according to OpenTable. By contrast, indoor dining levels were back to normal in Miami, Phoenix, and Nashville.

I saw the cruelty of geography play out across the street from me. If the criteria for choosing a locale had been feeding people in a pandemic, the Consulate, the restaurant I look at out my home office window, had providence on its side. In a city of restaurants occupying long and narrow spaces, theirs was wide, offering ample sidewalk space. The body-waxing place next door to the Consulate had closed shortly before COVID, enabling the Consulate to take over more of the sidewalk and stretch the size of the "streatery" they built. These sheds, tents, yurts, geodesic domes, and other dining structures popped up in cities and towns across the country and proved a lifeline for restaurant owners and a joy for consumers craving to dine out again without having to eat indoors. The Consulate could comfortably seat around forty-five people in its streatery. Taking over extra sidewalk space in front of the shuttered body-waxing place, they could set out more than twenty tables in good weather.

In contrast, there was a favorite place of ours, Vin Sur Vingt, a French wine bar on the next block over. Its owners had the misfortune of a large bike rack in front of their storefront, installed several years earlier by Citi Bike, New York's bike-sharing program. That left them with no room to construct a streatery to seat people during the eight-plus months New York City was closed to indoor dining. Vin Sur Vingt was just off the main avenue on a narrow side street. They had room to cram maybe a half-dozen tables on the sidewalk. The Consulate had been floundering pre-COVID but took off during the pandemic because of the draw of its streetside dining. Vin Sur Vingt, which had been thriving until the virus, struggled. The old adage of "location, location, location" took on a whole new meaning when the new rules for dining meant a small, intimate wine bar in the wrong storefront became a curse.

* * *

My worry at the start of this project was that writing about small businesses fighting to survive COVID meant chronicling the slaughter that the pundits were warning about. Would the book serve as a sad elegy to the great vanishing of small businesses around the country because of a pandemic?

Yet that's not what I found on the road in northeastern Pennsylvania. Starting in the spring of 2020, I checked in regularly with around a dozen small business owners. According to the doomsday warnings, three or four of them would go out of business. None did. There was a partial casualty: Posh, the restaurant in downtown Scranton owned by Paul Blackledge and Joshua Mast. Blackledge and Mast, who are both mentioned briefly in these pages, had moved from New York City to Scranton (Blackledge grew up there), a city that in its heyday was known as the "Electric City" because in

1886 it became home to the country's first electric-powered street-cars. They bought first one stately, run-down nineteenth-century building and then another, turning each into a wedding venue and catering hall. They opened Posh in the second property they purchased, a building large enough to include two upstairs ballrooms, each of which could accommodate 180 people. There were several more handsome rooms for parties of less than fifty people. The closing of Posh in February 2022 was sad (the food was quite good and the dining room elegant), but Blackledge and Mast were still in the fight. When I first spoke to Mast in June of 2020, their revenues were 5 to 10 percent of what they had been before the pandemic. The longer the pandemic stretched on, the more they feared they would not make it. Yet heading into 2022, they still owned both properties and continued to host and cater weddings, rehearsal dinners, showers, and the corporate functions that help keep them busy during the week.

I had contacted another few dozen small businesses in northeastern Pennsylvania and New York City. Only one, the Shop 2 vintage store, went out of business. In Hazleton, Mary Malone, the president of the local chamber, could name only two other businesses that had gone under since COVID, and both, she added, were casualties of more than a pandemic. Amidst all the uncertainty, two clothing stores had opened in town since March 2020. So did a barbershop near the corner of Broad and Wyoming. The story was the same in Old Forge. The restaurant Billy G's closed, but other businesses opened, including a scaled-down revival of the original Rossi's, by TJ's uncle Larry. (He sold his meats and other Italian delicacies, along with salads and other dishes that he hired Sha-Asia Johnson part-time to make.) In Wyoming County, the chamber's Gina Suydum also did not witness a rash of closings. A smattering of businesses had shuttered, but others had sprung up. Meat Hooks BBQ in Laceyville, for instance, an early casualty of COVID, reopened under new ownership. In Tunkhannock, Main Street looked more or less as it had before COVID, except for the deli across from the Dietrich Theater, which had been struggling before COVID and had closed shortly into the pandemic.

That, of course, represented just one corner of a single state. Yet I was hardly the only one happily surprised that the darkest predictions had not come to pass. Sarah Crozier is the communications director for the Main Street Alliance, a national organization with tens of thousands of members scattered across the country. Most of them are microbusinesses with fewer than twenty employees—the enterprises most vulnerable in a severe economic turndown. When we first spoke in the spring of 2020, Crozier was braced for the worst. We both were reading the same grim stories. One study reported that 41 percent of black-owned businesses were closed because of COVID. Another study projected that one-quarter of the country's independent restaurants would be permanently shut down by the fall.

Yet from her national perch, Crozier was also pleasantly surprised with what she was observing. "We saw a lot of businesses reopen in the second half of 2020," Crozier said, "and then saw a real economic boon in entrepreneurship and new businesses." Her main worry at the start of 2022 was the same one her group and its allies had been warning about since *before* COVID—corporate consolidation and further domination by the largest businesses.

"There's still a lot of questions around who were the real winners coming out of the worst of the pandemic," Crozier said. A small business may have survived, but she was concerned they would be weakened by an economic version of long COVID.

Luz Urrutia is the CEO of the Accion Opportunity Fund, a California-based microlender that makes loans in communities that generally do not have access to banks or other traditional funding sources. That included Latino-, black-, and immigrant-owned businesses, which the early studies showed were at the greatest risk of closure, along with women-owned enterprises. Urrutia also did not see the predicted casualties among the small businesses she worked with. The Accion Opportunity Fund, a nonprofit, offered coaching to 1,300 businesses, 83 percent of whom were owned by a person of color. All told, they had nearly 7,000 businesses in a loan portfolio that included eateries, auto repair garages, nail salons, and flower shops.

"Ninety-five percent of them are back on their feet," Urrutia said. She credited the grit of the entrepreneurs her organization tended to work with. "These businesses have a lot of capacity, a lot of stamina," she said. "They were hit with a real shock with COVID, but they're used to shocks."

The story was not nearly so positive in any big city where the local economy relies heavily on both tourism and commuters. WAMU, the public radio station in Washington, DC, broadcast a bleak account in March of 2021, "taking stock of the hundreds of businesses DC lost during the pandemic." I had deliberately avoided retail and restaurants in New York City, but that also spared me some of the worst carnage. Nearly two years into the pandemic, weekday ridership on the three main commuter railroads into New York City—the country's three busiest—was still less than half of what it was prior to the pandemic. Subway ridership had also been halved. I had looked beyond New York in part because rents were an order of magnitude higher than counterparts pay in most of the rest of the country, and that proved fatal for many businesses. Several thousand restaurants, bars, and nightclubs across the five boroughs had permanently shuttered by the start of 2022, and seventy-five thousand fewer people were working in those fields compared to early 2020. The hotel industry was similarly decimated. Fewer than twenty thousand of the fifty-five thousand jobs in the hotel sector had returned and 125 hotels, accounting for eighteen thousand rooms, were still closed. New York City's unemployment rate was 9.4 percent—more than double the national average.

College towns were similarly hard-hit. With students attending school studying in their childhood bedrooms, there were fewer people to shop in their stores and eat in their restaurants. A friend in Northampton, Massachusetts, estimated that there were two new vacancies on every block of the commercial districts she frequented. Ann Arbor created a COVID rescue fund with a goal of bringing back one hundred small businesses. Communities across the country where a large portion of the population had suddenly gone absent were similarly suffering.

A more precise count of small businesses will have to wait. The Census Bureau is unlikely to have data on business closures until 2023. Even then, most measurements will lump together a small business operator with one employee with those up to five hundred and also sometimes include the self-employed. (Under that definition, I'm a small business, and I'm not a small business.) Early in the pandemic, an abundance of academics conducted surveys or looked at alternative measurements of business exits such as business electricity accounts and commercial vacancies. Yet, as Sarah Crozier pointed out, "most places gave up tracking data." Among them was Harvard's Christopher Stanton, who had coauthored a study widely quoted early in the pandemic. "It's very hard to actually measure small business failures and closures," said Stanton, who returned to his normal study of management practices.

Complicating the task of taking a hard count is that closures are endemic to the small business environment, even in good times. Businesses go under; businesses are replaced. How many closures were the natural order of things, and how many could be attributed to COVID? A group of economists working for the Federal Reserve tried to capture the fluidity in a study released in April 2021. They calculated that roughly six hundred thousand establishments permanently close each year—8.5 percent of the country's registered businesses. The Fed researchers estimated that an additional two hundred thousand businesses went under in 2020, representing around 11.5 percent of the country's businesses. A bad year for small businesses but hardly the widespread catastrophe that was being predicted.

Pundits had predicted a spike in bankruptcies. "We are going to see a level of bankruptcy activity that nobody in business has seen in their lifetime," the CEO of a research firm that tracks bank-ruptcies told the *Washington Post* in May 2020. Yet business bank-ruptcies actually *fell* in 2020 compared to 2019. There were nearly three times more business bankruptcies filed in 2009 and 2010 as in 2020.

If there were a small business die-off of titanic proportions, my brother-in-law, Ron Caspert, certainly would notice. Ron is a certi-fied auctioneer and president of Caspert Auctioneers & Appraisers, which sells off the remains of failed businesses. Business since the start of COVID has been "on the slow side," he told me at the start of 2022. In the past, banks generally did not hesitate in foreclos-ing on a business in arrears on its payments. "But banks have not been playing hardball because it's a really bad look in the middle of a pandemic," Ron said. His great fear is what he described as a "tsunami" of small business closures once banks have no fear of a backlash against widespread foreclosures.

Robert W. Fairlie, an economist at the University of California, Santa Cruz, was another source of hard data. It was Fairlie who had published the study early in the pandemic showing that 41 percent of black-owned businesses were closed. (Actually, that figure had fallen to 19 percent by June of 2020, but media outlets contin-ued quoting 41 percent.) Rather than track closures, Fairlie tracked those business owners who described themselves as "active" in sur-veys. That might mean longtime business owners or people who had started one-person businesses the month before. By the last quarter of 2021, there were as many small businesses operating as at the start of 2020. During that same period, he found that there were several hundred thousand *more* black-owned businesses oper-ating in the US than there were in February of 2020. There were more Latino-owned businesses as well.

That was seemingly great news for anyone invested in the future of small businesses in the US—except those figures included entre-preneurs of choice, who saw the pandemic as their moment to start their own business, and also those who became self-employed out of necessity.

"We're seeing a lot of women starting new business[es] and in particular women of color," said Luz Urrutia of the Accion Opportunity Fund. "But that's not necessarily a positive thing. A lot of the folks we're seeing have started a business because they've been laid off or because their financial situation means they have to start a side business to support their family." (Research by the Kauffman Foundation, a nonprofit that bolsters entrepreneurship, found that roughly 30 percent of new entrepreneurs in 2020 were unemployed.) The same thing happened during the Great Recession: a blossoming of new businesses not because people saw opportunities but because they lost their jobs, and suddenly they were self-employed marketing consultants or baking wedding cakes in the hopes of bringing in cash.

"This was characterized as a boom in entrepreneurship after 2008," Urrutia said, "but the reality is that many of these people, without supports, weren't able to sustain what they started." In 2020, Americans filed paperwork to start more than four million new businesses. That represented a 25 percent increase over the volume of applications received in 2019 and a 75 percent increase over 2010. New business filings jumped to 5.4 million in 2021. "If this time is going to be a true entrepreneurial boom," Urrutia said, "you need organizations that help them grow and thrive and not just hope they do."

* * *

Any explanation of why the pundits got it wrong about small business starts with the creativity and fortitude of the individual business owners. I saw it every time I crossed the street to head to Central Park in the first months of the pandemic. Adding to its geographic fortune, the Consulate occupied a good corner, an asset its owners—four immigrants from the country of Moldova—used to their advantage. There, one block from Central Park, they set up a grill and gelato stand in the early days of the pandemic. When the city was stopping at seven each night so residents could bang pots and give essential workers their due, they transformed their restaurant into a sidewalk bar. They hung an American flag and blasted Sinatra singing "New York, New York," giving their small stretch of the avenue a slightly drunken 9/11 vibe. Once they had been granted permission to set tables out on the sidewalk and in the street, they invited musicians to play for patrons. Initially, they put tables in the parking spots in front of the restaurant. A flimsy metal-tube-and-tent set up followed, and eventually a sturdy shed complete with plywood floor, metal roof, electric lights, and piped-in music that set the restaurant back $40,000.

Some innovated, others didn't, but all of the survivors had the heart and muscle to keep their doors open. They might not have "pivoted," to use the word of the moment in every feature article about small businesses struggling to survive. But they persisted.

Big corporations pitched in, or at least some of them did. With their handling of PPP early in the pandemic, the megabanks had shown their true loyalties in the fight between big and small, but they also had a financial stake in helping small businesses survive the pandemic. The country's community banks saved truly small businesses, not the giants. But Bank of America, JPMorgan Chase, and Wells Fargo collectively deployed billions of dollars to help small businesses. American Express, Netflix, Google, and Adidas were among the big companies devoting gobs of money to strengthen and expand small businesses, and especially those owned by people of color.

Government deserves to take its bow. PPP was messy, inefficient, and, especially early on, skewed to bigger players. Frustrated EIDL applicants had their own support groups on social media, where they traded tales of an agency overwhelmed. But it's remarkable what happens when the US government sets aside nearly $1 trillion to help the country's small businesses. PPP helped more than nine million small businesses (that figure includes sole proprietors whose businesses were damaged by COVID). Nearly four million businesses borrowed a combined $349 million in disaster loans—a number far exceeding the cumulative amount the EIDL program had loaned out in its entire history. Kabbage, a small business payments and loan provider owned by American Express, has been tracking small business recovery through the pandemic. A 2021 Kabbage survey found that 84 percent of its respondents agreed with the statement that PPP saved their company. (That same data also found a divide between different-sized businesses. Thirty-four percent of the largest small businesses received PPP dollars but only 14 percent of the businesses with twenty or fewer employees that Kabbage tracked.)

Government moved fast. Jurisdictions permitted restaurants and bars to offer to-go alcohol sales. The rules were relaxed to allow restaurants to take over portions of the street in front of their establishments. And, unlike in 2008, government responded with considerable force. All that money pumped into the economy through unemployment supplements and stimulus dollars proved critical. One of the great unreported stories, Paul Krugman, the *New York Times* columnist, wrote in early 2022, was "America's extraordinary success in limiting the damage from a horrifying pandemic. In fact, there's a good chance that in retrospect we'll view economic management over the past two years as a policy triumph."

* * *

COVID-related challenges persisted, of course. In 2021, the country posted its fastest growth rate in decades but also its highest inflation rate in forty years. That put price pressures on all businesses, as did the constant supply chain disruptions. TJ saw it in his prices for steaks and other meats. Mark Monsey saw it in the furniture he sold. The Maloneys saw it in the price they paid for cacao beans.

Across the country, small businesses faced the same dilemma: Did they pass along their costs to customers, and risk losing them to an establishment that charged less, or did they absorb the additional costs as the price of doing business? The war in Ukraine brought about a steep increase in the price of oil and gas, which Mark had already been warned would increase even higher the price of the goods he bought.

There was also what the media dubbed the Great Resignation. More than thirty million people quit their jobs between the spring of 2021 and the start of 2022. The staff shortages Vilma and Glenda struggled with impacted a range of small businesses in both Hazleton and Tunkhannock. The restaurant Twigs had been open seven days a week before COVID but cut back to five days a week because of staffing issues. Even then, chef-owner Jerry Bogedin had trouble finding enough people. Down the street, the Bistro was now open only five days a week rather than seven and also trimmed its hours. The decision to go dark on Sundays was particularly hard, said Bistro chef and co-owner Maureen Dymond. That meant shutting down their popular Sunday brunch.

"I can't spread myself overly thin," Dymond explained. After a long sigh, she added, "I thought at fifty-seven years old, I'd be slowing down but it's not working out that way."

Spreading himself too thin was TJ's problem in Old Forge. He had envisioned the Devil's Pit, his backyard bar and barbecue joint, as a new profit center that could replace the lost revenues from all those pharmaceutical dinners and funeral luncheons that still had not returned. Yet his staff was already working too many hours, and it was not like in the old days, when he only needed to spread the word to find people to help him cook. There was his own workload to consider. What TJ called "my little passion project" would remain on hold until at least the spring of 2022.

Yet that was a manageable COVID-related problem rather than an existential one. He was disappointed but, TJ said, "welcome to running your own business." To operate a small business is to always feel the future is precarious. Staffing issues, rising prices, customers thinking you're charging too much for your food: that was the restaurant entering the third year of the pandemic but also his business since almost the moment he opened his doors. For TJ it felt like old times.

Acknowledgments

T hanks first to the small business owners, without whom there would be no book. I imposed on them for their time and attention at the worst possible moment, as they engaged in a fight for survival, and then kept coming back for more. My eternal gratitude to TJ, Vilma, Glenda, the Maloney brothers, and Joe, along with Mark, Tamara, and Paul and Josh. My thanks as well to all those other small business operators quoted within these pages, along with apologies to all those I spoke with but whose names are not included. There were too many compelling tales and not enough pages.

Hollis Heimbouch, editor extraordinaire, is the one who first planted the idea in my head of a book that explored the country's complicated relationship with small business: we fetishize mom-and-pop establishments as we drive past them on the way to the mall or the parking lot of some big-box behemoth. COVID-19 added an urgency to that battle. Thank you, Hollis.

And heartfelt thanks as well to Elizabeth Kaplan. Every author should be blessed with an agent like Elizabeth, whose savvy, smarts, and encouragement were vital to the success of this project. She has been my super-agent from the start, but never has she played so central a role in the shaping of one of my books. Hollis, Elizabeth, and also Wendy Wong served as my council of advisors dating back to the spring of 2020, when I first started reaching out to businesses. The three served as a video sounding board every step of the way, and then helped me tame an overly long first draft. Thanks as well at HarperCollins to James Neidhardt, for helping guide the book through the production process, and Janet Rosenberg, for saving me numerous times through the copy edit.

Local chambers of commerce proved a lifeline for small businesses through the pandemic and also for me. I'm indebted especially to Mary Malone in Hazleton and Gina Suydam in Tunkhannock, for their help connecting me to businesses in their community, and also Bob Durkin in Scranton. Doug Hoey and Leon Michos at the National Community Pharmacists Association also provided valuable help.

Credit and also kudos to Mike Powell, whose touching and evocative *New York Times* column, "This Working Man Was Ready to Retire. But the Virus Took Him," in May 2020, pointed me toward Hazleton once I decided to focus on northeastern Pennsylvania. Julie Kramer and Niko Triantafillou served as guides to the Scranton area and also played a matchmaker role with small-business people. Michael Sokolove helped me better understand Pennsylvania politics, both through his insightful writings and as a colleague. Thanks as well to my two translators, Aissa Cabrales and Arabellis Diaz, and also Fermin Diaz.

Randy Stross, business historian, writer, and friend, was the perfect reader for this manuscript. I'm in his debt for his many invaluable suggestions. Thanks as well to John Raeside, who has long played a special role in my writing life, along with Mike Kelly, Mike Loftin, Sue Matteucci, Jeff Cohen, Dina Harris, and Sarah Towers. Gratitude to Ellen Leander, my all-time favorite librarian, and also to my mother, Naomi Rivlin, who needs to be in the conversation among proofreaders as the GOAT. As always, she gets the last read.

And last but hardly least, my family. This book was conceived and researched during the worst of the pandemic, when the four of us—my wife, Daisy Walker, and our two sons, Oliver and Silas—

were living on top of one another in our New York apartment. I couldn't be prouder of Oliver and Silas for their good cheer through remote learning and the stresses of a lockdown in a city apartment, or happier for their support as their dad took on a new writing project. And then, of course, there's my Daisy, who does double duty as both life partner and my best reader, even if sometimes brutal ("No one cares!" "Cut it") with her feedback. This one is for the three of you, with my love and gratitude.

Notes on Sourcing

T his book is based primarily on interviews with the two-hundred-plus people I spoke with while working on this project. That includes more than sixty small business owners, only a portion of whom are quoted within these pages. But I also pulled information from a wide range of newspapers, magazines, TV and radio clips, and podcasts to round out my story. Below is an accounting of media accounts used in the writing of this book.

Any nod to sources I relied upon to inform this narrative starts with my daily diet of media, which is heavy on the *New York Times*, *Washington Post*, NPR, and the public radio show *Marketplace*. My daily consumption was dosed with the *New Yorker*, the *Atlantic*, and the *Guardian*, along with pieces from Bloomberg, CNBC, *Business Insider*, *Forbes*, and pieces I found as an avid consumer of Redburn Reads, the regular email blast by my old editor, Tom Redburn, which was always chockful of links and commentary to articles relevant to COVID, electoral politics, or anything else on his mind. I became a daily reader of the *Philadelphia Inquirer* and a frequent visitor at the websites of the Hazleton *Standard-Speaker*, the *Wyoming County Press Examiner*, and *Scranton Times-Tribune*. A shout-out as well to Harrisburg's *Patriot-News*' PennLive site, the *Pittsburgh Post-Gazette*, and Spotlight PA, a nonprofit investigative news site funded by news organizations around the state. From all of these I picked up insights, stray factoids, and the occasional quote.

Outside journalists have been traveling to Hazleton to chronicle goings-on there since at least the mid-2000s and passage of the city's draconian immigration ordinance. The articles and segments I want to call out start with an article by Michael Powell and Michelle García that ran in the *Washington Post* in 2006 under the headline, "Pa. City Puts Illegal Immigrants on Notice." Also worthy of note: Eleanor Klibanoff's "The Immigrants It Once Shut Out Bring New Life to Pennsylvania Town," on NPR in 2015; Michael Matza's 2016 article in the *Philadelphia Inquirer*, "10 Years After Immigration Disputes, Hazleton Is a Different Place"; Binyamin Appelbaum's October 2016 article in the *New York Times*, "In City Built by Immigrants, Immigration Is the Defining Political Issue"; NPR's Michele Norris, who wrote about Hazleton ("As America Changes, Some Anxious Whites Feel Left Behind") for a special issue on race that *National Geographic* published in 2018; and Ben Bradlee Jr.'s 2018 book, *The Forgotten: How the People of One Pennsylvania County Elected Donald Trump and Changed America*.

More recently, there was Charles Thompson's PennLive article, "Some Blame Latinos for Hazleton's COVID-19 Outbreak, Echoing Divisions That Once Roiled City."

Closer to home, Jamie Longazel, a son of Hazleton, wrote *Undocumented Fears: Immigration and the Politics of Divide and Conquer in Hazleton, Pennsylvania*, published in 2016. (Longazel is now a professor of law and society at John Jay College of Criminal Justice in New York.) Charles F. McElwee III has been writing engagingly about his ancestral home for the *City Journal* and the *Atlantic*, among other publications. The Greater Hazleton Area Historical Society & Museum, where McElwee is vice president, and Tom Gabos is president, provided a snapshot of downtown Hazleton in its heyday, when anthracite coal was still the area's main industry. I also relied on the trove of interviews with locals conducted by Sam

Lesante, the proprietor of a cable access station called SSPTV and the host of the eponymous *The Sam Lesante Show*.

A pair of books helped in my understanding of coal's impact on northeastern Pennsylvania. One, *The Face of Decline: The Pennsylvania Anthracite Region in the Twentieth Century*, published in 2005, was written by two academics: Thomas Dublin, a professor of history at Binghamton University, State University of New York, and Walter Licht, a professor of history at the University of Pennsylvania. The other was *Remembering Lattimer: Labor, Migration, and Race in Pennsylvania Anthracite Country*, by anthropologist Paul A. Shackel (published in 2018). Also helpful were a pair of terrific nonfiction books: *Coal: A Human History* (2016), by Barbara Freese, and *Big Coal: The Dirty Secret Behind America's Energy Future* (2007), by Jeff Goodell.

There has been much good journalism shining a light on Amazon, which looms large both in Hazleton and over the retail landscape more generally. Alec MacGillis's excellent 2021 book, *Fulfillment: Winning and Losing in One-Click America*, was one place to gain insights, along with anything about Amazon running under the bylines of Karen Weise, David Streitfeld, or Farhad Manjoo in the *Times*. Wiese's May 2020 *New York Times* article, "'Way Too Late': Inside Amazon's Biggest Outbreak," focused specifically on the Hazleton plant. There were Jim Dino's articles in the *Standard-Speaker* about Amazon (and the industrial parks generally) as they contended with COVID in the spring of 2020, along with (all in May 2020) Lesley Stahl's *60 Minutes* piece on Amazon; Josh Dzieza's "A Seventh Amazon Employee Dies of COVID-19 as the Company Refuses to Say How Many Are Sick," in the *Verge;* and Ezra Kaplan and Jo Ling Kent's "Eighth Amazon Warehouse Worker Dies from COVID-19," on the NBC website.

Helping to inform my writing about Old Forge were *Our Town Old Forge*, a 2018 documentary appearing on WVIA, the Scranton area's public television station, and "The Early Days of Old Forge: Pieces of History," by Margo L. Azzarelli, appearing in the

Wilkes-Barre *Times Leader* in 2015. I also relied on the entertaining *Wise Guys Love to Cook: Stories and Recipes from My Time with the Mob*, by Bob Rinaldi. The statistic about the enormous jump in pizza sales during the pandemic was from an article written by my old buddy Julie Creswell ("Pizza Was the Restaurant Hero of 2020," in the *New York Times*, in February 2021). On the topic of bars and restaurants, I want to call out Gabrielle Hamilton's terrific article about her Manhattan eatery, Prune, in the *New York Times Magazine* ("My Restaurant Was My Life for 20 Years. Does the World Need It Anymore?"); Jack Nicas's equally excellent "One Bar. Twelve Weeks. Seventeen Lives in Lockdown," appearing in the *Times*'s Sunday Business section in June 2020; and Patric Kuh's first-rate 2019 book, *Masters at Work: Becoming a Restaurateur*.

I never had a chance to interview Governor Tom Wolf, despite repeated attempts over the nearly two years I worked on this project. For his background, several articles proved especially useful. I loved "Perfect Stranger," by Steve Volk, a profile of Wolf appearing in *Philadelphia* magazine in 2014. Also in 2014, the year he was first elected governor, there were "As Tom Wolf Seeks the Pennsylvania Governor's Office, Political Life Comes Full Circle," by the *Pittsburgh Post-Gazette*'s James P. O'Toole, and "Tom Wolf Runs as Gentleman Politician," by Steve Esack at the *Morning Call*. I also want to call out "'Clear as Mud': How Pa.'s Chaotic Coronavirus Waiver Program Hurt Small Businesses," by Charlotte Keith and Angela Couloumbis, published by Spotlight PA in June 2020; the *Economist*'s Lexington column in June 2020, "How Pennsylvania's Governor Is Battling the Pandemic"; and Charles Duhigg's May 2020 *New Yorker* article, "Seattle's Leaders Let Scientists Take the Lead. New York's Did Not," which offered an interesting primer on the best practices among public officials during a pandemic.

There was a lot of great reporting on the Paycheck Protection Program by a wide range of outlets, from Yahoo! News to Bloomberg to the *American Prospect*. Of special note was Stacy Cowley's coverage in the *New York Times*, including "Banks Gave

Richest Clients 'Concierge Treatment' for Pandemic Aid" (cowritten with Emily Flitter) in April 2020, and "The Small Business Administration's Gaffes Are Now Her Job to Fix" in May 2021 (the source for the SBA budget being less than what the Defense Department spends in a day). I also relied on Zachary Warmbrodt's coverage of PPP for Politico; a column Eleanor Clift wrote for the *Daily Beast*, "How Susan Collins' Small Business Bill Helped Bail Out Big Ones," in May 2020; an April 2020 NBC News article by Gretchen Morgenson, Rich Gardella, and Andrew W. Lehren, "Firms with Trump Links or Worth $100 Million Got Small Business Loans"; the *Wall Street Journal*'s "PPP Small-Business Loans Left Behind Many of America's Neediest Firms," by Yuka Hayashi, Ruth Simon, and Peter Rudegeair, in June 2020; and "The Failures and Future of the Paycheck Protection Program," which WBUR's *On Point* broadcast in February 2022. The background on Oklahoma congressman Kevin Hern was reported by Timothy L. O'Brien, in his Bloomberg article in April 2020, "A 'McCongressman' May Get a Coronavirus Bailout for His Business."

On the CARES Act, the American Rescue Plan, and other aid the government provided during the pandemic, I relied on my usual diet of media, including Jonathan O'Connell and Aaron Gregg at the *Washington Post* and Ben Casselman and Jim Tankersley at the *New York Times*. Gregg and Erica Werner cowrote "SBA Slashes Disaster-Loan Limit from $2 Million to $150,000, Shuts Out Nearly All New Applicants" about the EIDL program in May 2020. The *Times'* Stacy Cowley wrote "How a Relief Fund for Restaurants Picked Winners and Losers" in December 2021, about the Restaurant Revitalization Fund. The invaluable OpenSecrets, a nonpartisan research organization, was my source for lobbying data woven into the book.

The sections about Steven Mnuchin were helped by three great Mnuchin profiles, all appearing in 2020: "Steven Mnuchin's Deal Staved Off Catastrophe. Can He Make Another One?," by Jason Zengerle in the *New York Times Magazine*; "Steven Mnuchin Tried to Save the Economy. Not Even His Family Is Happy," by James B. Stewart and Alan Rappeport in the *New York Times*; and "The High-Finance Mogul in Charge of Our Economic Recovery," by Sheelah Kolhatkar in the *New Yorker*.

Jonathan J. Bean, a history professor at Southern Illinois University at Carbondale, wrote a pair of books about the SBA: *Beyond the Broker State: Federal Policies Toward Small Business, 1936–1961*, which was published in 1996, and *Big Government and Affirmative Action: The Scandalous History of the Small Business Administration* (2001). Also of note was Alexander Sammon's article "Everybody Hates the SBA," appearing in the *American Prospect* in May 2020, and the writings of University of North Carolina professor Benjamin C. Waterhouse. The 2018 book *Big Is Beautiful: Debunking the Myth of Small Business*, by Robert D. Atkinson and Michael Lind, was also a source for understanding how small business is perceived by elected officials and the public.

At the *Washington Post*, there are three more articles that I want to call out: Heather Long's "Small Business Used to Define America's Economy. The Pandemic Could Change That Forever," appearing in May 2020; "The End of Small Business," by James Kwak, published in July 2020; and "America's Biggest Companies Are Flourishing during the Pandemic and Putting Thousands of People Out of Work," by Douglas MacMillan, Peter Whoriskey, and Jonathan O'Connell, in December 2020. In the *New York Times*, there was "Wealthiest Hospitals Got Billions in Bailout for Struggling Health Providers," in May 2020, by Jesse Drucker, Jessica Silver-Greenberg, and Sarah Kliff; "Large Companies Take Bailout Aid in Dubious Gains," by Jessica Silver-Greenberg, David Enrich, Jesse Drucker, and Stacy Cowley; "Lawsuits Swell as Owners, from Gun Shops to Golf Courses, Demand to Open," by Neil MacFarquhar, in April 2020; and "Start-Up Boom in the Pandemic Is Growing Stronger," by Ben Casselman, in August 2021. Other *Times* reporters whose bylines graced the top of articles that helped in the writing of this book: Emily Cochrane, Patricia Cohen, Michael Corkery,

Emily Flitter, Amy Haimerl, David Leonhardt, Eric Lipton, Sapna Maheshwari, David McCabe, Ben Protess, Nelson Schwartz, Jeanna Smialek, and Kenneth P. Vogel.

I loved Francesca Mari's article "What My Dad Gave His Shop," appearing in the December 2020 issue of the *Atlantic*. High praise as well for the collected works of the *Atlantic*'s Ed Yong and his coverage of the pandemic. It was Yong who offered the "a thousand times smaller than a dust mote" line. Deep respect as well for the writings of both Derek Thompson and Annie Lowrey. Thompson wrote "The Pandemic Will Change American Retail Forever," in April 2020, and "We Can Prevent a Great Depression. It'll Take $10 Trillion," in May 2020. Lowrey authored "The Small-Business Die-Off Is Here," also in May, and "The Pandemic Business Boom," in August 2021.

The Plague Year, by Lawrence Wright, was my favorite of the first batch of COVID-19 books I read. Other key sources about the pandemic included the COVID Tracking Project, Yelp, Kabbage, Womply, and the Census Bureau's Small Business Pulse Survey. Ally Schweitzer and Mikaela Lefrak were the reporters on the WAMU story "Taking Stock of the Hundreds of Businesses D.C. Lost During the Pandemic." Katherine Eban's "Painful Prescription," appearing in *Fortune* in 2013, was an early effort at exposing the PBMs as a behind-the-scenes drivers of healthcare costs.

There also have been a lot of insightful reporting on the take-over of the economy by giants. David Dayen's 2020 book, *Monopolized: Life in the Age of Corporate Power*, includes several pages about PBMs. Dayen is also the author of "The Hidden Monopolies That Raise Drug Prices," a 2017 article appearing in the *American Prospect*, where he now serves as executive editor. Also of note are works by Matt Stoller and Stacy Mitchell. Stoller is author of the 2019 book *Goliath: The 100-Year War Between Monopoly Power and Democracy*, and publishes BIG, a Substack newsletter on the same topic. Stacy Mitchell wrote the 2006 book *Big-Box Swindle: The True Cost of Mega-Retailers and the Fight for America's Independent*

Businesses. Mitchell, who is codirector of the Institute for Local Self-Reliance, also wrote "Amazon Doesn't Just Want to Dominate the Market—It Wants to Become the Market," which appeared in the *Nation* magazine in 2018. There was also Barry C. Lynn's illuminating article "America's Monopolies Are Holding Back the Economy," appearing in the *Atlantic* in 2017.

Finally, chocolate. My education in the finer points of high-quality dark chocolates began inside Sol Cacao's production facility and continued with a "Guided Craft Chocolate Tasting with Roni-Sue" (hosted by Rhonda Kave, the chocolatier at Roni-Sue's Chocolates in Lower Manhattan) that included samples of Sol Cacao's Peru and Colombia bars among her samples. I then moved on to the video library at John Nanci's site, Chocolate Alchemy, which is focused on "the art and science of bean to bar chocolate." *Confectionery News* was useful in its coverage of the chocolate industry and the palm oils, emulsifiers, and other additives many large producers use in their chocolates. There was also Stasia Bliss's 2013 article in the *Guardian Liberty Voice* that asked, "Does Your Chocolate Contain Wax?" If you're eating a mass-produced chocolate bar, apparently the answer is likely a yes.

About the Author

GARY RIVLIN is a Pulitzer Prize–winning investigative reporter and the author of nine books, including *Katrina: After the Flood*. His work has appeared in the *New York Times*, *Newsweek*, *Fortune*, *GQ*, and *Wired*, among other publications. He is a two-time Gerald Loeb Award winner and a former reporter for the *New York Times*. He lives in New York with his wife, theater director Daisy Walker, and two sons.